Social Partnership in the European Union

Social Partnership in the European Union

Edited by

Hugh Compston
Lecturer in European Politics
Cardiff University

and

Justin Greenwood
Jean Monnet Professor of European Public Policy
Robert Gordon University
Aberdeen

First published 2001 by
PALGRAVE
Houndmills, Basingstoke, Hampshire RG21 6XS and
175 Fifth Avenue, New York, N.Y. 10010
Companies and representatives throughout the world

PALGRAVE is the new global academic imprint of
St. Martin's Press LLC Scholarly and Reference Division and
Palgrave Publishers Ltd (formerly Macmillan Press Ltd).

ISBN 0–333–77520–1

This book is printed on paper suitable for recycling and
made from fully managed and sustained forest sources.

A catalogue record for this book is available
from the British Library.

Library of Congress Cataloging-in-Publication Data
Social partnership in the European Union / edited by
Hugh Compston, Justin Greenwood.
         p. cm.
     Includes bibliographical references and index.
     ISBN 0–333–77520–1
     1. European Union. 2. Corporate state. 3. Functional
representation. 4. Economic and Monetary Union.
     I. Compston, Hugh, 1955– II. Greenwood, Justin.
     JN30 .S63 2000
     306'.094—dc21
                                              00–066553

10   9   8   7   6   5   4   3   2   1
10   09 08 07 06 05 04 03 02 01

Printed in Great Britain by Antony Rowe Ltd, Chippenham, Wiltshire

Contents

List of Tables

Acknowledgements

We would like to express our appreciation of the funding from the European Commission DG Employment and Social Affairs and Cardiff University that enabled us to carry out this research. We would like in particular to thank Daniel Vaughan-Whitehead of Directorate D for his advice and assistance. We would also like to thank the administrative staff at Cardiff University whose assistance was vital, especially Bridget Bradley, Graham Edwards, Laura James, Mike Joynson and Helen Muir. The opportunity to discuss the dynamics of social partnership with Gerda Falkner was also valuable. Thanks are also due to those who made time to be interviewed for this project. Most of all, however, we would like to thank the contributors to this study who worked with us throughout and produced their contributions on time.

HUGH COMPSTON
JUSTIN GREENWOOD

Notes on the Contributors

Ann Branch is writing a DPhil thesis on European integration theory and the European social dialogue at Nuffield College, Oxford. Publications include 'Trapped in the Supranational–Intergovernmental Dichotomy: a Response to Stone, Sweet and Sandholtz' (with Jakob C. Ohrgaard), *Journal of European Public Policy*, vol. 6/1 (1999); 'The Impact of the EU on National Trade Unions', in R. Balme, D. Chabanet and V. Wright (eds), *Collective Action in Europe* (forthcoming); and 'The European Union and National Trade Unions: Living Up to Expectations or Better than Nothing?', *La lettre de la Maison française d'Oxford, Action collective, représentation des intérêts et espace public en Europe* (forthcoming).

Hugh Compston teaches politics in the School of European Studies, Cardiff University, and researches in the area of comparative public policy and political economy. Among recent publications are *The New Politics of Unemployment: Radical Policy Initiatives in Western Europe* (editor, 1996); 'Union Power, Policy-Making and Unemployment in Western Europe, 1972–1993', *Comparative Political Studies* (December 1997); and 'The End of Policy Concertation? Western Europe since the Single European Act', *Journal of European Public Policy*, vol. 5/4 (1998).

Jon Erik Dølvik is a researcher at the Institute for Applied Social Science (Fafo), which is affiliated to the University of Oslo. His current area of research is comparative labour relations and employment policies in the context of globalisation and regionalisation. Recent publications include 'Redrawing Boundaries of Solidarity? ETUC, Social Dialogue and the Europeanisation of Trade Unionism in the 1990s', doctoral dissertation (1997), ARENA-report 5/97/Fafo-report 238; *Making Solidarity Work? The Norwegian Labour Market Model in Transition* (ed. with A.H. Steen, 1997); *An Emerging Island? ETUC, Social Dialogue and the Europeanisation of Trade Unions in the 1990s* (1999); and 'EMU: Re-nationalization and Europeanization of Industrial Relations – Two Sides of the Same Coin?', in A. Martin and G. Ross (eds), *EMU and the European Model of Society* (forthcoming).

Justin Greenwood is Jean Monnet Professor of European Public Policy at the Robert Gordon University, Aberdeen. His career research specialism is 'interest representation in the European Union'. Books include *Representing Interests in the European Union* (1997), *Organised Interests and the New Global Order* (ed. with Henry Jacek, 1999), *Collective Action in the European Union: Interests and the New Politics of Associability* (ed. with Mark Aspinwall, 1997), *European Casebook on Business Alliances* (ed., 1995); and *Organised Interests and the European Community* (ed. with Jurgen Grote and Karsten Ronit, 1992). He has also published articles in journals such as *Political Studies, Parliamentary Affairs,* the *Journal of Common Market Studies, West European Politics,* the *International Journal of Public Administration,* and the *European Journal of Political Research,* and is the editor of *Current Politics and Economics of Europe,* the only EU studies journal to be published in the United States. His work has been funded, inter alia, by the European Community/Union, the British Academy, the Carnegie Foundation, and firms and business associations, and he currently leads the International Political Science Association (IPSA) Research Committee on Politics and Business, and the European Consortium for Political Research (ECPR) Standing Group on European Level Interest Representation.

Daniela Obradovic teaches in the Faculties of International Law and Political Science at the University of Amsterdam. Her main publications deal with European institutional law and the role of interest groups in the formation, implementation and enforcement of European Union policies.

Jelle Visser is professor of empirical sociology and chair of sociology of labour and organisation at the University of Amsterdam, where he directs the Centre for Research on European Societies and Industrial Relations (CESAR). He is also associated with the Max Planck Institute for the Study of Societies in Cologne, Germany, where he directs with professor Wolfgang Streeck a research project on the 'Europeanization of Interest Organizations'. He has worked as consultant to the Organisation for Economic Co-operation and Development in Paris and is currently consultant to the International Labour Organization in Geneva. Recent books include *Trade Unions in Western Europe Since 1945* (with Bernhard Ebbinghaus, 2000), *'A Dutch Miracle': Job Growth, Welfare Reform and Corporatism in the Netherlands* (with Anton Hemerijck, 1997) and *Industrial Relations in Europe: Traditions and Transitions* (with Joris van Ruysseveldt, 1996).

Tina Weber is currently working as a Senior Research Manager at ECOTEC Research and Consulting Limited in Birmingham, which has involved providing research and consultancy advice to organisations such as the European Commission, various employer associations and trade unions, and the British Department of Trade and Industry. Her main research interests lie in the area of the European sectoral social dialogue and the impact of European Community legislation and policy actions on the Member States, and she has recently completed a PhD thesis on 'The Politics of the European Social Dimension: a Comparative View of Trade Union Demands in Britain and Germany' (award pending, Edinburgh University). Publications include *Costs and Benefits of the European Works Councils Directive*, DTI Research Series (forthcoming, spring 2000); *Selecting Best Value – A Manual for Public Authorities Awarding Contracts for Guarding Security Services* (1999); *Women's Working Conditions in Different Sectors of the European Economy* (1998); *New Employment Opportunities in the European Cleaning Industry* (1997); 'Policies and Practices towards Older Workers' (with Gill Whitting, Jane Sidaway and Joanne Moore), *Labour Market Trends* (April 1997); and *Policies and Practices towards Older Workers in France, Germany, Spain and Sweden* (with Gill Whitting, Joanne Moore and Jane Sidaway, May 1997).

Introduction

Hugh Compston

The aim of this study is to determine the extent to which explanations of the development and operation of social partnership at EU level can be explained in terms of the logic of self-interest, as opposed to factors such as the influence of ideas or of cultural or ideological values. By social partnership (or policy concertation) is meant the co-determination of EU policy by means of agreements struck between EU institutions and European-level employer organisations and trade union confederations. At inter-sectoral level this essentially means the procedure using which the Council may transpose agreements struck between the peak European-level private sector employer confederation UNICE, its public sector equivalent CEEP and the peak European trade union confederation ETUC into the form of Directives. This is not the only current definition of social partnership, but we use it as our focus because it represents a fundamentally different form of policy-making to determination of public policy by EU institutions alone, and is therefore of major political significance. Theorists have often accorded interest groups a prominent role in European integration; social partnership as introduced at Maastricht in 1991 represents a new level of involvement of employers and unions in EU policy-making. This study is intended to set out an explanation of its development and operation by providing analyses of the positions and actions of employers, trade unions, the Commission and Member States and using these to construct a definitive account of why social partnership arose in the way it did and how it has functioned since 1991. Particular attention is paid to the relationship between the dynamics of social partnership and the debate over the desirability, nature and consequences of EMU.

1

The purpose of this introduction is threefold. First, it sets our analysis in context by briefly describing the main forums in which the social partners, defined as organisations that have the ability to participate in collective bargaining (Commission of the European Communities, 1998a, p.4), have been involved in EU policy-making, namely the Economic and Social Committee, the Standing Committee on Employment, Tripartite Conferences, the Social Dialogue, meetings with the Troika of Presidencies, and the Macroeconomic Dialogue. Second, it describes the procedure introduced at Maastricht whereby the Council may transpose social partner agreements into the form of Directives, which we call the 'social partnership procedure' for short. The final section outlines the research design and format of the study.

Social partners and EU policy-making

The body prescribed by the Treaty of Rome for sectional interests to be represented in the EU's decision-making process is the Economic and Social Committee (ESC), in which employer representatives, worker representatives and other interests (such as small and medium business, professional groups, farmers, consumers and environmental groups) each constitute a third of the membership.

As a means through which employers and trade unions participate in EU policy-making, however, the ESC has severe limitations: it is not a forum in which co-determination of public policy takes place. Its 222 members are nominated by national governments and appointed by Council rather than being representatives of national- or EU-level employers' organisations and trade union movements (Economic and Social Committee, 1999). The role of the ESC is strictly advisory, its principal task being to give Opinions on proposed legislation and other matters referred to it by the Commission, the Council and, under the Amsterdam Treaty, the European Parliament. The ESC also has the right to formulate Opinions on its own initiative. Opinions are adopted by majority vote, but efforts to produce large majorities have often led to bland lowest common denominator reports. Consultation is mandatory only for a limited number of issues, although the Commission and Council often refer other matters to the ESC as well. Finally, the ESC is consulted fairly late in the policy-making process, when it tends to be difficult to influence the content of legislative proposals. As a consequence, the ESC is generally considered to be rather ineffective, more a sounding board for the Commission and Council than an avenue through which influence can be exerted, although the Committee Secretariat claims that around two-thirds of Committee proposals are accepted by the Commission and find their way into texts adopted by Council (Barnouin, 1986, pp.81–3; Nugent, 1991, pp.215, 217; Economic and Social Committee, 2000, p.2).

The Standing Committee on Employment (SCE) is the only permanent formal body in which consultation and dialogue take place between Council, the Commission, employers and unions, but it is not a forum for co-determination of policy either. The Committee is chaired by the Labour Minister of the country holding the Council Presidency and was originally set up in 1971 to carry out the recommmendations of a Tripartite Conference on employment and social affairs held in Luxembourg in April 1970, although it was not given any decision-making powers on these matters. Soon after its inception a dispute arose between Council and the ETUC concerning the procedures for the selection of worker representatives, which resulted in an ETUC boycott of the SCE between 1973 and 1974, but this was resolved in January 1975 when the ETUC was allocated 17 of the 18 trade union seats, with the French CGT (*Confédération générale du travail*), CFTC (*Confédération français des travailleurs chrétiens*) and CGC (*Confédération générale des cadres*), which were not members of the ETUC, alternately occupying the remaining seat (Barnouin, 1986, pp.86–9; Commission of the European Communities, 1984, p.13).

As a forum for co-determination of EU policy the SCE has been impeded by lack of agreement on the causes of unemployment, the restriction of its purview mainly to relatively narrow labour market issues (Barnouin, 1986, pp.86–9; Commission of the European Communities, 1984, p.13), and the absence of Economic and Finance Ministers from its meetings. For a long time the social partners did not actually meet Ministers until after conclusions were agreed through a process of alternate meetings between the Chair, the Commission and the social partners, on the one hand, and the Chair, the Commission and Ministers, on the other, which progressively refined a draft based on an initial Commission paper. The only example of public policy resulting from SCE negotiations appears to have been certain parts of a 1975 Directive on collective redundancies (Commission of the European Communities, 1995, p.15).

The increased emphasis on employment issues during the 1990s, exemplified in events such as the incorporation of an Employment

Chapter into the Treaty of Amsterdam, the approval by the 1997 Luxembourg Employment Summit of a coordinated employment strategy involving specific guidelines for Member States, and the conclusion of an Employment Pact by the 1999 Cologne European Council, has led to more extensive consultation of the social partners on employment issues, but this has mostly taken place outside the SCE. The perceived limitations of the SCE led the Commission to propose extensive reforms, and on 9 March 1999 the Council approved a reorganisation intended to make it the main mechanism through which the Council, Commission and social partners consult on employment issues and discuss the EU employment strategy. Among the changes were the exclusion of all but European-level organisations, and imposition of a new requirement that the composition of each social partner delegation covers the whole economy. It is too early to evaluate the effects of these reforms, but it is already clear that co-determination of EU employment policy is still not part of its remit (OJ L 072, 18/03/1999, pp.0033–0035).

The first two Tripartite Conferences between employers, unions and Council were held in 1970 and 1974 and dealt with social issues. The first Tripartite Conference with economic Ministers present was convened in November 1975 as a result of ETUC pressure, but although a consensus was reached on the nature and causes of the economic situation, agreement was not obtained on the appropriate remedies. At the second Conference in June 1976 targets were agreed for employment and price stability and an agreed economic strategy was adopted as the official EU medium-term economic programme. In addition, a small steering group composed of representatives of employers, unions, the Commission and the Council Presidency was set up to monitor progress, the role of the SCE was strengthened, and the Economic Policy Committee of representatives of national governments and central banks was scheduled to start discussions with the social partners on economic policy. Progress towards the targets set by the programme was not forthcoming, however, and the ETUC accused governments, employers and the Commission of failing to implement the decisions of the Conference. A further Tripartite Conference in June 1977 made little further progress, with increased conflict developing between unions and employers. Meetings with the Economic Policy Committee were marred by the fact that government representatives remained completely silent. The November 1978 Conference was equally unproductive. Since meaningful contact with Council was the *raison d'être* for the ETUC seeking these Conferences, these experiences led to its withdrawal from the process (Barnouin, 1986, pp.90–5). The next Tripartite Conference did not take place until 1996, when one was convened in Rome by the Italian Presidency to stimulate action on unemployment, but again no policy decisions resulted (*Bulletin EU* 6-1996, Annexes to the Conclusions of the Presidency (6/108)). Tripartite Conferences have not been a forum for the co-determination of EU policy.

The social dialogue between employers and unions was launched in January 1985, when the Commission President, Jacques Delors, convened a meeting of the leaders of the ETUC, UNICE and CEEP at Val Duchesse to try to find common ground between employers and trade unions on economic and social issues. It was given legal status by Article 118b of the Single European Act, which stated that 'the dialogue between management and labour at the European level could, if the two sides consider it desirable, lead to relations based on agreement'. In November 1985 working parties were set up on macroeconomic issues and on new technologies, and agreement was reached on supporting the Commission's Cooperative Growth Strategy for More Employment. This was reaffirmed in joint opinions reached in November 1986 and November 1987, but the Strategy was rendered ineffective by the lack of practical backing by Member State governments (ETUC, 1991, p.50). A relaunch in January 1989 resulted in the formation of a political steering group and the creation of working parties on the labour market and on education and training, while the Commission agreed to submit an annual Employment Report to the Social Dialogue and to the Standing Committee on Employment before forwarding it to Council, and undertook to consult the social partners at regional level on structural policy. A number of joint opinions, joint declarations and working documents date from this period, but no collective bargaining or co-determination of EU policy took place.

The turning point for the social dialogue and for EU-level social partnership came on 31 October 1991, when UNICE, CEEP and the ETUC agreed to propose to the Intergovernmental Conference (IGC) not only that consultation be mandatory on relevant legislation but also that a procedure be established whereby the Council was given the power to transpose agreements between EU-level social partners into the form of Community law, as an alternative to leaving implementation of these agreements to the social partners themselves or passing legislation in the 'normal' way. The text of the 31

October Agreement was inserted virtually unchanged into the Social Protocol adopted at Maastricht in December 1991 by all Member States apart from Britain, and the resulting social partnership procedure became operational in November 1993 and was incorporated into the Treaty of Amsterdam in 1997. The text of the relevant Articles is reproduced in Appendix 1. During the 1990s the procedure was used at intersectoral level to pass Directives on parental leave in 1996 (Council Directive 96/34/EC), part-time work in 1997 (Council Directive 97/81/EC) and fixed-term work in 1999 (Council Directive 99/70/EC). The text of these Directives is set out in Appendices 2–4.

The introduction of the social partnership procedure was accompanied by a reorganisation of the committee structure of the social dialogue. In March 1992 the Macroeconomics Group was reactivated and discussions on EMU, as well as on the general economic situation, led to agreement on a joint opinion on economic policy and employment in July 1992. In October 1992 a central Social Dialogue Committee was established as the main forum for the negotiation of inter-sectoral agreements and to facilitate intensified consultation by the Commission on economic and social policy. This met regularly through the 1990s and issued a number of non-binding joint declarations on issues such as employment. The Education and Training, Labour Market and Macroeconomic Working Groups also issued a number of non-binding joint opinions, joint declarations and working documents. The growing prominence of the social dialogue, and especially its new capacity to submit framework agreements to the Council for translation into Community law, led organisations other than UNICE, CEEP and ETUC to demand to be included, and in January 1999 UEAPME, which represents small and medium-sized business, was officially accepted into the social dialogue as a European-level social partner.

Alongside the social dialogue the Commission has also been developing a broader 'civil dialogue' on social policy involving meetings and discussions between EU institutions, national authorities, the social partners and non-government organisations. This is designed to inform the 'third sector' about EU-level developments and to give this sector an input into EU policy-making. However, there is little evidence that it has had much impact on EU social policy since it was launched in 1996, and it has certainly not involved co-determination of EU policy. Despite its potential importance, therefore, it is not a focus for analysis in this study.

Another development during the 1990s was the increased consultation of the social partners on employment issues. During this period the European Council repeatedly called on the social partners to contribute to the EU employment strategy by negotiating agreements on wage restraint, work organisation, training and job creation. The 1997 Luxembourg Employment Summit instituted regular meetings between the social partners and the Employment and Labour Market Steering Group, and between the social partners, the Commission, and the Troika of Heads of State or Government of the Member States holding the current, past and future Presidencies. The 1999 Cologne Economic Summit set up a new 'macroeconomic dialogue' between the social partners and the Commission, national employment, economic and finance ministers, and the European Central Bank. This is intended to help ensure consistency between the monetary, fiscal and wage pillars of the 1999 Employment Pact, although the six-monthly meetings of participants are informal and have no power to issue recommendations to Member States.

While most attention has focused on the inter-sectoral social dialogue, similar types of consultation and dialogue have been taking place at sectoral level for decades. The first sectoral committee was the European Coal and Steel Community's tripartite Consultative Committee set up in 1955, and from 1963 Joint Committees comprising equal numbers of representatives from employer and employee organisations were established in the areas of agriculture, road transport, railways, inland navigation, sea transport, civil aviation, telecommunications, sea fishing and footwear. Informal groups were established in the areas of hotels, insurance, banking, retail, wholesale and intermodal transport. However, the first European-level collective agreement to regulate conditions at sectoral level was not concluded until September 1990, when a framework agreement was reached between the ETUC and CEEP on rail and energy distribution (DGV, undated). In 1998 the Joint Committees were replaced by Sectoral Dialogue Committees (COM(96)448 final).

At inter-sectoral level the social dialogue is clearly the preeminent forum through which the social partners are involved in the EU policy-making process, and the only one through which they are involved in the actual co-determination of EU policy. All the other forums – Economic and Social Committee, Standing Committee on Employment, Tripartite Conferences, meetings with the Troika of Presidencies and Macroeconomic Dialogue – are limited to consultation only, as are the many advisory committees on which the social partners are represented, such as the six committees that advise the Commission on Social Security for Migrant Workers, Freedom of Movement for Workers, European Social Fund, Vocational Training, Safety, Hygiene and Protection at Work, and Equal Opportunities for Women and Men (Commission of the European Communities, 1998a, pp.6–9).

The social partnership procedure

The legal basis of the social partnership procedure is set out in Articles 137–139 of the Treaty of Amsterdam, which are identical to Articles 2–4 of the Social Protocol agreed by eleven of the twelve Member States at Maastricht. These state, first, that the Commission should consult management and labour on the direction and content of proposals in the social policy field. The social partners may then request nine months to negotiate an agreement on the issue, a period that may be extended if the social partners and Commission all agree. If the social partners succeed in reaching an agreement on the issue itself, Article 139 states that this may be implemented either in accordance with the procedures and practices specific to management and labour and the Member States or, in areas covered by Article 137 and at the joint request of the signatory parties, by a Council decision on a proposal from the Commission. Article 137 covers health and safety, working conditions, information and consultation of workers, the integration of persons excluded from the labour market, and equal labour market treatment of men and women. Council decisions are taken by Qualified Majority Voting (QMV) apart from several areas in which unanimity is specified, namely social security and social protection of workers, protection of workers where their employment contract is terminated, conditions of employment for third-country nationals, financial contributions to the promotion of employment and job creation, and the representation and collective defence of workers and employers, including co-determination but excluding pay, the right of association, the right to strike and the right to impose lockouts, which are specifically excluded from the provisions of Article 137.

Although consultation may lead to social partner influence on EU policy, the social partnership procedure is the only mechanism through which the social partners actually co-determine the content of EU policy. Although the procedure is sometimes referred to

as a mere implementation mechanism, the contents of the resultant Directives are influenced not only by the social partners in
their negotiations to reach the agreements on which the Directives
are to be based, but also by the Council and, to some extent, by
the Commission. Although there is an accepted convention that
Council may not amend social partner agreements presented to it
for ratification, it does have the power to reject them and to request the Commission to put forward a new legislative proposal
through the 'normal' legislative procedure. As will become clear in
this study, the negotiating positions of the social partners are influenced by their perceptions of the likely content of the legislation
that Council would pass using the 'normal' legislative procedure if
a social partner agreement were not struck. Finally, the Commission not only retains the power of initiative in this procedure but
also has the power to assess the representative status of the contracting parties, their mandate, the legality of each clause in the
agreement in relation to Community law (such as whether it falls
within the required range of policy), and the provisions relating to
small and medium-sized business.

Investigating social partnership

The overall aim of this study is to discover whether the genesis
and use of the social partnership procedure can be explained purely
in terms of self-interest, or whether an adequate explanation needs
to include other types of causal factors as well. In the only mono-
graph published in Europe during the 1990s that deals with the
social partnership procedure, Gerda Falkner's book *EU Social Policy
in the 1990s: Towards a Corporatist Policy Community* (1998), it is
argued that while the actions of the Commission and the social
partners in relation to the setting up of the social partnership procedure can be explained satisfactorily in terms of self-interest, the
social partner agreement of 31 October 1991 was contingent on
the expectation of UNICE that Member States would extend QMV
to additional areas of social policy at Maastricht despite the fact
that it was against the economic interests of the poorer Member
States to do so. Falkner argues that this positive attitude of Member States towards QMV has to be understood as the result of a
long-term process of joint preference formation leading to the acceptance by all but the British government of the principled idea
that it is normatively desirable to build an expanded EU social

dimension as a means of preserving the 'European social model' (Falkner, 1998, p.202). Is Falkner right? In part our analyses are designed to answer this question.

To test the self-interest theory of social partnership, the actions of each of the main policy actors are examined separately before being synthesised into a single account of the development and use of the social partnership procedure. To this end, chapters were commissioned on each of the major policy actors involved: employers (Ann Branch and Justin Greenwood), trade unions (Jon Erik Dølvik and Jelle Visser), the European Commission (Daniela Obradovic) and Member States (Hugh Compston). The chapters on trade unions, employers and Member States all share a common format dictated by the research design. First, the actions and rhetoric of the relevant policy actor(s) in relation to social partnership are described, focusing mainly on the period since the passage of the Single European Act in 1986. This is then followed by an analysis of the extent to which the positions and actions of the relevant policy actor(s) can be explained by the logic of self-interest, accompanied by an analysis of the extent to which the residual – the positions and actions that arguably cannot be explained purely in terms of self-interest – can be explained in terms of other factors, such as institutional, cultural or ideological norms. Particular attention is paid to the perceived relationship between social partnership and EMU. The chapter on the Commission and European Parliament focuses on the relationship between the social partnership procedure and the powers of these institutions.

The chapters on the policy actors' positions and actions in relation to social partnership at inter-sectoral level are followed by a chapter by Tina Weber in which the state of play of social partnership at sectoral level is described and a comparison made between the experiences of three contrasting sectors: maritime transport, in which an agreement was reached to implement the provisions of the Working Time Directive; road transport, in which negotiations on this issue failed; and the private security industry, in which common interests have provided a strong driving force for joint actions.

The concluding chapter by Hugh Compston and Justin Greenwood summarises and synthesises the results of the investigation, focusing on the extent to which the political dynamics of social partnership can be accounted for in terms of self-interest.

1
ETUC and European Social Partnership: a Third Turning-Point?

Jon Erik Dølvik and Jelle Visser

The paradox of European trade union strengthening

There is no shortage of studies or indicators of European trade unions and union activity showing their decline during the final years of the twentieth century. After decades of growth in membership, organisational development and influence in national economic and social policies, reaching maximum levels in the 1970s, trade unions in Europe, like union movements in other world regions, have recently experienced a difficult phase in their history (ILO, 1997).

In 1996 the average level of union density in Western Europe was 12 percentage points below its post-war peak of 44 per cent in 1979 and 5 points below the level of 1970 (Ebbinghaus and Visser, 2000).[1] The return to labour quiescence, begun in the late 1970s (Shalev, 1992), has continued since. In the EU the number of working days lost as a result of labour conflicts has dropped from 85 million in 1979 to an annual average of under 20 million in the 1980s and under 10 million between 1990 and 1996 (calculated from ILO data). During the 1980s and 1990s, the rate of increase in real wages slowed down markedly in all European countries, ending the steep rise in real compensation of workers in preceding decades. Lower real wage increases reflected reduced productivity growth in the 1980s, and a lagging of wage increases behind productivity in the 1990s. This development is expressed in a fall in wage shares (or a rise in profit shares), showing a sharp reversal of trends around 1980. In 1970, at 66 per cent, the average adjusted wage share in the EU was slightly above the trend level of the 1960s; it rose to a peak of 70 per cent

11

in 1975 and 68.5 per cent in 1980. In 1990 the average wage share in the EU was just above 63 per cent, but continued to fall to 60 per cent in 1997 (Commission of the European Communities, 2000).[2] Finally, in the 1990s the average level of unemployment in the EU was 10 per cent, a full point above the already high level in the 1980s, two-and-a-half times the 4 per cent average in the 1970s and almost five times the 2.2 per cent average in the 1960s. Europe's employment deficit is sadly illustrated by the fact that, according to Eurostat data, between 1991 and 1999 not a single job, net of losses, has been created in the EU, though experiences are widely different across Member States (Commission of the European Communities, 1998c). In the 1990s the EU employment ratio slipped to 63 per cent in 1998, a full point below the level of 1980 and eleven percentage points below the USA, which increased its employment level from 66 to 74 per cent in the same period.[3]

At first, the setbacks of the 1980s were interpreted as a 'return to normality', correcting the 'excessive' trends in union power, militancy and wage growth during the 1970s (Baglioni and Crouch, 1990). But the data for the 1990s suggest deeper shifts, related to changes in the organisation of firms, work, class structure and power relations, affecting the social and economic basis for institutions like trade unions and sectoral collective agreements. In spite of persistent cross-national variation in levels of unionisation and strike activity (Ebbinghaus and Visser, 1999; Wallerstein *et al.*, 1997; Western, 1997), the aggregate trends in the EU and in most Member States indicate a receding tide in collective action of labour, if measured by its immediate results for workers (jobs, wages or social equality; on the latter see OECD, 1998), its expression (strike action) or resources (membership levels).

It is therefore paradoxical that, after rather inauspicious beginnings, the final years of the twentieth century have witnessed a remarkable vitality and strengthening of European-level union organisation within the institutional framework and multiple practices of social dialogue in the European Union. Europe's social partners – unions and employers – have gained a role as co-decision-makers in European social legislation, constraining the role of the Council of Ministers and in part displacing the European Parliament (Falkner, 1998). The establishment of Europe's Economic and Monetary Union in 1999 has furthermore encouraged a range of union initiatives to coordinate collective bargaining within and across national borders, complemented by a new macroeconomic dialogue between the

European Central Bank (ECB), the EU Ministers of Finance, the Commission, and European-level union and employers' organisations.

These developments have in many respects surpassed the expectations of observers in the scientific community and in the labour movement. The heterogeneity of union interests, the diversity of national traditions and institutions, employer opposition to European-level industrial relations, the shifting balance of power in favour of capital, union decline and decentralisation of labour relations within Member States, the regulatory conundrum of EU labour relations and the absence of a European state add up to an impressive list of obstacles against European union action and labour relations (Rhodes, 1995; Streeck and Schmitter, 1991; Visser and Ebbinghaus, 1992). The central aim of this chapter is, therefore, to explain why and how European-level union activity has become a reality after all – a task which we cannot accomplish without an analysis of the substance and meaning of the evolving European model of social dialogue and social partnership.

The formative years

The European Trade Union Confederation (ETUC) was founded in 1973, almost three decades after the end of the Second World War and 15 years after the start of the European Economic Community. Until the attenuation of the Cold War and the waning of America's ideological influence in the late 1960s, global or international union alliances based on religious and ideological cleavages had taken precedence over attempts to build regional union structures based on worker solidarity defined within a European identity. Moreover, without much need or space for a European social policy, there seemed little demand or basis for European Union activity.

During the 'Golden Age of Capitalism', lasting until the early 1970s, a 'rather miraculous mix of *pax Americana*, credit, capital and labour compromise, oligopolist competition, and structural and cyclical state intervention together created the Fordist growth regime' (Boyer, 1996, pp.44–5). Just as American supremacy relieved Western Europe from having to provide its own military solidarity, economic growth and (assumed) cross-national convergence in wealth and income conveniently took away the need to think or do a great deal about European social solidarity. EC social policy during this period was based on 'benign neglect' (Mosley, 1990). A similar characterisation applies to European (Community) trade union solidarity.

Until well into the 1970s, international trade union activity was foreign policy, a residual activity in national union offices, far removed from everyday practice, conducted by second-echelon union officials and staff with linguistic and diplomatic skills in far-way offices (see Tudyka *et al.*, 1978).

The first serious investment in a truly European trade union organisation coincides with a discordant phase in the European Community, when cross-national diversity in economic policy and performance increased in response to international financial instability and economic recession (Hodges and Wallace, 1981; Tsoukalis, 1992). Around 1973, European trade unions were at their maximum strength, measured on each of the indicators mentioned above. Social and regional policy had appeared on the European agenda during the negotiations over the first enlargement leading to the accession of Denmark, Ireland and the United Kingdom. In 1972 the Council set out the course for the adoption of the Commission's first Social Action Programme two years later. In 1974 the Regional Development Fund was put into action. These developments made it more important for unions to become effective in lobbying within the EC institutions, in addition to whatever unions were doing within their national states and home capitals.

The opening of the Bureau of the Social Partners in 1973, as a liaison office within the Commission, gave the unions an incentive to present themselves as a European agent for information exchange and gave the Commission an instrument to privilege European or transnational representation even though the rewards were small (Platzer, 1991, p.101). During the five 'tripartite conferences' with Labour, Economics and Finance Ministers, employers and the Commission, that took place between 1974 and 1978, representatives from ETUC and UNICE (the European peak association for employers) were invited alongside union and employer representatives from Member States. Though the talks ended in failure, the exercise worked as a 'catalyst' and 'much-welcomed integration push' for the unions, giving the ETUC media exposure and a bigger profile in Brussels (Platzer, 1991, p.61).

Another indicator of the growing importance of the European Community as policy arena was the gradual reform of the international sectoral union secretariats into European committees (Stöckl, 1986). In spite of the meagre results of the Commission's attempts to promote a European social dialogue in several sectors of the economy through the establishment of Joint Committees, many of the regional industry committees adopted a European identity and loosened their ties with the international movement. Reforms of this type happened among the metalworkers (1971), in agriculture (1971), PTT (Post, Telephone and Telegraph) (1973), printing (1973), building (1974), public services (1974), textile (1975) and food and catering (1975) (Ebbinghaus and Visser, 2000). In most cases these sectoral organisations were adopted or recognised by the ETUC, but without granting a membership status involving rights and obligations. The ETUC remained a weak confederation, a network of national trans-sectoral peak associations of trade unions.

Attempts to make the ETUC into a mere lobby organisation, pressure group or coordinating agency within the institutions of the European Community, with a corresponding geographical limitation of its membership, had successfully been resisted by Nordic and British unions during the negotiations leading to the ETUC's founding. As a consequence, the ETUC could develop into a truly regional organisation, representing workers from the North Cape to Asia Minor, from Ireland to Poland, with a membership base that has widened far beyond the confines of a European Union of 12, 15 or, in the near future, 21 Member States. In 1998 the ETUC represented 68 national confederations from 29 countries. Just over half, 36, came from the 15 current EU Member States. Together, these unions claim a membership of more than 50 million, which may rise to an estimated 60 million, from 33 countries, with the admission of more new members from Central and Eastern Europe agreed at the 1999 ETUC Congress in Helsinki. The ETUC has been consistently ahead of EU enlargement.

The ETUC has also been successful in expanding its membership beyond the boundaries of ideology, politics, religion, occupational status and the divide between public and private sector. The ETUC is the only international union association encompassing all ideological currents of unionism – the 'free' Socialist, Christian and previously Communist unions. Within the EU, and beyond, it is the European voice for labour, representing around 90 per cent of all union members in Europe (varying from around 84 per cent in Germany, Britain and Italy to 97 per cent or more in Sweden and Ireland) (Ebbinghaus and Visser, 2000). Of course, we cannot but note that two-thirds of Europe's wage and salary earners are not union members – although roughly half of them are covered by collective agreements negotiated by the unions (Traxler, 1996).

A union network without commitments or authority

According to Falkner (1998, pp.192–3), the birth of the ETUC was one of two turning-points in the formation of a European social policy community. Before 1974, she claims, 'EC social policy was scarce but even more so was the involvement of private interests therein. In an eclectic and purely non-binding manner, various – mostly national – interest groups were asked to give their opinion.' With the foundation of ETUC, alongside the European peak association of employers UNICE (1958), 'the core of a rather stable network was thus established', even though a 'multitude of specific lobbies' persisted and access to EC policy-making 'was not yet exclusive'.

That ETUC's foundation would be the beginning of a partnership was not quite obvious at the time, however much the Commission engaged itself in assisting the new organisation. The organisation was extremely weak, without the experience of joint European action, deprived of financial and staff resources, lacking authority over or commitment from its affiliates, with ill-defined and often contested relations between sectoral and trans-sectoral union activities and responsibilities, and utterly dependent upon its sponsors in the Commission and in DG V, the Social Affairs Directorate (Goetschy, 1996; Dølvik, 1999, p.67). ETUC became a reality nevertheless, with meetings and conferences, papers and statements, mostly put together by the European Trade Union Institute, which had been founded in 1978 with financial support from the Commission. In short, ETUC became an arena for the Europeanisation of national unions, for national unions and their officials to find out what Europe was all about and what it could do for them. In the 1970s and 1980s it was never an actor, least of all unified, capable of decisions that could influence or condition the policy choices of affiliates, the course of social and economic policy within the Community, or employer behaviour in Europe to any significant degree.

While 1973 may have been a turning-point in European social policy, it was a watershed in post-war European economic history (Hobsbawm, 1994; Van der Wee, 1986). With the hardening of the crisis that followed the collapse of Bretton-Woods and the oil price hike, the optimistic liberal convergence view made place for Europessimism. The failure of the first plans for monetary union added to the malaise and there was a notable reversion to protectionism combined with social resistance to economic adjustment in declining sectors. The 'economic relevance of the European Community was considerably reduced as a consequence' and it was a major achievement that 'the incomplete customs union of the 1960s did not come crashing down' (Tsoukalis, 1992, p.41).

The first attempt at cross-sectoral social dialogue in Europe, modelled after the *Konzertierte Aktion* (Concerted Action) in Germany (1974–6), had been the result of union pressure, especially from Germany (Kohler-Koch and Platzer, 1986). It ended in failure when the unions, frustrated by the fact that talks were just talks and had no noticeable effect on policies in Brussels or at home, refused to attend another conference in 1978. Unions and employers, in Brussels and in most Member States, were deeply distrustful and held diametrically opposed views on economic and employment policy. This first exercise in cross-sectoral social dialogue collapsed when its main sponsor, the German union movement, withdrew its support after the last meeting had ended with an intra-German fight between DGB (Deutscher Gewerkschaftsbund) and ETUC chairman Vetter and the conference chair, Economics Minister Lambsdorf. ETUC explained that, in the fight against unemployment, 'action is certainly required on the European level and Tripartite Conferences should play an important role in reaching a broad consensus on the measures which have to be taken. But it is completely unacceptable for governments to use these conferences just as listening posts. . . .'[4] ETUC did not reject concertation and its critique was addressed to the governments rather than to the employers. Clearly, the ETUC feared that its own lack of unity on the issue of working time reduction might be used against them in the national arena.[5]

In the late 1970s, experiences with concertation and social dialogue within Member States did exist, but they were hardly inspiring. The German unions had ended their talks with the employers and a Social Democratic government in a dispute over new legislation on co-determination (Streeck, 1984). The 'Social Contract' between the Labour government and the unions had collapsed in Britain and by 1978 Italian energies towards political bargaining within the framework of Communist support for a government of national unity had been spent (Regini, 1984). At this time, corporatism, or tripartism, went through a difficult phase, with miserable economic results, in Belgium and the Netherlands (Visser and Hemerijck, 1997; Van Ruysseveldt and Visser, 1996). There was little from which proponents of social dialogue in the EC could have taken inspiration. Positive experiences, which might have been drawn from social partnership in Austria or from the Swedish Model, itself in transition, were far removed from the European centre. Hence, the process of mimicking, and horizontal policy learning across countries through peer pressure and benchmarking, which would play such a big role in European social and employment policies in the 1990s (Visser, 1999), was absent.

In the decade after 1973, there was little of tangible interest in European social policy that mattered to the unions or their members. Arguably, Vredeling had been the most important project for them, but that was dead by 1983. In the early 1970s, unions from both sides of the Atlantic, with the help of their international trade secretariats, had tried hard to bargain with multinational companies through world company committees. These attempts had ended in failure and European unions came thus 'to regard EC legislation on worker participation as welcome and, indeed, indispensable assistance for their international organising activities, in that it promised to force multinational companies to enter into at least some kind of industrial relations at the European level' (Streeck and Vitols, 1995, p.244). The limited competencies and unanimity requirement of the articles (100 and 235 of the Treaty), empowering the Council to adopt measures to implement the Common Market, ruled out progress. Only three modest directives were adopted, dealing with information rights of workers in case of collective redundancies, transfer of ownership, and bankruptcy. In addition, after a decade of insignificance, Article 119 of the Treaty became the basis for a series of incisive rulings by the European Court of Justice and initiatives by the Commission in favour of equal opportunities for men and women. However, with the change of government in Britain in 1979, it became impossible to get any social policy proposal approved in the Council (Teague, 1989b). Later, under the provisions of the Single European Act (SEA 1986, Article 118A), the basis for minimum social policy legislation was widened and qualified majority voting became possible on issues concerning health and safety. The Commission tried a 'treaty base' game and moved issues related to working conditions under qualified majority voting, but this never got very far (Rhodes, 1995).

Creating a social partner

The Single European Act (1986) had broken the stalemate of Eurosclerosis through a forward leap in economic integration. By

1990, judging by most indicators, the European economy was in much better shape than ten years before. There was even considerable job growth, but most European economies were now saddled with high levels of unemployment that proved all but transitory. The growth revival went hand in hand with the unfolding of the capitalist market system and the success of trade liberalisation, culminating in the GATT and WTO agreements, the completion of the European Internal Market in 1992, the shift to an anti-inflationary monetary regime under ERM and the establishment of EMU in 1999 – all of which had the effect of intensifying competition among European producers in product, investment and labour markets. The changes of 1989 brought the industrialised countries in Central and Eastern Europe back into the capitalist world, creating new market outlets and nearer locations for low cost competition.

Unions supported the 'market making' process with a 'yes, but' strategy, because they believed that economic integration would lead to political integration – a goal that they had supported from the very beginning – and because they were convinced or seduced by Delors' promises of a social dimension (Busch, 1996; Martin and Ross, 1999). In February 1988, preparing its 6th Stockholm Conference, the ETUC executive committee published its first-ever 'European social programme'. This programme endorsed the single market project, but called for a stronger social dimension through EC legislation, supplemented by European collective agreements with employers through the social dialogue.

Delors and the Commission worked hard to keep the unions on board. In his addresses to the Stockholm Conference and to the TUC Annual Conference later in the year, he tried to raise union interest in the European project. He defined social partnership as an essential ingredient of the social dimension – together with social and economic cohesion, and European minimum standards, foremost in the area of health and safety (Ross, 1995a, p.43). In January 1985, one of his first acts as Commission President had been to convene a so-called Val Duchesse discussion among the social partners, having assured himself of employer support beforehand. On a small and rather informal or secretive basis such talks had taken place in 1984, chaired by the French Socialist Prime Minister Beregovoy. In a similar fashion Delors used his personal prestige to get everybody to the table. Another lesson learnt from the 1970s failure was that the sessions were well prepared and that the press was kept outside. Hence, an atmosphere of informal bargaining, with various working groups and some permanence, was created. It was hoped that, once under way, concertation would generate its own momentum, for instance by adding more layers and occasions for joint talks (Grote, 1987, p.249). This is the kind of 'corporatist dynamic' that was described by Schmitter on the occasion of an OECD conference on 'Social Dialogue and Consensus' in Paris two years earlier: a process through which 'actors become better informed about each other's intentions, more respectful of each other's capabilities and willing to trust each other's commitment' (Schmitter, 1983). This process does not presuppose consensus or necessarily lead to consensus on policy objectives or solutions. It does, however, help to 'build up' a policy community in which actors recognise common norms of behaviour and each other.

A new provision, Article 118b, was inserted into the SEA, stating that 'the Commission shall endeavour to develop the dialogue between management and labour at the European level which could, if the two sides consider it desirable, lead to relations based on agreement'. Meetings did take place and produced some 'joint opinions' on economic policy and training in 1986, but the dialogue process was soon in trouble again. One reason was the near stalemate in European social policy-making; the other was the refusal of employers, always assured of a blocking vote in the Council, to go beyond the phase of mere talks. For the unions, the Val Duchesse dialogue had seemed to open the road to European collective bargaining that they had tried ten to fifteen years earlier in the multinational companies and in sectoral dialogue, but had found so thoroughly blocked. ETUC and DGB chairman Breit, whose statement during the first social dialogue session of 1989 is quoted by Platzer (1991, pp.172–3), defended the 'fuite en avant' approach with which the ETUC leadership approached the social dialogue.

We need clarity about the social dialogue, what it is, what it can do, and what it should do. One often assumes that the trade unions aspire to change the 'social dialogue' into an instrument that enables European collective bargaining. . . . We know for sure, that the legal, organisational and political conditions for the negotiation of European collective agreements are absent. The same is true for the 'social dialogue'. But that does not mean that European collective bargaining and European collective agreements must be excluded for ever. In contrast, this remains the objective of the unions. . . . The ETUC is prepared, in the context of the social dialogue, to take on obligations and negotiate agreements which are less than collective agreements but more than non-obligatory exchanges of opinion. We will not make progress with social relations in the Community if UNICE and ETUC retreat on the basis of a restrictive interpretation of their mandates. The constitution of the ETUC gives us the legitimacy and the mandate to reach obligatory framework agreements with the employers, provided that the required partners are available. These framework agreements can become the basis for directives and legislative proposals of the Commission in matters of social policy. . . . A European social dialogue without the dialogue at the national, regional and not least the sectoral level would easily, though not necessarily, remain a purely abstract exercise without practical use. . . . We should try to make the forms of social dialogue more effective.

Hence, the ETUC was bound to be disappointed by UNICE's refusal, and so was the Commission. For Delors, the dialogue process was first of all a 'confidence-building' exercise, very much in the sense of Schmitter's characterisation of 1983, generating mutual trust and joint norms of conduct. Social dialogue, partnership, co-responsibility and decentralisation, not to Member States but to transnational organisations, were very much in accordance with his personal views and philosophy, as was his belief in a European Social Model based on the genuine participation of, and bargaining between, unions and employers, quite different from the etatist traditions in his native France (see Delors, 2000). Through the dialogue process, the actors might become 'agents with the power to deal', even though 'there was a considerable distance to travel here, since neither the ETUC nor UNICE, essentially Brussels lobbies, was empowered to negotiate' (Ross, 1995a, p.45).

Delors succeeded in politicising the issue of social policy stalemate in the Council and raised expectations concerning the outcome of the 1990–1 Intergovernmental Conference (Falkner, 1998, p.73). Under pressure from a 'pro-harmonisation coalition' (Falkner, 1998, p.65) of trade unions with the Socialist-Christian majority in the European Parliament, eleven Member States, without the UK, signed a 'Social Charter' of fundamental social rights. The Charter was non-obligatory and added little to what most countries had already signed up to under international law. However, it made the European Social Model a generally accepted reference point in debates and helped to shape the second Social Action Programme (1989).

After more prodding by the Commission, the social dialogue was re-started in 1989. A steering group of top-level representatives from ETUC, UNICE and CEEP was regularly convened by the Director-General of DG V. In addition to talks about training and the evolution of the EC labour market, this group was regularly consulted on upcoming EC social policy legislation. In late 1990, ETUC and CEEP signed a largely symbolic 'European Framework Agreement' on training and development in the rail transport and energy sector. Preparing the IGC of Maastricht, the Commission had at an early stage invited the social partners to discuss the role they wished to be given in the new Treaty. Under pressure of the 'negotiate or we'll legislate' position of the Commission, UNICE signalled at the April 1991 social dialogue meeting for the first time that they might be prepared to jump, accepting negotiations as the lesser evil compared to legislation, even though it meant conceding something which they never wanted. This led to the agreement of 31 October 1991, which was almost literally copied into the Maastricht Social Agreement (MSA), setting the rules for social policy-making in the future, and allowing the UK to opt out. Under the MSA rules the social partners must be consulted in case of new Community legislation and can signal that they wish to start negotiations and conclude an agreement, which pre-empts or becomes the basis for Community legislation or implementation through customary procedures negotiated by the social partners. Until the last moment, UNICE's signing had been uncertain. Its general secretary explains that:

> in the end, what prevailed was the pragmatic conclusion that the new IGC would almost certainly extend the scope of qualified majority voting in social affairs, that the Commission had already demonstrated, with its 1989 Action Programme, that it had an insatiable appetite for legislation often of questionable quality, and that the Council would now be in a position to pass it. If employers were unhappy about this, they had only one remedy; to secure the option to step in and negotiate as reasonable a deal as they could with ETUC.
>
> (Tyszkiewicz, 1999, pp.44–5)

UNICE president Ferrer defended the agreement as a means of obtaining more flexible regulation, respecting differences in national traditions (cited in Falkner, 1993, p.90).

UNICE's general secretary added that 'without the learning period provided by the "joint opinion" phase this outcome might not have been reached' (ibid.). This accords with the union view that a small group of negotiators who knew each other well 'had worked together for months, circumvented possible veto points and produced a social fact that was to set the premises for further developments' (Dølvik, 1997, p.179). In 1985 private employers had promised Delors to participate in the social dialogue process as the small price to be paid for Commission support for their main project of market liberalisation. It must have been their best bet to keep union protest muted. ETUC had embraced the social dialogue as a step on the way to European collective bargaining *and* legislation as the two means to prevent being 'whipsawed' by employers in a game of 'regime competition' or 'social dumping'. Given their weakness in national labour markets and polities in most countries and the fickle shows of international solidarity, unions had no credible 'exit' option. Hence, they chose to stay 'loyal' to a dialogue process even when it gave them a much smaller 'voice' than hoped. Their belief about what would be best for the defence of the economic and social interests of workers in an era of international trade liberalisation and union weakening was mixed with reasons of institutional self-interest:

> The ETUC was a weak organisation that depended more on the Commission for support than on its national union constituents. Bargaining results in Brussels could make the ETUC vastly more important, and generate more constituent support . . . ETUC understood that the Commission's original approach could well provide the incentives for real bargaining which the employers had always denied.
>
> (Ross, 1995a, p.151)

Union leaders went with Delors even when he could not deliver on promises of EU social policy, because they 'were aware that they were unlikely to get a better deal or a more sympathetic leadership than from him' (Ross, 1995a, p.38).

The ETUC saw the agreement of 1991 as a major breakthrough. According to its new general secretary, the social dialogue and the agreement 'responded to a core demand of the ETUC . . ., to further the social dimension by means of legislation and collective agreements' (Gabaglio, 1992, p.14). Unlike his UNICE counterpart, he was careful to avoid an 'either legislation or bargaining' position. Under pressure of internal critics, he stated roundly that European collective bargaining should be complementary to minimum rules fixed by law and national bargaining.

From arena to actor

Falkner (1998, p.192) considers the agreement of October 1991 on the future of social partner participation in EC social policy-making as the *second turning-point* in the formation of the European social policy community. The agreement made social partnership into a political fact – not least because it was resented by the European Parliament. It squarely put the social partners on the map of the EU institutions. From this point on, the ETUC turned from a privileged participant into a *de facto*, if not *de jure*, monopolist with co-decision powers, which could pre-empt, or narrow, the powers and options of the Council of Ministers, the Commission and the European Parliament, if only it succeeded in striking a deal with employers. This is, as Falkner rightly claims, neo-corporatist concertation pure and simple, i.e. 'a mode of policy formation in which formally designated interest associations are incorporated within the process of authoritative decision making and implementation' (Schmitter, 1981, p.295). Whatever the difficulty in implementing such an approach, the logic of influence that it implied was bound to change the ETUC from a network into a proper organisation.

As a result of preparations begun in 1990, and in anticipation of the expected centralisation of European economic and social policies, the Brussels Conference of May 1991 had voted in favour of reforms which aimed at turning the ETUC from an (intergovernmental) arena into a (supranational) actor. Through the intended streamlining of its decision-making procedures, extending qualified majority voting, allocating more resources and staff to the centre, and integrating the sectoral European unions (Dølvik, 1997), the ETUC responded to the 'logic of influence', establishing itself not just as the 'voice of labour' but as the authoritative voice, capable of entering into agreements with third parties and making binding commitments on behalf of its member organisations. However, ETUC's 'logic of membership', based on the conundrum of deep-seated national traditions and persistent cross-national diversity, prevented bold moves or easy implementation (Ebbinghaus and Visser, 1997). Thus, the decisions of 1991 would be contested after Maastricht and became a matter of dispute between the Brussels centre and several member associations, giving rise to shifting coalitions of national member organisations and rivalry between the trans-sectoral and sectoral affiliates.

The 1991 reforms had become possible when the calls for a stronger 'federal' or 'supranational' centre, traditionally backed by unions from the three Benelux countries, the three Italian federations and the French CFDT (*Confédération française démocratique du travail*), gained support from the German DGB. The *volte face* of the British TUC, after its 1988 Conference, from an anti- to pro-European player, weakened the forces that would greet the federal approach with scepticism. In 1991, with a new and more professional leadership installed in the ETUC Secretariat, a constellation more conducive to change was created. With the support of the Commission, privileged access to the EU institutions and a new role under the Maastricht Social Agreement (MSA), the new 'supranational' Secretariat had gained a strategic position as 'gatekeeper' and 'co-legislator' in the EU social policy community. This could only enhance its internal authority and pave the way for further organisational reform, left unspecified during the 1991 Congress (for instance, the matter of a mandate to ETUC officials for the purpose of bargaining). However, the Secretariat had to rely on an unstable coalition of forces. The backing of the DGB had been crucial in the 1991 reforms, but at home the DGB was under increased pressure from its affiliates to retract its steps. Thus the Secretariat's attempts to proceed with further 'supranationalisation' failed when the DGB yielded to affiliate pressure and gained support from the traditionally Euro-sceptical coalition of Nordic trade unions.

Heralded as a watershed in social policy-making, the MSA had given rise to doubts among the representatives of the Nordic and German unions, and from the European Industry Federations (EIFs). Their scepticism had been fuelled by concerns over the British 'opt-out', which, in principle, meant that 'regime competition' on social policies and labour law was now institutionalised in the heart of Europe. The show of popular discontent against the decisions of Maastricht during the Danish and French referendums in 1992, and UNICE's widely publicised opinion that it had only signed the October agreement as a means to dilute EC social policy regulation, did not help the cause of supranationalists in the ETUC. A renewed struggle over the further path of trade union Europeanisation ensued.

At stake was the issue of social partnership itself – the involvement of ETUC in social policy-making, the role of law and collective bargaining, the relationship between trans-sectoral and sectoral dialogue, and between peak associations and their affiliates, combined with anxieties over the encroachment on national sovereignty and traditions by ill-conceived European regulation (Dølvik, 2000). While several Continental affiliates wanted to strengthen the supranational authority of ETUC, the key German actors were opposed to a strong confederal centre at the European level (as they were at home). The Nordic unions did traditionally accept confederal leadership, within the national domain. They were deeply suspicious of any supranationalisation in Europe and wanted an overhaul of the ETUC statutes. After a compromise was brokered in 1993 – delimiting the leeway for the ETUC Secretariat by requiring an explicit case-by-case mandate for the pursuit of European negotiations while confirming the primacy of national collective bargaining and the objective of transnational coordination at the sectoral level – a multi-tiered pattern of union integration under strict control of the constituent national unions (peak associations and affiliates) seemed to be evolving.

Although considered as a setback by some unions with federalist leanings, this conflict had raised the stakes and led to a stronger involvement of affiliates in European issues and in the ETUC. Thus, the Nordic unions, which had come close to rejecting the agreement of 1991, could not avoid being drawn into active participation, not least because qualified majority voting within the ETUC and the possibility of European framework agreements made a position on the sideline a potentially risky strategy. Hence, they became very active in establishing a proper 'bargaining order' within the ETUC and, once drawn in, became supporters of negotiated European legislation (Dølvik, 1997). European collective bargaining, a ritual term during much of the 1980s, was again on the agenda – the issue now became how and under what conditions this could be achieved in a way that would be compatible with national legacies. By pulling reluctant affiliates and broader national union circles into this discourse, a learning process evolved which brought increased coherence, seriousness and realism into the process of trade union integration.

From dialogue to bargaining

A watered-down proposal on information and consultation rights in multinational firms – a heritage of the ill-fated Vredeling draft – became the first test for the European social partners. They failed to reach agreement, blaming each other. None of the parties wanted to be seen as wrecking the social dialogue or reneging on their promises implicit in the agreement of 31 October. According to Falkner this is in itself a significant fact, showing the 'normative validity' of the social policy model that they had staked out in 1991 (Falkner, 1998, p.106). Without Britain, and with Portugal's abstention, the Council adopted the European Works Council (EWC) directive in 1994. The directive applies to some 1200 cross-border operating large companies, which were given until 1999 to negotiate their own arrangements with worker representatives, or else accept minimum standards. A little over 600 companies did negotiate a 'voluntary' agreement. The information and consultation rights in these agreements are quite limited and in no way comparable with the consultation and co-determination rights in domestic firms in Member States outside Britain, Ireland and Portugal. Where (mandated) workplace representation under national legislation exists, the EWC serves as a form of deterritorialisation of representation, extending some provisions to representatives from locations in other countries while retaining the dominance of national structures (Streeck, 1997). It offers many opportunities for information exchange at grassroots levels and has revitalised expectations within sectoral federations that one day soon they will enter into European collective agreements, at company or sectoral level.

The next attempt by the social partners was successful because both sides, and the Commission behind them, wished to prove that they were capable of playing the role they had claimed under the MSA (Falkner, 1998, p.117). With the 1996–7 IGC approaching and with the threat of a sceptical, if not hostile Parliament, the social partners feared that another failure might mean the end of their co-legislation powers. The Commission gave more leeway to negotiators than in the case of EWC negotiations. This and the fact that the British employers' federation held only an observer status, without veto rights, in these negotiations, facilitated a positive outcome (Falkner, 1998, p.128). In December 1995 a framework agreement on parental leave was reached, intended 'to promote the reconciliation between professional and personal life'. In substantive terms it was a bleak agreement. Apart from establishing the individual right to three months' leave for family reasons, which was a notable improvement in countries like the UK, Portugal, Greece and Ireland, it left nearly everything to national regulation. For ETUC general secretary, Gabaglio, it was 'a point of departure', another hurdle taken on the road to European collective agreements. 'By and large, the importance of the Parental Leave Agreement is therefore in its existence rather than in its contents' (Falkner, 1998, p.122).

In June 1997, just before the Amsterdam IGC, the social partners reached a framework agreement on part-time employment. The contents are again very modest and the reactions among ETUC affiliates are mixed. For the ETUC's Women's Committee, the DGB, one of the French confederations, and some Industry Federations, this was reason enough to reject the deal, while for example the British, with no such rights, were quite enthusiastic, and the Nordic unions saw some useful potential in the deal. That the majority went ahead proves that the negotiating team of ETUC has a mandate and that decisions in the ETUC are possible even if its largest and most powerful affiliate is opposed. From ETUC's point of view, the principal benefit of the agreement lies, again, in the confirmation of the social dialogue just prior to the IGC. It consolidated the contractual model and was another proof that the 'quasi-corporatist procedures' of MSA can work (Falkner, 1998, p.142). As a result of the learning process within the ETUC, this agreement left room for additional European bargaining at the sectoral level as well as additional bargaining for the national social partners.

In March 1999 the ETUC, after notable concessions, reached agreement with UNICE and CEEP on fixed-term contracts, to be followed up by negotiations on the rights of employees working for temporary work agencies. Mainly establishing the principle of non-discrimination against employees on fixed-term contracts, the agreement (subsequently made into a directive) calls on the Member States to prevent abuse by defining objective reasons for use of such contracts, maximum limits on the number of renewals, and a maximum total duration of successive contracts (EIRO, 1999). The agreement improves social protection for fixed-term employees in some countries and was approved by a clear majority of ETUC affiliates. Its meagre content created no great enthusiasm, however, and the misgivings of the DGB were shared by many ETUC affiliates. It was therefore agreed that the ETUC should evaluate the experience with social partner negotiations, the conditions under which such negotiations are to be preferred to legislation, and how they can be improved. This is a signal that the ETUC is no longer willing to negotiate at any price. Since the legacy and institutions of social dialogue are now considered well established, ETUC affiliates are turning their attention more to the content than to the form of EU social regulation, and seem to be taking a more instrumental approach to the choice between negotiations and legislation.

Due to blockage by a minority of UNICE affiliates, it proved impossible to negotiate the other half of the Vredeling draft directive and agree on minimum rules on consultation and information for workers in domestic firms. The new UK Labour government's decision to join the 'Social Chapter' of the Amsterdam Treaty has added extra votes in the Council against such legislation. Still, under the Maastricht rules, without the UK, the Council did endorse a directive on 'posted workers', laying down the rule that workers contracted to work abroad should be entitled to wages and benefits, and pay social contributions, under the laws and contracts of the host country. This further example of deterritorialisation can be seen as a successful attempt, especially by Germany, to defend the integrity of national standards and regulations, while allowing diversity across Member States to persist.

ETUC approaches to social partnership

As an umbrella coalition of national confederations and European Industry Federations, the ETUC cannot be treated as a unitary actor with straightforwardly defined views on European social partnership. Fuzzy concepts like social dialogue and social partnership have in important European countries been unknown phenomena until they started filtering down from the European level. They were contested concepts, causing confusion and alienation in ETUC member associations. For example, unionists in the UK, used to an adversarial, voluntarist tradition of independent collective bargaining, a weak peak association, and no legacy of social concertation, continued to have great difficulty understanding what consensual social dialogue was actually about. In another key country, Germany, *Socialpartnerschaft* is a familiar concept, but the notion of tripartite negotiations on labour standards 'in the shadow of the law' was met with suspicion by key industry unions, among them the powerful IG Metall. To them it seemed to conflict with the constitutional principle of *Tarifautonomie* or bargaining free of state sponsorship or interference. For many, social partnership smacked of an *etatist* variant of corporatism. In the Nordic countries, many unionists found it difficult to draw a distinction between negotiated legislation within social dialogue institutions, plain collective bargaining and the domestic forms of incomes political exchange they were used to. In some Southern countries it sometimes brought back ambiguous memories of the corporatist past. In short, social partnership and social concertation always meant different things to different people, and never went uncontested. The appreciation of and responses to the European social dialogue by national unions is doubly conditioned, by its effects on social and economic interests of workers, employment and the location of firms, and by its impact on domestic institutions, including the integrity of national bargaining systems, trade unions, labour law and social security. In other words, the evolving ETUC approaches to social partnership must always strike a balance between common European institutional (self-)interests and diverse domestic institutional (self-)interests.

The particular mode of negotiated legislation enshrined in the social partner agreement of 31 October 1991 and the MSA took its inspiration from the Belgian model of social regulation.[6] This model is unique in Europe. There are examples of 'negotiated legislation' in other countries, for instance in the Netherlands (the recent overhaul of dismissal law, based on the Flexibility and Security agreement in the Foundation of Labour), in Spain (labour market flexibility), Italy (in the 1970s and 1990s), as well as failed attempts in France and Italy (working hours, in recent years). But the model chosen in 1991 was rare and mostly unknown to the majority of trade unions.

Consequently, a long drawn-out process of inter-union debate, struggle, mutual learning and compromise, which cannot be considered as finally settled, followed. Strategy debates in trade unions are nearly always couched in terms of the historically contested relationship between class struggle and cooperation, between conflict and partnership, and between collective bargaining and legislation as the two main methods of advancing workers' interests (direct action, as the third method, having already been buried in the archives). And so they do in the European union movement.

The variety of definitions and views of social partnership in the European union movement reflects not just differences in political appreciation and ideological position common to all or most trade union movements. They also mirror the stubborn diversity of national industrial relations systems. The construction of a European-wide system of labour market regulation has different implications for national unions and union practices. Possibly accentuated by development of sector-based European coordination of collective bargaining, the form of European regulations, and their transposition in national jurisdictions, is a delicate issue as it may upset domestic power balances and practices of mandating, prerogatives of negotiation, division of competencies between national centres and affiliate unions, or long-established methods of membership control. Or there may be a question of mandating in the first place, as was the case in the TUC and the DGB. Touching on sensitive matters of institutional union interests at the national level, these problems may have been resolved or 'papered over' for the time being, but they remain contentious in countries like Denmark, Germany and the UK, and will be in the Netherlands as a consequence of the formation of mega-unions with the potential and incentive to replace the confederation (Streeck and Visser, 1998).

An additional problem is that the two legs on which the ETUC tries to walk are sometimes out of step. The national confederations have always been the principal leg on which the ETUC stands. This reflects the formation process of the organisation and the traditional weight of intergovernmental practices, and hence of national lobbying or regulation, in the European Community. But since the reforms of 1991, the ETUC has officially incorporated, and assigned (near) equal status to, the European Industry Federations, the European networks of sectoral unions. Their weaker role, not least if measured by the meagre resources on which they try to get by, reflects the weakness of the sectoral dialogue from its beginnings in the 1960s, the absence of a partner to play with on the employers' side in most sectors, especially in manufacturing, and the stalemate in European-level collective bargaining. Thus, the European trade union (and employer) structures have paradoxically been weakest at the sectoral level where national unions are strongest, and they are strongest at the peak level where national unionism has been most weakened. Yet, negotiating the structures for information and consultation in major multinational firms in the context of the European Works Council directive of 1994, assisted by welcome financial aid from the Commission and Parliament, has lifted the profile of the European Industry Federations. The increased interdependencies between policies and national wage setting practices under EMU have given impetus to more realistic initiatives at transnational wage coordination within unions. Several EIFs, and some national sector unions behind them, question the potential of the political mode of trans-sectoral social dialogue promoted by the ETUC Secretariat and the national confederations. They advocate a 'bottom-up' approach anchored in the works council structures in the European MNCs and a sectoral dialogue combined with transnational wage coordination. They believe that this will bring more grassroots support, clout and control to the process, and more resources and power to them. Although views differ on whether these paths are alternative or complementary – most unionists profess to support the second interpretation – the distinction points to an important source of ambivalence prevailing in influential union circles as regards the particular mode of social partnership evolving at the EU level (reflected at the national level in union debates over whether to engage in social pacts).

The seductive appeal of the social partnership rhetoric has been instrumental in bolstering legitimacy and support around union claims for recognition and influence in the EU polity, but there has always been concern among the affiliates that the ETUC representatives might become co-opted by the EU institutions and risk prejudicing union autonomy. Some scholars have argued that autonomy has been lost and that the price paid by the unions may have been too high (Martin and Ross, 1999). In their view, the European form of social partnership has induced a flawed pattern of trade union Europeanisation, concentrating too much on the peak ETUC level and the Euro-company level, while committing unions to dubious European ideas and a particular economic approach to political integration 'pursued despite its social costs and rising popular disenchantment'.

> ETUC insiders, committed but critical 'Europeans' to begin with, must have understood in the later 1980s that accepting the resources by the Commission was one way to generate the prominence and strength which they needed to promote their urgent messages about the importance of transnational organization and action. They could then rely for additional support for their goals on the more 'European' contacts in different national movements. In return for these resources, however, the ETUC was drawn into a coalition to advance the initiatives of those supplying them, particularly the Delors Commissions.
>
> (Martin and Ross, 1999, pp.355–6)

According to these scholars, the deal turned sour, however, when 'the Commission was unable to produce anywhere near as much as it had promised'. In their view, the European trade union movement was doubly wrong-footed. First, because it had read its institutional self-interest wrongly, because it had restructured itself along lines 'that were only partly its doing and not always clearly to its advantage'. Second, because the ETUC had become dependent on a coalition which left it no other option than supporting, albeit critically, the EMU, which, in its present design, so Martin and Ross assert, is 'arguably inimical to the interests of European workers and unions'.

In view of what has been achieved, however, this interpretation seems overly critical, hedged on a too static view of the EMU project and a simplification of union strategy formation (see Dølvik, 1997, pp.467–72). In view of the soft stance of the ECB on the Euro, the recent upturn in growth and employment in all but a few countries (mainly Germany and Italy), the extension of the social dialogue process to economic and employment policy since the 1999 Cologne summit, and the vitalisation of union cooperation at the sectoral level, the ETUC approach has clearly brought some leverage. Because of these developments, internal criticism of the policy choice in favour of the Single Market and EMU, embedded in the overall social partnership approach, has been muted, and scepticism has become less pronounced with the passing of time. Besides the British TUC, even Danish and Swedish affiliates now consider supporting EMU membership, hardly, we believe, because they have been 'seduced' by the modest outcome of the social dialogue. The current discussion in the ETUC concentrates not on the question of whether or not to invest in the social dialogue, but rather on the question of how union participation in the various layers of EU social and macroeconomic dialogue can be given a stronger underpinning and more clout by developing ways of mobilising and by establishing closer links between the activities of national (sectoral) unions and their representatives at the European level. This debate is increasingly focused on developing a European system of industrial relations where social dialogue is complemented by Europeanisation of collective bargaining, a deterritorialisation of the right to strike, and integration of concertation on economic and employment policies (ETUC, 1999b).

Contrary to the pessimistic scenarios, we have reason to speculate that the leap into the Economic and Monetary Union will become a third turning-point in the evolution of an EU social policy community, now concentrating more strongly on employment, wage setting and labour market governance. Its qualitative change is a shift in focus, on the union side and in the Commission (DG II and V), from legal minimum standards towards coordination of national collective bargaining at the sectoral level, which, if it succeeds, might in turn become a fresh input and give more body to ETUC's participation in cross-sectoral social dialogue and macro-economic concertation (with the Finance Ministers and the ECB). By creating closer ties between union participants in peak level social dialogue, national unions and the EIFs, the unions' role in the shallow structures of EU social partnership might become more solidly embedded in a multi-tiered European pattern of trade unionism, bearing greater resemblance to national antecedents of industrial relations and encompassing both the national and EU levels. To what extent the trade unions will prove capable of transforming the hitherto rather toothless European mode of social partnership in this direction remains to be seen, but the Europeanisation of monetary, employment and wage policies currently under way in both EMU and non-EMU countries is likely to change and revitalise the European social dialogue, just as it has done at the national level where social partnership and social pacts have been rediscovered as assets in bolstering the national capacities for policy response to uncertainty, change and competition (Hassel, 1999; Pochet, 1998; Visser, 1999).

With these qualifications in mind we should leave no doubt that the ETUC has been and is a persistent advocate of social partnership at the Community level. For the majority of European trade unions it seems that social partnership has become a positive catchword synonymous with the defence and renewal of the European social model (see Table 1.1). Carrying considerable symbolic value, social partnership is a concept that is hardly distinct from words like 'social dimension', social Europe, social dialogue, espace social, Sozialunion, social cohesion, social responsibility, social solidarity, and information and consultation. In this broad and vague sense the call for social partnership has almost become an ETUC trademark. Based on a fuzzy blend of values and ethics, belief in Europe's social model, methods of how to best solve conflicts and notions of legitimate governance, the social partnership idea has been instrumental in promoting social policy and union involvement in the European project in difficult times, when the world was mostly moved by the rhetoric

Table 1.1 ETUC Definitions of Social Partnership

Term	Meaning
National social partnership	Mode of societal governance in which social, employment and economic policies in particular are shaped through consultation, bargaining, conflict and compromise between labour, capital and the state.
European social partnership	In practice a looser, vaguer mode of consultation on EU policies than at national level, and consensual co-decision on a limited set of EU framework social policy regulations; in principle ETUC wants to extend consultation to issues covered by national precedents.
National social partner	Employer and trade union organisations that are mandated to sign nation-wide collective agreements and publicly recognised as participants in political exchange with the national government.
European social partner	Mutually recognised European-level employer and trade union organisations whose members have the power to negotiate at the national level and/or have been part of the Val Duchesse social dialogue.
Subsidiarity	Pragmatic principle indicating that (1) European action is justified mainly on issues with a genuine transnational character and/or where such action can create a clear 'value-added'; (2) negotiated solutions are to be preferred to statutory labour market regulation. Should not be misused as a pretext for halting integration in the name of protecting national sovereignty.
Representativity	Members of participants in EU social dialogue must be recognised, representative bargaining agents in most Member States. The social actors decide themselves whom they recognise as representative counterparts.

and realities of money, markets, individualism and neoliberalism. Albeit alien to many unions, and contested, the concept of social partnership was sufficiently vague to become accepted in an 'ecumenical' union movement such as the ETUC. Because of its vagueness, there was hardly a danger that one current, or some coalition of national unions against others, would instrumentalise it. Moreover, by presenting themselves as the 'enthusiastic' social partner, the unions could expose the stubborn unwillingness of employers and gain an easy advantage in public opinion.

The vagueness of the social partnership concept, the multiplicity of actors and the variety of contexts in which it is used in ETUC circles precludes any unequivocal definition of its meaning. If we restrict ourselves to official ETUC language, as comes across in the policy documents and declarations of the 1999 Congress, the term is actually not that much used. The key phrase is *social dialogue*, which is seen as the main method of promoting, adapting, reforming and modernising, through negotiations, 'the basic values and institutions of the European social model . . . on the basis of balance between economic efficiency, competitiveness and the rights of working people' (ETUC, 1999a, p.5). Faced with the challenges of unemployment, cohesion, EMU and enlargement, the ETUC wants relevant parties – the public authorities and the social partners – to be involved and mobilised. The need for pacts, partnerships and consultation is frequently invoked to underpin these union demands. It should further be noted that, in contrast to employers' associations, which want no more power for Brussels than needed for a common market, the ETUC approach to social partnership is embedded in a comprehensive notion of European polity-building, associated with demands for Political and Social Union, and European economic governance. Although union views on such issues may vary considerably if one travels from one country or one affiliate to the next, the ETUC understanding of social partnership is not confined to being a way of adopting certain minimum standards in the labour market but is part of a vision of European state-building in which unions have a central societal role to play as promoters of human rights, democracy and social justice. Against this backdrop, Table 1.2 tentatively summarises the ETUC understanding of social partnership.

Although the ETUC wants to extend the reach of social partnership consultation and co-regulation to a broader set of policy issues, including welfare policy, economic policy, industrial policy etc., and transform current forms of consensual co-decision by establishing rights of European-wide collective action, it is worth underscoring that the ETUC adheres to the principle that social regulation at EU level should be of framework, minimum character. That is, the ETUC does not want European regulations to replace national regulations, but rather sees the former as a way of protecting the latter against regime-competition by developing a multi-tiered system of European framework regulation, leaving ample room for negotiated adjustment by the social actors at lower levels.

Conclusion

The internally contested process of ETUC integration and support for EU social partnership reflects an interplay between common European and competing national economic and institutional *interests*, and *values, ideas and identities* of even more diverse character, varying across national boundaries and between actors at national and European levels. This process is mediated by the *institutional* dynamics at the European level that have tended to influence and re-shape notions of interests and ideas. EU-level institution-building has changed the preferences, interests and ideas among ETUC players *and* – more limited and in recent years – among national union leaders, drawing them into what may broadly be called the European social policy community. In terms of its contents, the European unions, again reflecting their diversity, defended an open and broad concept of partnership – easily stretching the conceptual and practical boundaries between dialogue and bargaining. The narrow concept of social partnership – the exchange of views which may on rare occasions result in negotiated minimum standards – held by employers and most EU governments was rejected by the European trade union movement from the outset and never matched its ambitions.

While the ETUC approach to EU social dialogue has been driven by a perceived common interest in protecting labour rights and promoting more employment growth oriented macroeconomic policies at the supranational level, underpinned by the ideational devotion of key affiliates to the building of a United Europe, it has been conditioned by difficult intermediation between sometimes competing institutional self-interests in the national and European arenas. The particular modus of European social dialogue was inspired by traditions of policy concertation in the Low Countries, but its evolution has, together with the EMU programme, spurred a recent revival of national social pacts in several countries. Against the trend, this has strengthened the role of the national (cross-sectoral) peak federations in societal governance (Fajertag and Pochet, 2000). It is a telling example of the growing interpenetration between the European and national institutional structures for policy-making. The impact of European integration on trade unions has been ambiguous. While the Single Market and EMU have contributed to the erosion of traditional union power resources at national level, the most important contribution of social partnership at the European

Table 1.2 ETUC Rationales for European Social Partnership

Rationale	Explanation
Social justice, equity, cohesion	Ensuring representative influence of the weaker part in working life and civil society in EU policy-making; defending and adapting the European social model; providing a social benchmark in global capitalism.
Democracy, legitimacy	Establish a channel of 'voice' for ordinary citizens and workers at EU level; compensate for the democratic and legitimacy deficit of the EU; fulfil the political vocation of the Community and ensure that social concerns are incorporated in the EU's global agenda.
Economic and political functionality	Ensure that all relevant interests are taken into account; promote learning and improve EU problem-solving capacity/quality; negotiated adjustment of the social model ensures optimal trade-offs between equity, efficiency and competitiveness; bolster EU support.
Subsidiarity	By defending the autonomy of organised labour and capital against unaccountable EU etatism, and bringing decisions closer to those they concern, decision-making efficiency, flexibility and quality are enhanced.
Economic and monetary union	Without concerted monetary, fiscal and wage policies there is a risk that the EMU will run into a deflationary trap and be bogged down by social and regional conflict.
Interest intermediation and conflict reduction	Organised actors are more trained in handling complex, pragmatic interest intermediation than states; reduces social and national conflict by building civil society ties across boundaries.
Employers	European dialogue educates national actors with antiquated social attitudes through peer learning; convergence of attitudes on both sides positively influences partnership at EU and national level.
Trade unions	Counter national decline by regaining role and resources at EU level; incorporate unions that are opposed to the EU; promote learning and dissemination of best practices; strengthen unions in countries where they are weak. Risk of co-optation.

Power relations	Wants to redress the structural EU bias in favour of capital interests and reap benefits of political support from EU institutions, but the consensual policy-style often provides business veto-groups with the upper hand. Danger of going native in Brussels and alienating domestic rank-and-file.
Dilemma of seduction and support	How to balance between showing responsibility to achieve access and recognition and preserving autonomy and clout to gain headway?

level has been to restore the legitimacy and credibility of trade unions as societal actors, not least in the national arena and against the trend of neoliberalism and union weakening. At the same time, social partnership has helped the unions to stress their role as weaker, indeed junior, but nevertheless indispensable partners in the reform and modernisation of welfare states and labour markets (Visser and Hemerijck, 1997; Ebbinghaus and Hassel, 1999).

Unions did not regain in Europe the power they lost at home. Yet, in view of the paradox stated in the introduction, we have argued in this chapter, borrowing from Alan Milward (1992), that Europe has come to the rescue of national unionism in economic and political lean times. Through their joint efforts at institution-building and social partnership at EU level, national trade unions have been able to draw on resources and engage in processes of mutual learning that have helped to create new roles, or strengthen old ones, at home. We don't want to be misunderstood, so we restate what we wrote in the introduction. Trade unions in Europe wield much less power in economic and political arenas than 20 years ago, during the days of Fordism and the Keynesian mixed economy. But without the strengthening of trade union cooperation and representation flowing from their role in developing European social dialogue and labour market re-regulation, they would have been in a worse position. Even as junior partner in European social partnership capitalism, itself a bleak variant of Rhineland capitalism without the underpinnings of sectoral bargaining and societal participation in corporate governance, the unions did condition European events during the 1990s more than in the 1970s and 1980s. They owed this to their (and the Commission's) persistent investment in social dialogue, and to their increasingly essential role as source of popular loyalty, voice and legitimacy in the transformation of European integration and economies. The increased priority given to employment issues at EU level cannot be attributed to trade union demands alone, but it would not have happened without the strikes in France, the discontent expressed by unions in other countries, the persistence of the ETUC to have the issue on the agenda of the European decision-making bodies, and the reward it could claim for its loyalty in a difficult phase of the European integration process.

2

European Employers:
Social Partners?

Ann Branch and Justin Greenwood

Introduction

In this chapter we focus on the perspectives and behaviour of European cross-sectoral employers' organisations in social partnership since 1985. In overview, this has evolved from a non-binding, consultative forum into an arena, since Maastricht, in which the social partners enjoy an institutionalised role in the policy-making process and can negotiate legally binding agreements on labour market issues. The quasi-legislative role accorded to them under the terms of European social partnership now enables their agreements to provide an alternative for Commission proposals, and allows them to effectively displace the Council and the European Parliament from their usual legislative functions, in the sense that the social partners are now entitled to determine the content of social legislation in their place and offer it to the Council of Ministers for ratification through passage of binding legislation. Three agreements have been negotiated so far.

Employers' actions were instrumental in bringing about this change. In particular, European-level negotiations only became possible when, in the run-up to the 1991 Intergovernmental Conference (IGC), private sector employers abandoned their long-standing opposition to the principle of bargaining at European level – something considered inconceivable prior to Maastricht – and consented to negotiate with trade unions. For public sector employers, the concept was relatively easy to accept, and indeed the representative organisation embraced it with some enthusiasm. Thus, in line with the remit of the book, we examine the extent to which this evolution can be explained in terms of the logic of self-interest – defined as economic benefit and institutional power – and to what extent explanations couched in other terms, such as the influence of institutional, cultural or ideological norms not reducible to self-interest, are necessary.

The organisations examined are: representing mainly private sector employers: UNICE (the Union of Industrial and Employers' Confederations of Europe); UEAPME (the European Association of Craft, Small and Medium-Sized Enterprises); Eurocommerce (the European organisation for the retail and wholesale sectors) and Eurochambres (the European body for chambers of commerce and industry);[1] and representing public sector employers, CEEP (the European Centre of Enterprises with Public Participation). The primary focus is on UNICE because it is the main cross-industry European employers' body, it has been involved in the social dialogue from the outset, and, unlike CEEP, its role has been pivotal to the development of the social dialogue. Its mainly private sector constituency means that, unsurprisingly, its role in social partnership has been the most complex and difficult to define. In addition, UNICE is the principal employer body which negotiates agreements at European level. The other three private sector organisations are also examined more briefly, as they have all contested UNICE's representativity, claiming that they should be entitled to play a greater role in cross-sectoral dialogue. Furthermore, at UNICE's initiative Eurocommerce has actually participated as an 'expert' in the preparations for the three sets of negotiations, while UEAPME recently reached a cooperation agreement with UNICE and will be included in future negotiations. The role of CEEP is also given some attention, although in a more limited way because the nature of its constituency, together with its need for a role in European public affairs, makes its involvement in social partnership less complex than that of UNICE, although as is apparent later, not necessarily straightforward. Notwithstanding this latter qualification, unlike UNICE, CEEP has only rarely equivocated on a decision to negotiate on an issue in social partnership, reflecting the familiarity of its members with managing social goals alongside performance criteria as state enterprises. For CEEP members, there has been little that is unfamiliar about the content or style of social partnership. Whilst it shares with UNICE the natural caution about the costs imposed upon employers by social partnership, CEEP as an organisation appears to exude optimism about the future of social partnership and the opportunities it presents for them. Indeed, the very presence of social partnership is central to the continued prosperity of CEEP as an

organisation. Although social partnership is not restricted to negotiations under the Maastricht procedures, and includes consultative
forums such as the Standing Committee on Employment, troika
meetings and meetings with the Social Affairs Councils, the chapter concentrates on social partnership negotiations on the October
1991 agreement, parental leave, part-time work and fixed-term contracts as it is here that the most impressive developments have
taken place.

The chapter argues that although a considerable shift has occurred
in UNICE's attitude to social partnership over the years, namely
towards greater cooperation with the trade unions at European level,
this evolution has been driven mainly by economic and partly by
institutional self-interest. Above all, it contends that although UNICE's
strategy for pursuing its objectives may have changed in response
to a changing institutional environment and changing institutional
incentives, its fundamental *goal* – namely to minimise what it per-
ceives as the negative impact of European social legislation on
European companies – has not. Although institutional forces,
socialisation and learning have been important, the attitudes of
these organisations towards social partnership and social dialogue
are nevertheless instrumental. The shift in UNICE's position did
not, then, reflect a conversion to a new philosophy. Instead, its
attitude was one of 'realpolitik', namely a change in strategy in
response to changing political realities.

In the case of CEEP, institutional self-interest, together with the
relative familiarity of public sector employers with social partnership born of the entirely different relationship which managers in
public enterprises have with trade unions and national politicians,
help explain its apparently different role in EU-level social partnership. Unquestionably, CEEP's role, and interests, in EU-level social
partnership are different from that of UNICE, and as an organisation
the continued prosperity of CEEP is more dependent upon institutionalised social partnership than is that of UNICE. Historically,
the organisation was formed on the initiative of its southern members, and these continue to be powerful within it. CEEP lost a
significant number of its members as a result of privatisation, and
social partnership has been an important recruiting sergeant for it,
particularly amongst northern European members. Danish public
sector employers, for instance, only joined CEEP after the passage
of the social protocol annexed to the Maastricht Treaty. To date,
every single position of CEEP in the social partnership has been

endorsed unanimously in its General Assembly, and most of the work of CEEP is now devoted to the social partnership, and it is difficult to envisage it having an important role in European public affairs without it. But it is possible to overemphasise CEEP's apparently public enthusiasm for EU-level social partnership, and to overplay the seemingly different perspective it has from UNICE. One qualification is that there may be a distinction to be drawn between rhetoric and reality in that UNICE's 'tough guy' role in social partnership may suit CEEP rather well, allowing CEEP to maintain a softer public stance to social partnership whilst conveniently relying on UNICE to draw a line in the sand where necessary.

The chapter is organised into two main sections. The first examines the rhetoric of these organisations, and the second looks at why and how their positions have evolved. We draw upon 23 interviews, primarily in employer organisations conducted over a 16-month period that was completed in July 1999. Our interviews span those with practical experiences drawn from both the national and European levels, and with personnel ranging from middle ranking officials through to those involved at the very highest levels. Most importantly, we felt it important to undertake 'duplicate' interviews in the principal organisations, such that we both interviewed different respondents from the same organisation at a similar time. This provided considerable reassurance for the interpretation that follows. Thus, our interviews were confirmatory of similar points, and, when compared, enabled us to ensure that our lines of enquiry coincided. We have taken care to treat disparate points with caution, and to only draw upon those issues confirmed by both sets of interviews.

The rhetoric of European employers' organisations

The task of examining the discourse of social partnership – i.e. the key concepts and arguments – in relation to European employers' organisations and eventual self-interest explanations proved to be rather difficult as employers tend to avoid terminological dogmatism and potentially emotive jargon, possibly for fear of the uncertain repercussions they may have. Indeed, employers are aware of the way in which the Commission has tried – often successfully – to capitalise upon the rhetoric of national governments to promote social measures (Cram, 1997). As a consequence, the primary documentation contained virtually no direct reference to social partnership per se. Instead, most of the position papers were concerned with the European social dialogue. This reflects the fact that UNICE's main concern was to create the conditions in which Delors and Cockfield could succeed in their ambitious single market programme. The social dialogue and social partnership were never seen as ends in themselves, but as the means to an end, i.e. to the creation of a more competitive Europe. It was, therefore, necessary to rely mainly on interview material in order to form an idea of the significance attached by employers' organisations to certain terminology. Four main terms stood out: (European and national) 'social partnership'; (European and national) 'social partners'; 'representativity'; and, 'subsidiarity'. The usage of these terms supports the conclusion that the positions and actions of employers can be accounted for by self-interest, as the first three are used instrumentally to justify either the inclusion or exclusion of certain actors from the process, while 'subsidiarity' is used to promote employer interests vis-a-vis the policy-making process.

With regard to the concept of 'social partnership', a distinction needs to be drawn between UNICE and the other organisations. It was clear that UNICE preferred to avoid speaking explicitly of 'social partnership', partly because different nationalities understand different things by it. While for some of its members 'partnership' was a very broad concept, for others it had a very specific meaning, namely co-determination. It was clear that UNICE does not really think in terms of social partnership at all, but rather in terms of social dialogue. Another possible reason for avoiding the use of rigid jargon is that a coherent conception of 'social partnership' and 'social partners' might well, by implication, complicate the problem of representativity (discussed below) for the organisation even further.

Clearer views on social partnership emerged from the other organisations. This is not entirely surprising as – in contrast to UNICE – much of their energy has until now concentrated on tackling the problem of (at least partial) exclusion from the social dialogue and terminology has, therefore, been important to them as a justification for improving their institutional standing. For example, Eurochambres is excluded from certain social partnership forums, including the SCE, because it is not considered to be a proper 'social partner'. The official reason[2] for this is that its members are not 'social partners' at national level – in other words, they do not have the competence to negotiate with trade unions or the government, and in many countries membership of chambers of commerce and industry is compulsory. Both UEAPME and Euro-chambres agree that the definition of social partner at the national level entails these two aspects. But while both agree that European- and national-level 'social partnership' are fundamentally different in nature, only the latter argues that this should, as a corollary, entail a more 'modern' definition of a 'European social partner' (Eurochambres, 1998). More specifically, there is agreement that European social partnership involves consultations and negotiations on far more general issues than at the national level, where nego-tiations generally concern more detailed – and often quantitative – issues with a very direct bearing on companies. However, while UEAPME employs its rhetoric on social partnership to justify its own inclusion among the cross-industry organisations entitled to negotiate at European level and to exclude Eurochambres, Eurochambres in turn uses its rhetoric to reject traditional concep-tions and to be accepted as a 'full-blown' European social partner with a seat on the SCE.

For CEEP's part, the importance of its institutionalised role in social partnership for its own continued prosperity is reflected in its positive articulations of partnership, although the qualification between its need to present positive rhetoric whilst relying on UNICE to play the 'bad cop' role should be taken into account in reading Tables 2.1 and 2.2 below. Another key term to emerge – similarly primarily among Eurocommerce, UEAPME and Eurochambres – was 'representativity' (Eurochambres, 1996, 1998; Eurocommerce, 1998; UEAPME, 1997).

However, in the early years, 1985–93, there was no pressure what-ever from any employer body to take part in the social dialogue. UNICE, CEEP and ETUC, invited by Delors to the first Val Duchesse meetings in January and November 1985, met regularly from then on, and no other employer organisation objected or showed any interest in joining the talks. However, after the TEU entered into force in November 1993 and the Commission began drafting its paper on how the social chapter was to operate in practice, other employers' organisations began to show an interest. The exclusion of some of these organisations from the Maastricht procedures mean that 'representativity' has become an issue of key concern for them, primarily as an argument by UEAPME and Eurocommerce for in-clusion in social dialogue negotiations, and by Eurochambres for inclusion on the SCE. The term is frequently linked to concepts

Table 2.1 Employer Use of Terms Relating to Social Partnership

Term	Meaning
National social partnership	Discussions and negotiations on labour market matters on issues (often quantitative) with a direct bearing on companies (UEAPME, Eurochambres)
European social partnership	Different to, and broader than at national level. Involvement in drawing up of general, 'framework' EU economic and social policies (UEAPME, Eurochambres, CEEP)
National social partner	Employer and trade union organisations with the power to bargain with each other and/or the government (UEAPME, Eurochambres)
European social partner	European-level employer and trade union organisations whose members have the power to negotiate at national level and for whom membership is voluntary (UNICE, UEAPME, Eurocommerce, CEEP)
	(Eurochambres) Broader view of European social partners. Organisations with compulsory membership and no national bargaining role should not necessarily be excluded from or disqualified as 'European' social partners if they are representative
Subsidiarity	Two dimensions: (a) whether to act at EU or national level (CEEP); (b) by legislation or negotiation (UNICE, CEEP)
Representativity	Used by every organisation to justify their own position. UNICE claims it is representative of all sectors and firms of all sizes, while UEAPME and Eurochambres also lay claims to be cross-sectoral and more representative of SMEs than UNICE

such as 'democracy' and 'legitimacy' in that the social dialogue is considered to introduce a complementary dimension to parliamentary democracy, but only if it is as representative as possible – otherwise it is considered to lack legitimacy.

One key term that stands out for all the organisations was 'subsidiarity'. UNICE is very explicit on this subject, arguing that there are two dimensions to it: whether to act at EU or national level, or by legislation or negotiation (UNICE, 1994). This usage also supports the self-interest argument but at the policy-making level. If employers cannot persuade the Commission that action should not be taken at EU level, they then generally argue that they are the most appropriate actors, as they are closer to those who will be directly affected by legislative outcomes.

As part of the common investigative framework for analysing the perspectives of actors, we were also asked to examine the arguments for and against social partnership used or adhered to by the principal protagonists. The arguments in favour are summarised in Table 2.2, and again, they support the self-interest argument.

A striking feature for all the organisations is the absence of a clear link between 'Economic and Monetary Union' and social partnership anywhere in the documentation on social dialogue of these organisations, although they do call for discussions between employers and unions to cover macroeconomic policy as well as labour market issues. Both UNICE and CEEP want economic and labour market issues to be discussed together, so that the economic impact of proposed labour market measures would always be kept in mind. The ETUC for its part has concurred because the trade unions also saw advantages in ensuring that macroeconomic policy did not ignore labour market demands. Surprisingly perhaps, it was very difficult to identify arguments by employers' organisations against social partnership. This is, however, interesting in itself, revealing that European employers' organisations are highly pragmatic, and although they have traditionally been fiercely opposed to European negotiations, they now accept social partnership and the social dialogue as something they have to live with, and are trying to make the best of it. If anything, they are learning that it presents them with an opportunity to increase their influence over the policy agenda and decision-making process. They have also been reassured by the realisation that it may actually work to their advantage, as trade unions have effectively been co-opted into an essentially neoliberal economic agenda, while the emphasis on macroeconomics and the increasing involvement of the social partners in macroeconomic policy debates have helped to ensure that European labour market measures are no longer prescriptive, but framework in nature, with broad principles determined at European level and the detail left to be determined nationally, in line with the definition of directives in Article 249 (ex. Article 189) of the Treaty establishing the European Community. UNICE feels that the agreements negotiated by the social partners have respected this definition far more faithfully than any directives approved by the Council. In the light of the earlier discussion about CEEP, it is unsurprising that arguments against social partnership are not to be found either in its own position statements, or in discussions between CEEP officials and those outside the organisation.

Table 2.2 Employer Arguments in Relation to Social Partnership

Rationale	Explanation
Economic utility	Helps to ensure that EU policies take business needs into account and do not undermine competitiveness (UNICE)
	Fosters the success of the stability-orientation of macroeconomic policy, of structural reform and of the renewed cooperative growth strategy (UNICE, CEEP)
	Negotiated agreements contribute to ensuring greater flexibility in the workplace, which is necessary to restore European competitiveness and to create jobs (UNICE)
Improves policy-making	Improves the quality of policies because business needs, and the practical considerations of implementation, are taken into account (UNICE, CEEP)
Legitimacy	Increases acceptance of EU policies by business, improves understanding between European citizens and legislators, improves the 'social acceptability' of EU policies, helps to explain EU policies better to the general public (UNICE)
Democracy	Introduces a complementary dimension to parliamentary democracy (UNICE, CEEP)
	Enhances democracy, but only if it is truly representative (UEAPME, Eurocommerce, Eurochambres)
Subsidiarity	Social dialogue has played an essential role in improving the application of the principle of subsidiarity (UNICE)
Conflict reduction	Helps to achieve a good understanding and acceptance of the process of change in company restructuring (UNICE)
	Conflicts emerge when there is no communication and dialogue (Eurocommerce); learning to understand mutual positions is essential given the inevitability of social partnership (UNICE)
	Has helped business to develop in a peaceful way (UNICE)
Trade unions	Moderates trade union demands (UNICE)
	Co-opts unions into a neoliberal economic agenda (UNICE)
Substitute for lobbying	Ensures influence over legislation which would otherwise be inevitable and/or difficult to influence (UNICE, CEEP)
Single Market	Has helped to prevent any serious disruption to the Single Market (UNICE)
	Has helped to make the Single Market of benefit to everyone (UNICE)
Power	Organisations feel that social dialogue is necessary for their survival (CEEP) and development (UNICE)
	UNICE did not want to include other organisations in order to enhance its own power (UEAPME)
Brake upon social policy	European-level bargaining serves as a substitute for legislation which is 'misconceived, over-prescriptive or over-detailed' (UNICE)
	The reason for being involved is to put a brake on 'harmful' social policy (Eurocommerce, UNICE)

Certain arguments against social partnership which might have been expected from employers' organisations did not emerge at all. For example, there was no reference to social partnership giving trade unions too much power, to harming the economy by restricting market mechanisms, or to restricting managerial prerogative. If anything it was viewed as helping to dilute trade union demands and to prevent disruption to the Single Market, established for the pursuit of its objective of ensuring completion of the Single Market and the competitiveness of companies. This may be indicative of the fact that European social partnership is viewed as very different to national social partnership, addressing more general issues of broad principle, rather than detailed, quantitative matters. It may also be indicative of learning, or realising that the organisation's interests are now best pursued in a new arena as a result of interacting with other protagonists.

The evolution of employer positions and actions

This section examines the evolution of the European employer position from 1985 – when the new Commission President, Jacques Delors, launched the social dialogue – until the present day. As mentioned in the introduction, the policy-making landscape today is very different from that prior to Maastricht. This is interesting not only because the European social partners now enjoy a quasi-legislative role, but also because of how it happened. Indeed, it was only possible because of a considerable shift in the employer position. Retrospectively it is easy to forget the sheer scale of this shift, so it needs to be recalled that this was an extremely difficult issue for private sector employers, having been consistently and intransigently opposed to the very principle of negotiating with trade unions at the European level. When UNICE did alter its position, it was completely unexpected. Indeed, as late as 1991, the year of the IGC, no one – neither practitioners nor scholars[3] – expected these employers to agree to negotiations at the European level, not least because many of UNICE's members were seeking to decentralise collective bargaining at the national level. Many equated such a development with neocorporatism and concluded that the conditions for such a development at European level were, quite simply, lacking (Streeck and Schmitter, 1991; Visser and Ebbinghaus, 1992; Streeck, 1994; Rhodes, 1995). In particular, UNICE, CEEP and ETUC – because of the absence of a uniform membership in all

Member States – were relatively weak organisations, which lacked a clear negotiating mandate, and were incapable of ensuring the compliance of their members. Many of these doubts remained even after the Maastricht Treaty had been signed, with considerable scepticism as to whether the social partners would actually manage to make use of these procedures (Streeck, 1994; Rhodes, 1995). Since 1995, however, European employers and trade unions have managed to conclude three agreements, which have been given the force of law in the form of directives. Clearly then these developments require explanation. In particular, why did private sector employers shift position in 1991, and why have they consented to negotiations on three agreements so far with trade unions in spite of their long-standing opposition to the principle of European-level negotiations with trade unions?

The beginning: 1985–90

The social dialogue as it is now known dates from 1985 when Jacques Delors took over as President of the European Commission. Although there were some precedents for social dialogue at this time, they were generally viewed as ineffectual (Teague, 1989b; Carley, 1993). Delors – a former trade unionist himself – believed deeply in social dialogue and from the start had grander ambitions for it, hoping that the social partners would eventually reach binding agreements among themselves (Grant, 1994; Ross, 1995a; Tyszkiewicz, 1999). Within days of taking office, Delors invited the European social partners[4] to a summit meeting, the main purpose of which was to ask the social partners to talk to each other, in return for which he would halt the flood of draft directives on social matters to which employers were strongly opposed (Grant, 1994; Tyszkiewicz, 1999). The initial results of the social dialogue were widely viewed as disappointing. The main problem was that UNICE and ETUC failed to agree on the objectives of the working parties which had been established in the long-term hope of brokering productive dialogue. For private sector employers, the issue was to ensure that the Single Market and (later) the EMU objective of the EU would not be frustrated by trade union opposition and that Europe remained a forum for non-decision-making about employment-related matters. UNICE wanted the social dialogue to remain a forum for discussion about the problems arising from these policies, but made it clear that 'it was unwilling to enter into any dialogue which sought to establish binding agreements' (Teague, 1989b, p.70). The Secretary-General

of UNICE argued that 'dialogue should not be confused with negotiation of collective agreements', as they were 'an entirely separate
process, with different objectives' (quoted in *European Industrial
Relations Review*, 1992). UNICE considered, therefore, that the social dialogue was 'meant to be just talk' (Ross, 1995a, p.151).

In contrast, the Commission and ETUC viewed the dialogue very
much as 'preparing the groundwork for effective (legislative) action
in selected social policy areas' (Teague, 1989b, p.70) and as 'a pre-
liminary stage of Euro-bargaining' (*European Industrial Relations Review*,
1992). In the event, the viewpoint of private sector employers prevailed, with UNICE insisting that the final texts should be joint
opinions, as opposed to agreements. They argued that an agreement 'tied the partners to certain arrangements or actions, while
an opinion was an open-ended expression of a view or judgement
on a particular matter' (ibid.). Because of UNICE's position the joint
opinions had to be very loosely worded.[5] This inevitably led to
dissatisfaction amongst the trade unions.

It was against this background and after two years of inertia that
Delors launched the second phase of the social dialogue at a meeting
with the social partners on 12 January 1989. To inject new impetus,
the Commission introduced several innovations. One of the most
important developments of this period was the Commission's commitment to consult the social partners on the draft directives to be
proposed as part of its 1989 Social Action Programme (SAP): 'this
was a positive experience for all sides, demonstrating that on a
number of issues the views of employers and of trade unions actually coincide, and that this has a real influence on the Commission'
(Tyszkiewicz, 1999, p.10). The following period was more productive than the first and more joint opinions were issued, and CEEP
and ETUC reached a bilateral agreement concerning training in state-
owned companies.[6] In spite of the progress during this second stage,
however, disagreement over the objectives of the dialogue persisted
between UNICE and the ETUC: 'Discussion again revealed contra-
dictory purposes. UNICE sought to frustrate Commission legislative
purposes and to prevent any bargaining. ETUC, in contrast, wanted
as many concrete proposals as possible' (Ross, 1995b, p.377), while
CEEP had no apparent objections to the development of bi- or tripartite bargaining.

The turning-point: the 1991 IGC

At the beginning of 1991, legally binding European-level negotiations with trade unions still appeared to be a very distant prospect. Indeed, leading scholars dismissed this possibility because employers had the capacity to block developments which were contrary to their interests: 'by not delegating authority upward to the European level, employers were, and still are, able to confine institutions like the Social Dialogue to a strictly nonbinding, consultative status' (Streeck and Schmitter, 1991, p.141). Even the ETUC was taken by surprise, as 'as late as the morning of 31 October' officials of the ETUC 'would not have believed that the day would have closed with the conclusion of a document which provided for the possibility of European framework agreements' (Buschak and Kallenbach, 1998, p.171). This prospect looked even more unlikely because of the general trend in European industrial relations towards decentralised forms of bargaining away from national or regional level to company level, and because globalisation meant that the political advantage was perceived to have shifted permanently in favour of business.

However, behind the scenes, already in the first half of 1991, all UNICE member federations – with one or two exceptions – were convinced that the correct strategy was to accept binding negotiations with the ETUC in order to have the option of keeping matters out of the hands of the legislator, as it was clear that QMV in the social field would be extended. UNICE therefore decided to abandon its opposition to European-level negotiations and to work with the trade unions to draw up a set of joint proposals for the IGC. The Social Partners Agreement was adopted on 31 October 1991, and incorporated virtually verbatim into the Maastricht Treaty. The significance of this agreement was that it provided the European social partners with an institutionalised and quasi-legislative role in the policy-making process. What happened during 1991 to make UNICE change its position on the principle of European-level negotiations?

When the 1991 IGC opened, the Commission was keen to promote the social dialogue further, and invited the social partners to try to agree what role they wanted to play at the EU level and submit their conclusions in the form of an amended Article 118B. It was against this background that the Social Affairs Commissioner, Vasso Papandreou, invited the social partners to discuss the possible role they wished to be given by the new treaty (Tyszkiewicz, 1999). She speculated that an extension of QMV in the realm of social policy was a virtually inevitable outcome of the IGC and argued that the time had come for them to play a greater role and challenged them to do so.

The question within UNICE was would the IGC amend the Treaty rules on QMV in social policy or would the UK veto hold? No federation in UNICE welcomed centralised bargaining at EU level (although the British, the Greeks and the Portuguese were the most fiercely opposed), but it was pragmatically accepted as a lesser evil than giving the Commission, the Council and above all the European Parliament a free hand in social policy following an extension of QMV. Experience of what they perceived to be previously badly thought out and costly legislation led them clearly towards the final decision. The view of the largest camp was therefore the one which prevailed, namely that there was too much at stake to take risks and that the opportunity to give themselves a determining role in EU-level social policy decisions would probably never again present itself. The main advantage of the negotiation provisions was, then, that they would, at the very least, act as a brake on the Commission's determination to create a body of Community law covering employment matters. The political reality as they saw it was that the pressure for Community regulation of employment-related matters would increase and that the bargaining arrangements offered the best prospect of containing or diverting this pressure (Hornung-Draus, 1998; Tyszkiewicz, 1999). By 31 October 1991 all federations were in agreement with the formula jointly drawn up by the social partners.

The main reason for UNICE's abandonment of its long-standing opposition to European negotiations was, therefore, pragmatic. It was an exercise in damage limitation, rather than a conversion to the virtues of bargaining per se (Ross, 1995a, 1995b; Tyszkiewicz, 1999). Although UNICE's real preference was for no change at all in the treaty, the organisation had to deal with the prospect that some change was likely in view of the considerable pressure for extending QMV from most Member States, the Commission and the European Parliament.[7] UNICE was not, therefore, optimistic regarding the outcome of the IGC and was, in fact, convinced that greater QMV was inevitable (Hornung-Draus, 1998; Tyszkiewicz, 1999). Faced in 1991 with 47 new measures in the social policy field, stemming from the 1989 SAP, including twelve directives on employment-related issues, UNICE eventually concluded that 'if the Community and Commission acquired a wider legislative mandate, the barrage of legislation that it had confronted under the Social Charter would only intensify' (Ross, 1995b, pp.379–80), but this time many of the proposals would be subject to QMV rather than unanimity. In this context, the option of negotiated agreements began to look like an attractive alternative.

The fears over QMV were exacerbated by the strong expectation[8] – because of the unpopularity of the incumbent administration – that the British Labour Party would win the general election to be held in the spring of 1992. In this event UNICE expected the new government to agree to an extension of QMV in the social domain. Furthermore, if QMV was extended, UNICE expected the European Parliament, in which the Socialists had formed the largest group since 1989, to press hard for progress in the social field. The European Parliament had already, since 1989, exploited its limited powers to the full by attempting to promote progress on social measures by using its delaying powers to block progress on internal market measures (Ross, 1995a). Furthermore, employers did not feel that they could rely on their national governments to block reform. Above all, relations between the government most likely to block reform – the British one – and the CBI were at an all time low. So although the government told the CBI that it would block any reform in the social field, the CBI did not believe that the government would be prepared to wreck the entire treaty over this issue. Indeed, the political context of the time needs to be recalled – there was a very strong sense at the end of the Cold War and just after German unification that a new treaty was necessary for geopolitical reasons. It therefore seemed totally inconceivable – particularly against the background of the *quid pro quo* nature of bargaining in the EC – that the government would sacrifice everything over this dossier.

UNICE objected, therefore, to both legislation and collective bargaining but concluded that collective bargaining would deliver more favourable outcomes for companies than legislation. The Commission's practice of consulting the social partners about the 1989 SAP legislation was, in fact, important in this respect, as it had exposed UNICE to the advantages of consultation and subsequently helped to persuade it to reconsider the negotiation option (Ross, 1995b; Tyszkiewicz, 1999). As such, this had therefore been an important organisational learning experience for UNICE. Although UNICE would have to swallow its pride and abandon its previous opposition to European-level collective bargaining, the Commission's proposals had the advantage of helping it to limit Community social action. In other words, UNICE believed that the Commission's proposal for them to come up with their own proposals represented the least unpleasant alternative.

Post-Maastricht: 1993–9

The unexpected nature of this development was reflected in the fact that after Maastricht, no one was very clear about how the procedures would work in practice. Indeed, in 1991 UNICE had not really considered this issue, and the trade unions were equally uncertain about what the procedures meant and an intense internal debate subsequently flared up within the ETUC (Dølvik, 1997). As a result of ratification problems it took until November 1993 for the Treaty to enter into force. As soon as it did, however, the Commission took advantage of the provisions to try to break the legislative deadlock in the Council concerning certain social policy proposals.

European Works Councils (EWCs)

The first proposal to be submitted to the new provisions was the draft directive on EWCs that sought to establish information and consultation rights and structures for employees in multinational companies above a certain size. After a series of 'talks on talks' the social partners failed to agree to negotiate on this dossier. Whilst CEEP was perfectly content to reach agreement, UNICE's desire to water down the existing legislative proposal was, in fact, one of the main reasons for the failure of these talks, as UNICE's motives were well known to the trade unions. The ETUC Secretary-General, Emilio Gabaglio, repeatedly expressed his concern that employers' main intention was to dilute any eventual measure (Dølvik, 1997).[9] As a consequence, in spite of the long-standing calls by the ETUC for European-level negotiations, the trade unions were not really very keen to negotiate on this issue. In addition, the positions of national governments at the October 1993 Social Affairs Council, the position of the European Parliament, and the known enthusiasm of the forthcoming German Presidency to achieve a result on this dossier for electoral reasons (it faced a general election in October 1994) meant that trade unions knew they could obtain a more favourable result from legislation.

Indeed, UNICE was so concerned at the prospect of legislation that it ended up conceding all of the key principles demanded by the ETUC, including the controversial principle that information and consultation was a 'fundamental right', something which UNICE had consistently opposed in the past. Even this was not enough, however, to persuade the trade unions to negotiate. Although the blame for the failure of the breakdown in talks was pinned on the CBI when its Director-General, Howard Davies, withdrew from the talks because the CBI did not have time to consult its members before the deadline, it was, nevertheless clear that the ETUC never really had an incentive to negotiate on this issue (Falkner, 1996a; Dølvik, 1997).

Parental leave

The first negotiated agreement at European level was eventually reached in December 1995 on parental leave. When the social partners failed to negotiate on EWCs, widespread doubts emerged concerning their ability to negotiate in general. UNICE was not interested in free-standing negotiations initiated by the social partners themselves, which resulted in the ETUC appealing to the Commission to bring forward legislation on the grounds that UNICE needed a 'big stick' with which to be persuaded to bargain (Dølvik, 1997). A number of considerations dictated that parental leave emerged as the most appropriate, and politically straightforward, proposal with which to begin (ibid.). The social partners decided to negotiate immediately after the launch of the second consultation stage (5 July 1995), negotiations began a few days later (12 July), and were completed by 6 November.

Whilst CEEP's main reason for deciding to negotiate was a mixture of institutional self-interest together with a need for its members to adopt positions which would not offend their stakeholders, UNICE's main reason for deciding to negotiate was economic self-interest. As with EWCs, UNICE believed that negotiations would deliver a more favourable – i.e. less demanding and costly – outcome for its members than legislation: 'UNICE entered these negotiations mainly because it is convinced that agreements ... can meet the needs of companies and of their employees better than directives which would otherwise be proposed' (UNICE, 1995). In spite of UNICE's initial reservations about negotiations, there was surprisingly little conflict within UNICE; after all, most Member States already had more stringent legislation in this area. As for the countries with no existing provisions in this area, the fact that the agreement only provided for unpaid leave took care of most of their concerns.

Furthermore, most things – including all the difficult issues such as social security – were left to be determined at the national level.

It has been argued that another reason for negotiating was that all of the social partners had an institutional self-interest in doing so. During spring 1996 the Commission started to suggest that it was important for the social partners to demonstrate that they were capable of using the Maastricht procedures, with the implicit suggestion that otherwise they might be removed at the forthcoming IGC in 1996 intended to review the Maastricht Treaty (Falkner, 1996b; Keller and Sörries, 1998). Indeed, in a speech to the ETUC Congress in May 1995, the Commission President, Jacques Santer, emphasised that the social partners must now demonstrate that 'the European constitutional legislator was right to trust them and give them considerable co-regulatory power' (Agence Europe, 10 May 1995). In particular, many MEPs were not happy at being sidelined in the legislative process and questioned the democratic credentials of the social dialogue in view of the exclusion of various representative European organisations (Vilar, 1997). In interviews, however, all the respondents denied that UNICE was genuinely worried by the Commission's threats that the negotiation provisions would be repealed. It is true that some of UNICE's members did use this argument vis-a-vis their own memberships, but this was mainly as a persuasive tool, in order to convince them to back negotiations. So in spite of statements by UNICE's President that the agreement 'demonstrates the ability of the European Social Partners to meet their responsibilities and fulfil their role as set out in the Maastricht Social Protocol' (UNICE, 1995), which suggest a motivation based on institutional self-interest, UNICE's main concern appears to have been economic self-interest. Reaching an agreement did, nevertheless, help to consolidate the role of the social partners, whether or not that was the deliberate intention. Nevertheless, UNICE did take seriously the probability that if the 'horizontal' or multisectoral organisations such as UNICE and CEEP failed to perform, then this would lead to ever stronger pressure for sectoral negotiations, with the consequent risk of 'leapfrogging' tactics by trade unions, as well as a series of overlapping but not uniform agreements leading to confusion and high costs for business.

Part-time work

The second agreement concerned the issue of part-time work. Consultations were launched on the broader topic of atypical work in late September 1995 and formal negotiations began in October 1996. After eight negotiating sessions a compromise was reached in May 1997 and the agreement was formally signed in June.

The main problem was that the legal and contractual situation in the Member States was so different, that it became extremely difficult to arrive at an acceptable formula even when there was no fundamental disagreement on principle. A fairly major concession made by employers was that part-time workers should benefit, pro rata temporis, from equal treatment with full-timers, which they felt meant considerable cost increases in a number of countries. A major concession from the union side was their undertaking to identify and seek to eliminate existing legal and contractual obstacles to the use of part-time work. UNICE's motivations were very similar to those for parental leave, arguing that the agreement delivered a better deal – i.e. a less stringent and costly alternative – for employers than a Council directive would have done: 'by facilitating access to part-time work, this agreement constitutes a major step towards greater flexibility of work, which is necessary to the restoration of European competitiveness and to the creation of jobs' (UNICE, 1997a). Indeed, there was a perception and some subsequent tension within the ETUC that the trade unions had obtained a poor deal (Dølvik, 1997).

As with parental leave, although institutional concerns were not a prime motive, the agreement does also appear to have served UNICE's institutional self-interest as the IGC was still ongoing, and a second agreement was seen to consolidate the Maastricht provisions and to prove that it was not just a one-off success (*European Industrial Relations Review*, 1997a). This is reflected in UNICE's statement that 'the agreement bears witness to the capacity of the European social partners to assume their responsibilities and to play the role attributed to them by the Maastricht social protocol' (UNICE, 1997a). Furthermore, another press release issued on the same day urged the European Council to reach a successful conclusion in the IGC (UNICE, 1997b).

Sexual harassment

The Commission initiated the Maastricht social policy procedures on the subject of sexual harassment in July 1996, and launched the second consultation in March 1997. While the ETUC wanted to negotiate a binding instrument with UNICE, the latter turned down the offer in July. Although the organisation recognised the importance of tackling sexual harassment in the workplace, it rejected the need for a binding instrument at European level (UNICE, 1997c).

Whilst less reluctant, a similar view was held within CEEP, whose members recognised the cultural diversity of the concept in different national settings and the consequent difficulties of reaching agreement, and could not see how European-level legislation could really advance existing national legislation. Nonetheless, in its carefully worded response to the Commission CEEP avoided outright public rejection of negotiations, stressing that it did not wish to wash its hands of negotiations and its view that the EU social partners have an important role to play. It went on to propose research on the problem, and suggested a joint declaration from the social partners, emphasising its wish to be involved. In reality, however, the position of CEEP may have been very much closer to that adopted by UNICE than its public position suggests.

UNICE's reasons for turning down negotiations were again motivated by economic self-interest, and objections on the grounds of the principle of subsidiarity, namely the argument that the Commission had failed to demonstrate the need for action at the European level. Indeed, the Commission's own consultation paper showed that much progress had been achieved by the Member States in dealing with the problem by law and collective agreement since a previous Council resolution and no study had been carried out to find whether, since then, the situation at the workplace had improved or deteriorated. However, the Finnish and Greek employers were in favour of negotiations in order to avoid an excessively binding instrument at EU level. Wishing not to appear too negative, the Danes, Dutch and British recommended exploring the alternative possibility of initiating social dialogue with ETUC with the aim of preparing a non-binding joint recommendation of the social partners, while the Austrians and Italians were entirely opposed to the opening of negotiations on this subject. In brief, all the federations shared the same basic goal – to minimise the impact of such a measure on their members – but they disagreed as to the best strategy to achieve this.

In the end a majority of UNICE members felt sufficiently confident that a potential legislative measure on this subject would be blocked in the Council, and also that it was unlikely that the ETUC would agree to negotiate a non-binding instrument. In addition, UNICE did not want to establish a precedent which would make the Commission think that it could be bullied into negotiating on everything. The organisation therefore turned down the offer of negotiations.

National information and consultation

The next major issue to emerge was the dossier on establishing information and consultation procedures in national companies. In spite of the fact that negotiations did not take place on this issue because of UNICE, it is worth mentioning because it caused considerable internal problems which have a bearing on the remit of this chapter. The first round of consultations was launched in June 1997 and the second in November 1997 (*European Industrial Relations Review*, 1997c, 1997d). Each time UNICE emphasised the principle of subsidiarity, arguing that this was a national, not European matter. However, as the Commission was determined to push the measure, divisions arose among UNICE's members as to the most effective strategy. The dilemma with which UNICE was presented was: does one refuse to negotiate in order to defend the principle or does one accept, in order to limit the damage? While some UNICE members argued that negotiations were the most effective guarantee of damage limitation, others opposed them in the belief that UNICE should rely on a blocking minority in the Council. This second strategy was viewed as high risk by some members, as the positions of national governments on this 'young' dossier were not clear, having only been mooted for the first time in 1995.

Initially the minority opposed to negotiations within UNICE consisted of the usual three – the British, the Greeks and the Portuguese – but in March they were joined by the German BDA (*Bundesvereinigung der Deutschen Arbeitgeberverbände*), after obtaining confirmation from its government that, along with the British, it would oppose the measure. Nevertheless, some UNICE members still viewed this reliance upon governments as a high risk strategy, partly because only two opposing governments could definitely be identified – not enough for a blocking minority – and partly because Chancellor Kohl's government was widely expected to lose the general election later in the year, and the position which a Social-Democratic-led coalition would take was unknown. However, four members exceeded a blocking minority, so UNICE took the decision not to negotiate. However, to pacify those members who supported negotiations, it did not rule out negotiations completely, and the press release states simply that UNICE had decided not to proceed with negotiations 'at this time' (UNICE, 1998a).

After the appointment of a new President, the Belgian Georges Jacobs, the issue was reopened. Apparently as a result of a conversation on a plane trip with the Commission President, Jacques Santer, Jacobs managed to convince the Commission to give him some time to see if he could persuade his members to reconsider their decision (*European Voice*, 10–16 September 1998). This tied in with a leaked Commission draft of the legislative proposal, which was worrying for employers because of the low threshold it set for exempting companies (20 employees, rather than 50). But contrary to expectations, the majority within UNICE opposed to negotiations actually increased, rather than diminished, with the Swedes and Italians joining the others (*Financial Times*, 17–18 October 1998). One explanation was that by October the German BDA had received confirmation from the new labour minister that Germany would continue to oppose the measure on subsidiarity grounds. There was, therefore, greater confidence after the German general election in September that a blocking minority could be obtained in the Council. Another factor, however, was the feeling among some of UNICE's members that they were being bullied by the Commission, which was not respecting their autonomy. Domestic factors also played a role. For example, the real reason for the Italian shift appears to have been a reaction to domestic politics, as a new left-wing government had undermined an agreement between the national social partners on working time. In protest, Italian employers adopted a more negative stance to social partnership at every level. To sum up, in spite of internal disagreements within UNICE over strategy, the fundamental goal remained the same – to limit the damage from this proposal. CEEP's public position, on the other hand, was that it had no problem with the proposals and would have been happy to reach agreement.

Fixed-term contracts

The third negotiated agreement was reached in January 1999 on fixed-term contracts. This dossier marked a break from the others in that UNICE actually initiated the negotiations. However, the reason for this was that the organisation had already committed itself, along with CEEP, to examining the issue of fixed-term work when it was separated from part-time work under the atypical work consultations. UNICE was, therefore, conscious that the Commission would address the issue sooner or later and sought to pre-empt a Commission document which might play into the hands of the

trade unions. UNICE also wanted to avoid legislation as any legislative measure would probably have been issued after the entry
into force of the Amsterdam Treaty (May 1999) and therefore been
subject to the codecision procedure, with the danger for UNICE
that the European Parliament might exploit its enhanced powers
under this procedure to make the measure more stringent. Addi-
tionally, UNICE also hoped – wrongly as it turned out – that this
might delay the national information and consultation dossier on
the grounds that they could not conduct two sets of negotiations
at once. Again, the primary reason for the agreement was that UNICE
believed that this would deliver a more favourable and less costly
outcome for its members. In addition, the framework nature of the
two previous agreements helped to create a positive precedent and
persuade employers that a negotiated agreement would deliver a
preferable outcome to legislation. In particular, some members had
come to realise that the results of the previous negotiations represented an improvement for them over the prevailing situation at
national level.

Other employers

So far this section has focused on UNICE's role in the negotiations,
but has not discussed how UEAPME, Eurocommerce and Eurochambres
fit in. As indicated earlier, the position of these other private sector employers has so far been mainly driven by their concerns about
representativity and combating their exclusion. As a consequence,
the criticisms of all three organisations of the first agreement on
parental leave mainly concerned their exclusion from the negotiations (Reuters, 9 November 1995; Agence Europe, 28 November 1995),
with UEAPME going so far as to lodge a complaint with the Court
of First Instance that the agreement should not be binding upon
its members. UEAPME's problems with the agreement had only to
do with the principle of being excluded, rather than the actual
substance of the agreement. For its part, UNICE was reluctant to
incorporate additional organisations on the employer side where
there were already two (UNICE and CEEP) and was concerned that
this would weaken the employers' negotiating position (Hornung-
Draus, 1998).

The next agreement was criticised mainly by UEAPME, which was
again excluded from the negotiations (*European Industrial Relations
Review*, 1997c). UNICE did, however, respond to the concerns about
representativity by including Eurocommerce as an 'expert' (but not

as a co-signatory) in the negotiations. Eurocommerce was included along with the hotel (HOTREC) and industrial cleaning (FENI) sectors because of the large number of part-time employees in these sectors. Eurocommerce therefore had less reason to be discontent and felt that it had managed to water down certain provisions, for example the exclusion of casual workers. Nevertheless, although Eurocommerce views this status as 'a step forward', it still seeks equal status in negotiations with UNICE (Eurocommerce, 1998). As for UEAPME, it lodged a second complaint with the CFI, although again, they did not have any real problems with the content of the agreement.

By the time the negotiations on fixed-term contracts were near conclusion in December 1998, UNICE and UEAPME had settled their differences through a bilateral cooperation agreement that would co-opt UEAPME into future negotiations (UNICE, 1998b; *European Industrial Relations Review*, 1999).[10] Pressure had been growing on UNICE from the Commission and the European Parliament and some national governments to find a peaceful solution. As part of the agreement, UEAPME agreed to drop its complaint on part-time work as well as the appeal on parental leave. Eurocommerce was again involved in the fixed-term negotiations as an expert and lobbied above all for differential treatment between permanent and fixed-term workers if there were 'objective' grounds. Eurochambres does not aspire to a bargaining role, because its members do not have such a role at national level, so its grievances have been directed essentially at exclusion from forums such as the Standing Committee on Employment (SCE) on which it, unlike UNICE, UEAPME and Eurocommerce, does not have a seat (Eurochambres, 1996, 1998).

Conclusion

The main explanation for UNICE's positions and actions has, then, been a pragmatic one driven mainly by economic self-interest, but it has also served the institutional self-interest of employers by elevating their role in the decision-making process and by consolidating the *raison d'être* of their representative organisations. Although prior to 1985 private sector employers originally had little incentive for dealing with trade unions at European level, ever since the Commission launched the social dialogue it has provided employers with an interest in talking to them. The very first incentive was that the

Commission would stop bombarding employers with social directives if they talked to the unions. Similarly, during the 1991 IGC employers abandoned their long-standing opposition to the principle of European negotiations because this was the best way – in a changing institutional environment – of limiting the damage of European social legislation upon their members. Private sector employers knew that more QMV was inevitable and that they would no longer be able to rely on the veto of a single government in the Council. To sum up, they were forced to reconsider their strategy; however, their basic interest remained the same: to reduce as much as possible the passage of what it perceived to be unnecessarily costly and restrictive EU-level social legislation.

Since Maastricht, although negotiations have not taken place on all the dossiers which have been submitted according to the Maastricht provisions, interviews and press releases demonstrate that UNICE's logic has remained the same. The agreements on parental leave, part-time work and fixed-term contracts have all served UNICE's economic interest. Although not a primary motivation, the first two may have served, or at least did not harm the purpose of ensuring that the institutional privileges they had obtained at Maastricht would be preserved at the 1996–7 IGC. Similarly, UNICE's positions on EWCs, sexual harassment and national information and consultation were also self-interested. In the first instance, however, the 'baggage' of the dossier undermined the possibility for negotiations. UNICE was deeply divided over its strategy on national information and consultation, but the objective of both camps was identical: to obtain an optimal – i.e. least economically costly – outcome for members. One side believed that negotiations offered the best route, while others were more confident that a blocking minority could be obtained in the Council in order to undermine the measure altogether. The situation was similar with regard to the sexual harassment dossier. The evidence from UEAPME, Eurocommerce and Eurochambres supports this view that one of the main interests of employers in the social dialogue is that it serves as a partial brake on or dilution mechanism for what it perceived to be bad social policy.

This does not mean that other factors, such as institutions, were unimportant. The institutional environment, in particular changing institutional incentives were critical and formed part of a deliberate neo-functionalist-style strategy on the part of the Commission whose ultimate aim was to promote the suitable conditions for European collective bargaining (Branch, 1997). Undoubtedly, the actions of institutions have introduced a path dependency and had unintended consequences as neither UNICE nor the ETUC knew where the Val Duchesse social dialogue would lead then, nor were they absolutely certain about how the October 1991 provisions would operate in practice, and it was precisely fear of the unknown that was one of the major problems for UNICE.

Factors such as socialisation and learning have also been important. For example, the most important effect of the joint opinions was that the working groups in which they were drawn up 'provided – for the first time – a truly European platform for the exchange of experiences between representatives of national social partners' and offered them 'the opportunity to widen their horizon beyond their national system, to develop an understanding of other systems and traditions and to arrive at European common positions which were compatible with the different national approaches' (Hornung-Draus, 1998, p.231).

Furthermore, the evidence suggests that the more dealings individuals have with European processes, the more supportive they tend to be of them. Indeed, UNICE has learnt that 'often it can achieve a more sensible outcome by negotiating with European level trade unions than by leaving matters to the Commission, as many of the ETUC's officials are actually good economists'. Nevertheless, this remains an instrumental view of the social dialogue, as although a greater awareness has developed of each other's industrial relations systems, this has resulted, in the words of one respondent, if anything in 'greater pragmatism and probably awareness of the *limitations* of social dialogue'.

Several respondents stressed the view that UNICE viewed the social dialogue as a chance to be informed of the Commission's intentions, and one respondent described how social dialogue had worked to the advantage of employers by providing a 'wonderful platform from which to propagate the employer point of view because often European Parliament, Council and Commission representatives are present as observers'. As a consequence, if employers have good ideas, the social dialogue helps their views to prevail.

A distinction needs to be drawn between secretariats and members, as the former, who have more regular dealings with the European level, are almost always more enthusiastic than their memberships, and there is a sense that it is often necessary to educate their members who are unaware of the political stakes. Nevertheless, what this means is that it is necessary to educate their members about the effectiveness of the social dialogue as a 'lobbying platform', and to make them understand 'where power lies, and how the Treaty works'.

In addition, in some of the interviews we undertook as part of the process of writing this chapter, the enthusiasm of some of the protagonists in employer organisations was obvious, not so much for the concept per se but also for the possibilities for these organisations to engage in bureaucratic expansion. One respondent told us:

> it is difficult for us to balance the reluctant interests of our members with the chance for this organisation to be something... it is difficult to account for this, it is really intricate... my members are reluctant to make progress on the sectoral level, and yet at the other we want to take part at the intersectoral SD... there is a bit of a contradiction here... I cannot see how this will be resolved, but it is not a new question... it has been an issue since I have been working here.

It is not, therefore, possible to separate out 'learning effects' from economic and institutional self-interest.

While the impact of institutions and learning are interesting stories in themselves and worthy of independent investigation, they do not alter the fact that although UNICE's strategy for pursuing its self-interest has changed, its fundamental goal has remained the same. Individuals may be 'socialised', have 'gone native', support a 'proactive' employer position, or feel that the social dialogue has 'matured', but what this actually means is that they have learnt that the organisation's goals can now best be achieved through full participation in European processes and trying to assert control over the agenda, rather than responding purely reactively. Above all, UNICE views negotiations as an end point, 'primarily a tool in the process of shaping European social legislation', and not as part of a developing process, namely the beginning of European-level traditional collective bargaining, as the Commission originally hoped (Hornung-Draus, 1998, p.233). Similarly, UNICE has never viewed the social dialogue as a goal in itself, but as a means to an end, namely as a way of ensuring the success of the internal market and the competitiveness of European companies.

Although a few individuals may have been socialised one step further and have a personal, almost philosophical 'belief' in the virtues of 'European social partnership' and its benefits for 'society', these do not alter outcomes. This is because these organisations are highly constrained and do not exist for themselves, so they are prevented from 'running ahead' of their members, and have often deliberately taken steps to prevent their secretariats from talking them into places where they do not wish to go. Even CEEP has an extremely close monitoring system for its involvement in the social partnership, with virtually everything depending upon the agreement of the General Assembly, although this may be more related to the relatively small numbers allocated to CEEP in actual negotiations (typically six), with the result that each country represented within CEEP cannot be represented at negotiations. CEEP apart, therefore, the other organisations themselves retain an instrumental view of social partnership, rather than a belief in it per se. Indeed, UNICE has emphasised that its members have an issue-by-issue approach and will only negotiate when there is a specific proposal from the EU institutions. A view echoed by several respondents was that, 'it is right to say that we will not negotiate unless there is a specific legislative proposal from the Commission to have an agreement'.

Another reason for not overplaying social explanations is that there is little evidence of a unilinear evolution in members' views within UNICE, something which could reasonably be expected if explanations of this nature really were decisive. One reason for this is the magnetic pull of the domestic level, which often means that short-term considerations prevail. As an illustration, although UNICE's members now generally accept the principle of European negotiations, considerable fluctuations occur in members' positions within UNICE, often as a result of ongoing issues at the domestic level. For example, although the debates on 35-hour working weeks in France, Spain and Italy were completely unrelated to the European level, discontent with national developments spilled over into the European debate on employment. In Italy in particular, when a new government undermined the national agreement reached between Italian employers and trade unions on working time, Italian employers protested by reacting negatively to dialogue at every level.

The interviews also indicated that frequently the reason for non-linear shifts is the impact of personality upon short-term assessments of self-interest. Conflicts between senior individuals, rather than over issues, and differences of view between successive senior individuals, can also result in an evolution characterised by peaks and troughs rather than unilinearity. Equally, several respondents argued that the extent to which the social dialogue runs smoothly depends on the quality of communication within national federations, and that the skill of UNICE's secretary-general (and equally the ability of UNICE's national members to sell developments to their members) were also important factors. A view which emerged from several respondents who had been involved in the process for most of its existence was that some newer participants are less committed to social dialogue and do not understand why it is so important because they were not involved in the late 1980s when private sector employers had felt that they were being inundated by social legislation and that a new strategy was therefore necessary. One respondent was concerned that, if anything, this was resulting in centrifugal forces.

The picture of evolution in the other organisations is also rather 'messy'. In UEAPME and Eurochambres this is largely because so much of their efforts have been concentrated on securing access to social dialogue structures, so everything else has so far been secondary. Nevertheless, it is clear that Eurochambres has had to work hard at making its members understand the political stakes and in maintaining their interest in European issues. Similarly, although Eurocommerce's members are conscious that European negotiations could often work to their advantage, there is little genuine enthusiasm for them, and also a sense that the secretariat has to work hard at maintaining their interest. The primary interest of these organisations is domestic, and European social partnership is still perceived as a rather new, abstract and remote phenomenon.

Finally, UNICE's actions may have had unintended consequences, but these have, arguably, benefited UNICE, and do not therefore constitute evidence against a self-interest argument. Although UNICE refused binding negotiations with EU-level trade unions for as long as the Council's actions were limited by the unanimity rule, when an extension of QMV in social policy appeared inevitable, it rapidly concluded that the new arrangements could work to its advantage by introducing the type of framework social legislation originally intended by the Treaty of Rome in its definition of directives, which ' ... shall be binding as to the result to be achieved ... but shall leave to the national authorities the choice of form and methods'. However, UNICE considers itself fortunate in having the ETUC as a social partner, believing in European integration and supporting the internal market and EMU, seen as the policies which are already lifting the EU out of its long period of economic decline. So although the motivating force for UNICE has been self-interest, its perception of this has changed from one of hostility to cooperation with trade unions at the EU level, to a rapprochement and realisation that cooperation may have genuine benefits for its members.

3
The Impact of the Social Dialogue Procedure on the Powers of European Union Institutions

Daniela Obradovic

Introduction

The involvement of European management and labour associations in European Union decision-making through the social dialogue[1] procedure (Goldstein and Keohane, 1993, p.19; Garrett and Weingast, 1993, p.204) has been strengthened by its incorporation into the main body of the European Community Treaty at the 1997 Amsterdam European Council summit.[2] The EC Treaty, by virtue of Articles 138 and 139, formally set up a procedure for the structured involvement of European-level management and labour, i.e. social partners in European lawmaking. The social partners have to be consulted on any legislative proposal in the social field and may initiate a suspension of the legislation process by entering into negotiations with a view to concluding a European agreement.

The legislative procedure involving social issues is replaced by social partners' negotiations. The policy-making autonomy guaranteed to them in Article 137(1) of the European Community Treaty (EC) enables them to have wide freedom of action, which can be termed discretionary powers. Thus, the social partners not only influence Community policy but also make public policy in their own right. They act as private agents empowered to make public policy. By virtue of the Treaty they gained power to decide public policy, to make 'authoritative allocation' for society. This development indicates an increase in the capacity of the social partners to define European public policy. Their role is not simply to be consulted on particular issues but to determine public policy: essentially, it means sharing in the Union's authority. The Treaty provisions provide the social partners with an institutionalised public purpose as regards social issues in the Union. Organised business and labour become formally integrated in Union policy formation and responsible for many decisions discharged by the European Union institutions.

The social partners encroach upon the Union's institutions' powers throughout both stages of the social dialogue procedure: consultation with employers' and employees' organisations at the European Union level envisaged in Article 138 EC, and the negotiation phase described in Article 139 where these associations may conclude agreements which can be given binding legal effect. This results in the substantial decrees of powers of the Union institutions in social policy formation.

The main aim of this chapter is to examine the nature and scope of the restriction of powers of the European Union institutions within the social dialogue procedure. An assessment is to be made as to the limitation of the institutions' discretion which occurs as a result of endowing the social partners with social policy formation powers by virtue of the Treaty. Analysis is confined to the competence of the Commission and the European Parliament since the role of the Council is dealt with elsewhere in the book. Although the introduction of the social dialogue procedure significantly limits the legislative powers of both the Commission and the European Parliament, the consequences for their overall position in the Union decision-making structure are considerably different. Although the introduction of the social dialogue procedure expands the decision-making competence of the social partners at the expense of both Union institutions, it does not affect their roles in an identical manner. Indeed, the Commission and the European Parliament experienced quite different repercussions for their lawmaking powers as a result of the advancing role of the social partners in Union decision-making. While the Commission may benefit from the involvement of the social partners despite limitations upon its own legislative rights, the most significant loser has been the European Parliament, totally deprived of its prerogatives in this area.

The second purpose of this chapter is to examine the attitudes of these institutions towards the greater involvement of the social partners in the Union policy process. I argue that the evolution of the positions of the Commission and the Parliament towards the introduction of the social dialogue procedure in European lawmaking are conditioned by a degree of distributional power gains that they could obtain from the social partners' involvement in Union social policy formation. The attitudes of those institutions towards the participation of management and labour in the European policy process can be best understood in terms of the power distribution advantages arising from cooperation with the social partners. That helps to explain why the Commission created social partnership,[3] while the European Parliament, which suffered exclusion from Union social decision-making as a result of the introduction of the social dialogue procedure, became the fiercest critic of all the European Union institutions.

The restriction of the Commission's powers within the social dialogue procedure

The enshrining in Community law of autonomous unions and employers' organisations offers the potential for developing an increasingly significant role for the social partners in the Union policy formation process at the expense of the Commission's competence. Notably, the Treaty-based social dialogue procedure expands the decision-making powers of Union-level labour and employer organisations working in tandem, and simultaneously restricts the Commission competencies which it enjoys in other areas of Union decision-making. It limits the Commission powers guaranteed in the other areas of European decision-making in that it posits the challenge to its agenda-setting monopoly and restricts its right of amendment. Throughout all the other decision-making procedures in other areas of Community law, the Commission enjoys the monopoly of the right of initiative[4] and unrestricted power of amendment (Article 250(2)), which practically means that it can alter its proposal or even withdraw it at any point during the procedures leading to the adoption of a Community act. The only restriction is that this right should be exercised before the common positions are taken by the Council and the Parliament. In addition, pursuant to Article 250(1) Member States can only amend a proposal from the Commission unanimously. In contrast to this, the role of the Commission within the social policy formation process has been weakened under the social dialogue procedure.

The restriction of the Commission's agenda-setting competence

On the basis of Article 138 of the Treaty, the Commission has to consult the social partners every time prior to presenting a proposal in the sphere of social policy. It is obliged to conduct the two-stage consultations among the range of social partners before making proposals in the social field, and also if, after such consultations, it considers Union action advisable. The time limit for each consultation stage is six weeks, though the Commission may extend this deadline (Commission of the European Communities, 1998a, p.9).[5] First, the Commission shall, at the initial stage, consult under Article 138(2) of the Treaty both union and employers' organisations before submitting any proposals about social affairs, in order to obtain clarity as regards the direction of Union action. Under Article 138, the Commission has an onus to consult labour and management, so that actions taken in breach of such provisions should be sent back to the social partners for evaluation; when adopted without consultation, such actions will be invalid. The Commission (1993a, paragraph 6), for its part, has underlined that 'the social partners now have a right to be consulted', although it remains unclear whether collective organisations would be able to enforce such a right against the Commission. Nevertheless, without their consultation, no action can be taken by the Union institutions.

Should the Commission consider that Union action is necessary, it must, as the second stage (Article 138(3) of the Treaty), immediately request the opinion of the social partners on the substance of the planned proposal, and wait for an opinion or recommendation from the social partners for each further step. The Commission cannot proceed further within the social dialogue procedure if the European organisations of business and workers decline to grant their support for the Commission proposal at this stage. In all other areas of Union decision-making the Commission's initiative could be rejected only by the institutions, the Council or the Parliament.

During the second stage of the consultation, management and labour can ask to be allowed jointly to draft a proposal under the provisions of Article 139(1). The social partners may, at the second stage, as an alternative to action by the Commission, enter into a collective agreement. This means that, instead of leaving further action to the Commission, the social partners can decide to take up the issue themselves. They are free to engage in negotiation after the Commission has begun the second consultation.[6] As a safeguard to prevent any legislative obstruction by the social partners, however, this procedure has to be completed within a definite time period (nine months), which may be extended only through a joint decision by the Commission and the social partners based upon principles of autonomy and mutual recognition of the negotiating parties (Commission of the European Communities, 1998a, p.14). In the process of negotiations, the social partners are not bound by the scope and content of the Commission's proposal submitted in course of the consultation (Commission of the European Communities, 1993a, paragraph 31). The completed test cases of parental leave and part-time and fixed-term work revealed that adopted issues were only one component of the proposal suggested at the first stage of consultation (Keller and Sörries, 1999, p.121). In the first case, the package put forward by the Commission also contained educational leave; in the second and third cases, casual work was included and the principle of non-discrimination was restricted not only to 'employment conditions' but was extended to statutory social security.[7] So far, the general pattern has been that the social partners have concluded their agreements on some selected, consensual parts of the original package only.

This shows that the social partners in the social dialogue procedure assumed quite important agenda-setting rights under the social dialogue procedure, and encroached upon the Commission monopoly of initiative guaranteed in the other areas of the European Community policy formation process.

The deprivation of the Commission's amendment rights

Under the Article 139 procedure, management and labour are allowed to jointly reach agreements on social issues and then to seek, through a Commission proposal and a Council decision, to have these agreements enacted as European Union law. The Council cannot alter the agreement reached by the social partners (Commission of the European Communities, 1993a, considerations 38 and 42), as this would infringe the autonomy of the social partners guaranteed in Article 139 (though see Compston's introduction in this volume). The Council can adopt this agreement as it is concluded, or decline to endorse it. The Commission also took the view that the Council decision must be limited to making binding the provisions of the agreement concluded between the social partners, so that the text of the agreement would not form part of the decision but would be annexed thereto (Commission of the European Communities, 1993a, consideration 41). It also proposed the adoption of a decision on the agreement as concluded. Finally, the Commission announced that if the Council decided not to implement the agreement as concluded by the social partners, the Commission would withdraw its proposal (Commission of the European Communities, 1996c, consideration 30). Simultaneously, the Commission (1993, consideration 38) implicitly proclaimed that it also is not empowered to insert amendments or changes to the text, and maintains that it will always propose to the Council that the agreement should be adopted as it stands. The social partners, in their common proposals (ETUC, CEEP, UNICE, 1993, Section 10.3) for the implementation of the social dialogue procedure, also reject the view that modifications either by the Commission or the Council are admissible. Thus, under the social dialogue procedure the Commission is deprived of its amendment rights guaranteed to it elsewhere in the Treaty.

The Commission's residual powers in the social dialogue

In spite of the fact that the Commission's powers are increasingly encroached upon by the social partners in the social dialogue procedure, it still retains specific powers within it. The residual competence of the Commission within the social dialogue revolves around:

1 the right to trigger the social dialogue negotiations;
2 the right to license the European organisations to be consulted under Article 138(2);
3 the right not to suspend legislative process on the request of European labour and management organisations;
4 the right to submit a proposal to the Council if the social partners request the implementation of their agreements reached under the social dialogue negotiations through EC law;
5 the right to assess an agreement requested by the social partners to be implemented by EC law as regards the representativity of the signatory parties and legality thereof;
6 the provision of the balance of support for the parties or the right to intervene.

1. The right to trigger the social dialogue negotiations phase

In their independent negotiations, the social partners are in no way required to restrict themselves to the content of the proposal presented by the Commission during consultations under Article 138 or merely to make amendments to it (Commission of the European Communities, 1993a, paragraph 31). Indeed, the freedom of the social partners to conclude Community-wide contracts unrelated to Commission proposals is explicitly recognised in Article 12(2) of the 1989 Community Charter of the Fundamental Social Rights of Workers (1990), of which observance is guaranteed in Article 136 EC. Where the subject matter of such free-standing agreements covers the social policy categories identified in Article 137(1) and (3), they can also be implemented by a Council decision on a proposal from the Commission, if the social partners jointly request this.[8] However, although there is nothing in the text of the Treaty that prevents social partners from negotiating on any subject of their own choice, the social dialogue procedure can in practice be commenced only after the proposal has been tendered by the Commission. UNICE (1999)[9] has declared that it will only agree to take up bargaining in the case of the Commission's initiative since for UNICE, the goal is to determine decision-making, not to facilitate new social regulation (Hall, 1994, p.300; Ramsay, 1995, p.103).

2. The right to license European organisations to be consulted under Article 138(2)

The Commission is endowed with power to license European management and labour organisations for the purpose of their consultation stipulated under Article 138(2). On the basis of representativity criteria set out in the Commission's communication on the implementation of the social dialogue (1993a, paragraph 24),[10] it identifies 29 European social partners whose representativity in its view entitles them to be consulted under Article 138(2). However, the Commission points out clearly that the listed associations are not granted a representational monopoly and that it does not have any intention of using this list as the basis for official 'licensing' of the social partners. It expressed its intention to revise the list in the light of experience as the process develops. Although it did not revise the original list in its 1998 Communication on the development of social dialogue (Commission of the European Communities, 1998a, Annex 1), in practice it did not rigidly stick to the list. For example, it consulted 39 organisations on the matter of burden of proof in sex discrimination cases (Commission of the European Communities, 1996a, considerations 3 and 5).

Thus, in practice the Commission has the unlimited discretion to independently choose which associations to consult in the course of this procedure. The European organisations not designated by the Commission as meeting its representativity criteria are barred from participation in consultations within the social dialogue procedure. Without the Commission's endorsement, management and labour organisations operating at European level cannot claim any right under Article 138 EC.

While the Commission is empowered to designate the participants in the consultation stage of the social dialogue procedure, it cannot do so with regard to the negotiation process foreseen in Article 138(3). It is not allowed to decide which parties should participate in the talks. The social partners concerned will be those who agree to negotiate with each other (Commission of the European Communities, 1993a, paragraph 31). The Commission (1993a, paragraph 26; 1998, 12) recognised that only organisations themselves are in a position to develop their own dialogue and negotiating structure, and that it cannot impose on participants freely undertaken negotiations. The right of any social partner to choose its negotiating counterpart is a key element of the autonomy of the social partners (Commission of the European Communities, 1998a, pp.12–13). These limits on the Commission's licensing rights for the purpose of the implementation of the social dialogue procedure has recently been confirmed by the European Court of Justice in its UEAPME ruling.[11]

3. The right not to suspend legislative process on the request of European labour and management organisations

Although the social partners are entitled during the second stage of the consultation of management and labour on the social law proposal, under Article 138(4), to ask the Commission to suspend the legislative process in order to enable them to proceed with the negotiation on the subject, the Commission retains the discretion to approve or reject this request. The Commission can decline to do so if it considers interested parties to be insufficiently representative in terms of criteria set up in its communication on the implementation of the social dialogue procedure (Commission of the European Communities, 1993a, paragraph 24).[12] It announced in the aforementioned communication that it would judge on a case-by-case basis, taking into consideration both the character and the impact of the proposal and the possible effects of a collective agreement (Commission of the European Communities, 1993a, paragraph 30). However, the Commission has never rejected the possibility of stopping legislative activity on the request of the social partners.

4. The right to submit a proposal to the Council if the social partners request the implementation of their agreement reached under the social dialogue negotiations through EC law

If the social partners reach an agreement within the social dialogue negotiation procedure and decide to request the implementation of the agreement by virtue of EC law, only the Commission is entitled to propose the social partners' document to the Council. Article 139(2) states that agreement by the social partners 'shall be implemented . . . by a Council decision on a proposal from the Commission'. If the Commission is mentioned explicitly, it will have to play an active role in the social dialogue process, such that it must be granted discretion (Commission of the European Communities, 1993a, paragraph 30).

5. The right to assess an agreement requested by the social partners to be implemented by EC law as regards the representativity of the signatory parties, and its legality

The Commission's right to present an agreement to the Council concluded by the social partners implies the Commission's discretion to decide whether or not to propose the social partners' document to the Council. However, the Commission is not empowered to assess the agreement as regards its content, but only in terms of criteria listed in its 1993 Communication (Commission of the European Communities, 1993a, paragraphs 38 and 39). The reason for this is that the procedure set out in Article 139 is not designed to seek the Commission's approval for a collective agreement, since it guarantees the autonomy of the social partners, but rather to use the Union's legislative machinery to endow agreements with the legal standing that they otherwise would not have. Consequently, the Commission has no right to encroach upon the decision-making autonomy of the social partners in the negotiation procedure and amend the content of the agreement, as it already acknowledged (Commission of the European Communities, 1993a, paragraph 38), but only to examine whether the agreement in question meets the formal criteria required by EC law. The Commission is not needed to endorse the social partners' will, but, as the guardian of the Treaty, makes sure that the EC law requirements are observed by the social partners if they wish to implement their agreement by a Community measure.

Before any legislative proposal implementing an agreement is presented to the Council, the Commission carries out an assessment involving consideration of (1) the representative status of the contracting parties, (2) their mandate, (3) the legality of each clause in the collective agreement in relation to Community law, and (4) the provisions regarding small and medium-sized undertakings set out in Article 137(2) EC (Commission of the European Communities, 1993a, paragraphs 38–42). In addition, before proposing a decision implementing an agreement negotiated on a matter within the material scope of Article 137, but outside the formal consultation procedure, the Commission has the obligation to assess the appropriateness of Community action in that field (Commission of the European Communities, 1998a, p.16).

Among those tests, the representativity assessment is the most significant one. The Commission claims that this question of representativeness must be examined on a case-by-case basis, as it can vary according to the subject matter. The Commission may sanction non-representativeness of signatories by not submitting to the Council any collective agreement concluded by groups which it does not consider to be representative. It is emphasised in the Commission documents that it will not submit a legislative proposal to the Council, making the agreement binding if it considers that the signatory parties are not sufficiently representative in relation to the scope of their agreements (Commission of the European Communities, 1998a, p.16).

The Court of Justice confirmed this right of the Commission in its UEAPME judgement.[13] The Court held that if the management and labour organisations concerned address their joint request for the implementation of their agreement by a Community measure to the Commission under Article 139, the Commission thereupon resumes control of the procedure and determines whether it is appropriate to submit a proposal to that effect to the Council. According to the Court, the Commission must, in particular, examine the representativity of the signatories to the agreement in question. It is the duty of the Commission, held the Court, to verify that the signatories to the agreement are truly representative, because of the fact that democratic legitimacy of the measures adopted under Article 139(2) procedure derives from the representativity of the parties involved in the negotiations.[14]

6. The provision of balanced support for the parties or the right to intervene

Under the Treaty, the Commission is given the task of promoting the social dialogue. Moreover, Article 138(1) posits that the Commission shall not only promote consultation of the social partners, but also ensure balanced support for the parties. This ambitious task the Commission is entrusted with stands in sharp contrast with its pre-Maastricht assignments regarding the stimulation of the participation of the social partners in the Union policy process. Article 118b of the 1986 Single European Act only requires the Commission to 'endeavour to develop the dialogue between management and labour at European level'. Article 138(1) redefines the Commission's tasks of promoting the social dialogue by placing an obligation on the Commission, on the one hand to promote the consultation of management and labour (the social partners), and on the other hand to take any relevant measure to facilitate their dialogue by ensuring 'balanced support for the parties'. This means that the Commission is not only given the task of providing the arena where the negotiation takes place, but is also charged with facilitating the dialogue. Furthermore, the Treaty requires the Commission to redress the imbalance between the actors participating in the social dialogue. It is, in effect, given the task of controlling balanced input of management and labour in the Union social policy process.

The duty to ensure 'balanced support for the parties' in the social dialogue in reality means the right to intervene, which makes the Commission an active agent in this process. Indeed, in its documents the Commission emphasised that the relevant Treaty provisions 'assigned to ... [it] ... a dynamic role in promoting this dialogue, and entrusted it with the task of playing an active part in overcoming any difficulties or reluctance which might occur on the part of one or other of the partners and possibly impede progress' (Commission of the European Communities, 1993a, consideration 12). Obviously, by claiming its rights to engage in the social dialogue in order to eliminate impediments to this process, it announced in public its intention 'to continue to play its stimulating role while fully respecting the social partners' own willingness, though not disregarding the Commission's obligations and its prerogatives under the Treaty (Marin, 1988, paragraph 23).

I argue that the 'provision of balanced support' requirement is

not inserted in the Treaty in order to redress the imbalance between two sides of industry, but to provide the Commission with a
convenient tool for intervention and enable it to retain full control of the social dialogue procedure which would otherwise be
restricted due to the fact that it transferred some of its powers to
the social partners within this procedure. The reasons for this are
as follows:

1 the imbalance of interests is inherent in the original Treaty;
2 the Commission has not yet developed the capacities necessary
   to reshape the social dialogue by ensuring balanced support for
   management and labour.

The disproportionate influence of business interests at the expense
of workers' interests in the European Union policy process is well
elaborated in the literature (Streeck, 1994, pp.166–7; 1995, p.49).

The EU has often been characterised as reflecting a business agenda
(Green Cowles, 1995, p.552; Rein and Schon, 1991, p.262).[15] Huge
business resources, it is suggested, are readily translatable into political power. According to Harlow (1992, p.349) the imbalance of
interests on the European scene is written into the original Treaty.
The commercial, business and other corporate interests dominate
European politics. Indeed, in the substance of the agreements on
parental leave and part-time and fixed-term work there are notable
concessions to the employers' side which were absent in the Commission's original proposal. As far as the parental leave agreement
is concerned, most important is the provision to the effect that
Member States may permit an employer to postpone the granting
of parental leave 'for justifiable reasons related to the operation of
the undertaking'.[16] The exclusion of casual workers from the part-
time agreement,[17] the guarantee of the discretion of a Member State
to discriminate against particular categories of workers for 'objective reasons' in both part-time and fixed-time work agreements,[18]
the exclusion of social security from those agreements,[19] and the
non-regulation of initial recourse to fixed-term contracts by the
agreement on that subject further illustrates the weaker position of
labour in the European social dialogue. The constant and long-term
decline in trade unions' powers (Lecher, 1994, p.87; Hepple, 1994,
p.iii) raises the problem of an imbalance of interests in a more
pressing way.

For business, it is much easier to pursue its preferences in an
international arena than it is for labour. Class interests of labour
seek supranational protection against 'competitive deregulation' of

national systems, while among capital, class interests are to remove barriers to mobility of capital and labour across national borders, without in the process having to accept 'market-distorting' re-distributive intervention or the development of welfare state-like international institutions. As has been pointed out by Streeck (1996, pp.90–1), closer inspection of the strategic options available in a transnational system of interest politics reveals that capital finds it structurally easier than labour to pursue its transnational class interests, since it can do this by either not acting at all, or continuing to act exclusively at national level. Labour, on the other hand, can pursue its transnational class interest only if it manages to define positive common objectives; build a transnational capacity for collective action; and overcome the logic of non-decision inherent in the intergovernmental system. It is this differential significance of action and non-action that governs the transnational class politics of European social policy, and accounts for its result. Here capital is privileged by the fact that it can achieve its class interests by non-action, while the class interests of labour depend for their realisation not just on their own transnational organisation, but also on the willingness of labour's opponent, capital, to organise itself as an interlocutor capable of negotiating binding agreements. Unlike the class political interests of capital, those of labour require positive political decisions and central regulations capable of suspending social system competition.

The Commission is not capable of redressing this structural imbalance between parties involved in the social dialogue. It does not have the capacities necessary to reshape the social dialogue by ensuring balanced support for management and labour, as the Treaty requires (Streeck and Schmitter, 1991, p.142; Vobruba, 1995, p.312).

In order to redress this structural imbalance the Commission should be:

1 an autonomous political actor;
2 endorsed with redistributive powers necessary for redressing the imbalance in question;
3 standing above and beyond sectional interests.

However, none of these conditions is fulfilled at the present stage of European integration.

The Commission can hardly be regarded as an autonomous political actor. The first problem is that the Commission cannot really act as a corporate actor. As Cram (1997, pp.155, 157) has pointed out, the Commission is in fact not a 'monolith' but rather a 'multi-organisation' with fierce internal conflicts (Christiansen, 1997). It is composed of Commissioners, cabinets and Directorates General, each with distinct preferences and distinct policy networks forming around them. Although some scholars (Peters, 1992; Dang-Nguyen *et al.*, 1994, p.494; and Cram, 1997, Chapter 6) do argue that the Commission is an internally differentiated corporate actor with autonomous action capacities, there is no empirical evidence that the Commission can exercise its discretion without constraints. On the contrary, there can be little doubt as to the determination of the Member States to limit the Commission's discretion at every stage of policy-making. Political initiative comes from the heads of state or government in the European Council; political mediation takes place in the framework of the Committee of Permanent Representatives of national governments (COREPER); formal adoption is the prerogative of the Council of Ministers; and implementation is in the hands of national administrations (Majone, 1996, pp.61–2). Thus, although the Commission enjoys a certain degree of discretion in its actions and capacity to be engaged in political exchange in the European policy process, it is exceedingly difficult to demonstrate Commission independence in empirical research since its autonomy is subjected to specific conditions that vary across issue-areas, and over time (Pollack, 1997, pp.116–17).

Second, as shown by Majone's empirical research (1996, pp.63–6), the Commission is not capable of pursuing distributional policies, but only regulatory tasks. Redistributive policies transfer resources from one group of individuals to another. This requires the direct expenditure of public funds. Thus, the size of distributional programmes is determined by budgetary appropriations which are borne not by the Commission but by groups who have to comply with the regulations. The action of the Commission is, on the one hand, restrained by insufficient resources for altering the imbalance between the parties to the social dialogue. Although, it provides financial support for the European labour organisation, the Commission has very limited resources at its disposal for a 'political exchange' with the trade unions (Rhodes, 1993, p.317). On the other hand, the Commission, as explained above, does not possess unconstrained political powers to force specific groups to comply with its redistributive decisions. Its discretion regarding the allocation of resources is still tightly controlled by the national governments.

Third, at present there is no evidence that would support the thesis that the Commission can be regarded as a sufficiently centralised and autonomous state bureaucracy that could develop and defend notions of public interest and policy. It is argued, in essence, that the Commission is being left in the case of the social dialogue, to judge what is in the public interest. But the public interest can only be evaluated through a political agreement: the Commission is not appropriate for this task since in the European Union the political arrangements are still made by the Member States, and not by the members of the Commission. What is more, the Commission has interests of its own, which it can best pursue by using its discretionary powers to support particular interests. It might use its powers to pursue its own preferences (Mazey and Richardson, 1999, pp.200–16; Cram, 1997, Chapter 6; Wendon, 1998, p.343). The outcome is that the Commission tends to be captured by the special interest groups. This is not to suggest that the public servants concerned are acting improperly; only that the public whom they are serving is a rather narrow segment of the whole.

Defining its duty to ensure 'balanced support for the parties' in the White Paper, the Commission limits itself to the role of moderator and service station for social partners[20] in the social dialogue process (Commission of the European Communities, 1993b, section 56). In doing so, it confirms the lack of a European political body capable of being engaged in the redistributive process implied by the imposition of 'the provision of the balanced support' requirement. The Commission restricts its task to the provision of the arena where the negotiation takes place, and not to exercise authoritative attribution over conflicting interests.[21] Consequently, the Commission states that 'among the different measures which may facilitate the dialogue, mention can be made of working groups and the provision of technical assistance deemed necessary to underpin the dialogue' (Commission of the European Communities, 1993a, paragraph 6 of the summary). Similarly, Bercusson (1994, p.25) finds that, though Article 138(1) requires the Commission to take any relevant measures to facilitate the dialogue, this would seem only to indicate administrative support.

Although some authors claim there are many indicators that the Commission is busy in all of these areas (e.g. Falkner, 1998, p.171 and Chapter 4 and section 5.1), this type of technical assistance cannot be considered to be an effective mechanism for redressing the structural imbalance of parties participating in the social dialogue. These types of measure are specifically designed to provide the Commission with a legitimate means for intervention in the social dialogue process. As pointed out by Falkner (1998, p.127), although the Commission cannot directly participate in the collective negotiations[22] and it is not formally represented at the bargaining table, it supplies the social partners with a document that constitutes the starting point and basis of their talks, and often plays the role of secretary to the 'neutral umpire', or chairperson. Thus, the Commission uses its role to provide technical support for the negotiations as a convenient tool to intervene in the social dialogue process, in spite of the fact that formally it is barred from participating in the social partners' talks. In this manner the Commission obtains compensation for the partial loss of its agenda-setting and amendment rights through the social dialogue procedure.

The Commission's remaining discretionary rights in the social policy formation process

Apart from possessing residual competence to the right of initiative within the social dialogue, the Commission is endowed under Article 137 with the discretion to look into the possibility of proposing a legislative instrument to the Council and the European Parliament if (1) the social partners do not open collective negotiations, (2) if the negotiations fail and (3) if an agreement's provisions are deemed insufficient by the Commission and the Council (Commission of the European Communities, 1993a, paragraph 34). The Commission has resorted to this option on several occasions after the social partners declined to negotiate on particular issues. It proposed legislation in the cases of the works councils and of the reversal of the burden of proof in sex discrimination cases, which were subsequently adopted by the Council.[23] The Commission also issued its proposal on the obligation of firms to inform and consult works councils on a national level (Commission of the European Communities, 1998b), since the social partners failed in 1997 in their attempts to arrive at a joint response here.[24] The Council has not yet discussed this initiative.

However, although Article 137 provides the legal framework for a social policy proposal to remain in the Commission realm, this is not the option preferred by the Commission. This is because the Council retains amendment rights that enable it to detract from the Commission's original proposal. The Commission tries to avoid this by granting its support for the social dialogue procedure and transferring some of its agenda-setting powers to the social partners. A Commission's counter-proposal to the social partners' agreement may have little chance of adoption in the Council in its original version. Indeed, every draft legislation initiated by the Commission under the Article 137 procedure after the social partners failed to reach an agreement on the issue has been subjected to extensive changes by the Council.[25] Contrary to this, the agreements negotiated by the social partners within the social dialogue procedure almost replicated the proposals submitted by the Commission at the beginning of the social dialogue procedure. Although, as we showed above, those agreements usually reduce the scope of the original Commission's proposals, they introduce only minor adjustments to the content of the text. The parental leave agreement reassembles the original Commission's proposal on the matter (Cullen and Campbell, 1998, p.278).[26] The part-time and the fixed-term work agreements also broadly mirror the previous Commission initiatives dating back to the 1990s.[27]

Moreover, Article 137(2) of the Amsterdam Treaty introduces the co-decision procedure as an alternative to the social dialogue procedure. This procedure removes the Commission as the middle-man between the Council and the Parliament, allowing direct bargaining between the two bodies, providing the Parliament with a possible veto of the final product – and removing the formal agenda-setting power of the Commission in the process (Earnshaw and Judge, 1995; Garrett and Tsebelis, 1996). This means that the Commission's proposal under Article 137 procedure could be amended not only by the Council but also by the European Parliament, which considerably decreases the Commission's chances of pursuing its own preferences.[28]

To conclude, the Commission monopoly of initiative on social issues envisaged under the Article 137 procedure should be considered mainly in terms of an incentive for the social partners to have recourse to negotiation under threat of forthcoming legislation.[29] It is much less a mechanism for the Commission to preserve its monopoly of initiative within social policy, and to counter-balance the expansion of the social partners' public policy-making. This is due to the fact that this alternative avenue imposes a lot of constraints upon the Commission's powers, since the Council and the European Parliament can insert amendments to the Commission's original legislative text and change it substantially under this procedure. Throughout this legislative procedure, the Commission is confronted with the Council's and the Parliament's demands, and that is precisely what the Commission intends to bypass by giving its support for the social dialogue.

Assessment of the Commission role in the social dialogue

Although the extensive inclusion of the social partners in the Union social lawmaking framework greatly affected the powers of the Commission, it still retains the greatest control over this field. The pivotal role assigned to the social partners in social decision-making did not deprive the Commission from exercising a quite substantial influence in this area. The Commission has partially handed over its legislative powers to the representatives of business and labour throughout the social dialogue procedure, but it has retained informal means of influence due to the insertion of its 'provision of balanced support' task in the legal framework of this procedure.

The social partners encroached upon the Commission's agenda-setting and amendment rights, and constrain its monopoly of initiative. Due to this it is very difficult to agree with the view arrived at by some scholars (e.g. Falkner, 1998, p.126) that the Treaty actually extended the Commission's powers of initiative in the social dialogue procedure. The practice that the social dialogue procedure cannot be triggered without the Commission's proposal owes to the unwillingness of UNICE to be engaged in negotiations not initiated by the Commission, and not to legal constraints arising from the Treaty stipulations. Furthermore, the Commission's monopoly of initiative within the social dialogue procedure is confined only to the situation where the social partners request the autonomously concluded agreements to be implemented by a Council decision and it is not applicable should the signatory parties decide to implement the agreement themselves. However, the Commission retained some of formal legislative powers in this procedure. The most important of these competencies are the licensing rights reflected in its authorisation to assess the representativeness of the social partners for the purpose of consultation, and in the case when they request the implementation of their agreements by Community law.

However, the most important channels of Commission influence within the social dialogue are of an informal nature. The Commission retains an informal right to intervene within this procedure as a result of the Treaty empowerment to provide balanced support for the parties. As was shown, the Commission is incapable of redressing the structural imbalance of the parties involved in the social dialogue since it has insufficient autonomy to be involved in the redistributive policies presumed for the provision of the balance in question. The imposition of this duty upon the Commission is intended to provide the legal avenue for the Commission to retain its control over European social legislation and remain a political entrepreneur[30] in this field. Thus, while the Commission ceded some of its formal authority to the social partners throughout the social dialogue procedure, it reclaimed some of its powers by securing the right to intervene.

Accounts of the Commission's attitude towards the social partners' involvement in Union decision-making

Despite the restriction of its powers under the social dialogue procedure, the Commission (Commission of the European Communities, 1993a, consideration 49(2); 1996a, p.1; 1998a, p.15) has demonstrated its unreserved support for social partnership. The reason for this is because the Commission could enhance its influence despite transferring some of its powers to the European employers' and employees' associations. This is because the Commission's position towards the participation of management and labour in the Union policy process is determined by the degree of distributional gains it can obtain from cooperation with them. Its positive attitude towards the social partners' involvement in European social policy formation arises from the potential gains that could be secured through the implementation of the social dialogue procedure.

The Commission can benefit from the institutionalisation of the social dialogue. It is able to strengthen its own position in relation to the Council by restricting its amendment rights. Here, the interests of the Commission and the social partners partly coincide relative to the position of the Council. Under the social dialogue procedure the Council is not entitled to amend the agreement which in any case usually reflects the Commission position because negotiated agreements have invariably been designed and initiated by the Commission. The Commission may gain from the involvement of the social partners if its own proposal is constrained by the Council's amendment rights. Has this right been a constraint in the past? The findings of the empirical studies suggest that the amendment right has almost always been used by the Council (Addison and Siebert, 1994a, p.16). If the Commission's ideal point is outside the Pareto set of the Council and it shares a common interest with the social partners, regulation closer to its ideal point may become attainable. These possible distributional gains may help to explain why the Commission was willing to transfer some of its own agenda powers to the social partners (Boockmann, 1998, p.243). In this case, the interplay of actors facing different constraints in the political process allows for mutual benefits at the expense of a third party, the Council. This is the reason why the thesis that social dialogue restricts the legislative powers of the Commission is reconcilable with the thesis that the involvement of the social partners in European social policy-making helps the Commission to push for an expansion of its competencies (Cram, 1997, Chapter 6). The formal transfer of some of its legislative powers to the social partners throughout the social dialogue procedure could be considered a powerful selective incentive aimed at encouraging their participation in European social policy formation. This enables the Commission to create an alternative institutional venue capable of making legislation, and in that manner effectively reduce the Council influence (Wendon, 1998, p.343) which still prevails over that of the Commission in the Union classical decision-making procedures (Pollack, 1997).

The exclusion of the European Parliament from the social dialogue

In contrast to the position of the Commission in the social dialogue procedure, the European Parliament is deprived of any influence whatsoever in this process. The social partnership concept as operationalised in the social dialogue procedure renders the European Parliament redundant in the area of social affairs subjected to its regulation. The Parliament is bypassed in social decision-making due to the introduction of the social dialogue procedure.

The absence of the Parliament from the social dialogue consultations and negotiations

The European Parliament has no role in the lawmaking procedures set out in Article 138 of the Treaty. The consultations concerning the Commission proposal for social policy legislation are directed only towards the social partners and not towards the European Parliament. In addition, the Treaty does not give the EP a right to be consulted if a social partner agreement is to be turned into EC law. Under Article 139, the Commission is not legally required to consult the European Parliament on requests made to it by the social partners concerning implementation of a framework agreement by means of a Council directive. However, in its Communication concerning the application of the social dialogue procedure, the Commission expresses its intention to inform the European Parliament and to send the text of the agreement, together with its proposals for a decision and the explanatory memorandum, so that Parliament may, if it so wishes, deliver its opinion to the Commission and the Council (Commission of the European Communities, 1993a, considerations 34 and 35). In accordance with this undertaking, the Commission kept the Parliament informed about the various phases of consultation of social partners on the parental leave, part-time and fixed-time work issues. It also forwarded the proposals for directives on these matters to the Parliament. Although these drafts were sent to the Parliament for information, it was permitted no real input on the substantive outcome. Thus, apart from being informed about the consultation with social partners pursuant to the Commission undertakings in its Communication on the social dialogue procedure, the European Parliament has practically no role to play in lawmaking procedure under Articles 138 and 139. Moreover, the experience of the European Works Council Directive[31] does suggest that the Commission takes the social partners' views in the priority to suggested amendments of the European Parliament even when negotiations under the Article 139 procedure failed and the legislation was passed under Article 137(2) (Falkner, 1996b, p.5).[32]

During the negotiations on the Amsterdam Treaty, the European Parliament expressly called to be formally involved in the social dialogue procedure, as the lack of assent of the European Parliament, in its view, is a violation of the institutional balance that is a principle of Community law. However, this request was not acted upon. The only consolation for the Parliament was that it was granted a power of co-decision under the Article 137(2) procedure, which could be initiated by the Commission for social legislation. But, although the Parliament has a co-decision right in some matters under the Article 137(2) procedure when the social partners decide not to negotiate on a particular matter, it will be systematically excluded from legislation on social issues whenever industrial representatives succeed in reaching a negotiated result.

Is the participation of the EP indispensable for achieving democratic legitimacy for Community decisions?

While some authors (e.g. Betten, 1998) point out the consequences for democracy arising from the bypassing of the Parliament, the

Court of Justice does not find the involvement of the Parliament to be an indispensable precondition for the legitimitisation of the legislation. It is of the opinion that the democratic legitimacy of EC measures could be derived from the participation of truly representative management and labour organised at European level equally successfully as from the involvement of the European Parliament in Union decision-making.[33]

In its view the implementation of a social partner agreement through EC law has the effect of endowing that agreement with a Community foundation of legislative character, without recourse to the classic procedures provided for under the Treaty for the preparation of legislation, which entail the participation of the European Parliament. As the case law makes clear, the participation of the Parliament in the Community legislative process reflects at Community level the fundamental democratic principle that the people must share in the exercise of power through a representative assembly.[34] In that regard, Community measures adopted pursuant to this classic procedure derive their democratic legitimacy from the European Parliament's participation in the decision-making process. In contrast, the procedure referred to in Article 139 EC does not provide for the participation of the European Parliament. However, in the absence of the participation of the European Parliament in the legislative process, the principle of democracy on which the Union is founded and the participation of the people are assured through the parties representative of management and labour who concluded the agreement. In this case democratic legitimacy of the measure derives from the representativity of the parties to the agreement. Thus, legitimacy could be achieved, in the Court's view, only if the signatories to the agreement are truly representative. That means that the truly representative social partners could equally successfully be the source of democratic legitimacy of Community measures as the European Parliament. Consequently, since the principle of democracy, i.e. the participation of the people, could be assured in the Union either through the participation of the European Parliament, or through the participation of truly representative associations of the two sides of industry, the indispensability of the Parliament's involvement for democratic decision-making has been rejected by the European Court of Justice.

The evolution of the opinion of the European Parliament towards the inclusion of the social partners in Union decision-making

The evolution of the opinion of the European Parliament towards the inclusion of the social partners in Union decision-making clearly shows that it has been exclusively driven by institutional self-interest. In this process, the Parliament has been transformed from the unreserved supporter of the social partners' participation in Union lawmaking to fierce critic of the social dialogue procedure. This change of position corresponds to the degree of distributional gains and benefits that it could expect from cooperation with the social partners. That is to say that the evolution in the Parliament's attitude to social partnership over the years, namely towards the greater involvement of European business and labour associations in Union decision-making, is determined by the contribution of that involvement to its potency or impotency in the European policy process.

First phase: the Parliament's support of the inclusion of the social partners in Union decision-making

In the mid-1980s when the social partners did not have any formal, Treaty-based legislative powers in the Community policy process and when the social dialogue was only a forum for discussion, the European Parliament was very open to relations with the social partners. Not only did it not compete with them for distributional gains within the Community decision-making structure, but the social partners in that period could be mobilised in support of the Parliament's campaign for a greater role in EC policy-making. For example, in the mid-1980s the ETUC called for more control by the European Parliament.[35] Organised interests were also important to the electability of the members of Parliament, who could benefit from their resources for collecting information needed by MEPs. Consequently, the European Parliament expressed at that time its conviction that management and labour must be given a greater role in the European social policy formation (European Parliament, 1988b, consideration 9).

Although the Parliament clearly takes the position that the parliamentary system is the best way of converting the will of the people into prescriptive decisions (European Parliament, 1988a, 1991), it did not, in that period, regard the inclusion of the social dialogue procedure in European lawmaking as a practice in collision with democracy (Bercusson, 1996, p.73). On the contrary, it expressly emphasised the need for the involvement of the social partners in Union policy-making. In its Resolution on the role of the social partners in the labour market, the European Parliament (1986, considerations E and F) expressed its conviction 'that the role of workers' and employers' organisations and dialogue between the social partners are part and parcel of the European identity and essential preconditions for European integration' and 'that the goal of European integration cannot be achieved without consensus between the sides of industry'.

Phase two: the ambiguous position of the EP towards the institutionalisation of the social dialogue procedure

After the institutionalisation of the social dialogue procedure by the Agreement attached to the Maastricht Treaty in 1992, the Parliament did not develop outright hostility towards it. Rather, its position regarding the role of the social partners in Union lawmaking can be described as an ambiguous one. On the one side, the Parliament, in principle, regarded the institutionalisation of the social partners' decision-making powers as a step towards greater involvement of citizens in Union policy formation (European Parliament, 1996c). On the other hand, it deplored the weakness of its role in the legislative process in the whole social sphere (European Parliament, 1994a, consideration B) and called for its own active incorporation in the process of the adoption of the decision-implementing agreements concluded by the social partners (European Parliament, 1994a, consideration E).

The Parliament stated that the social dialogue and an enhanced role for the social partners constitute an essential condition for the achievement of the social dimension of the internal market (European Parliament, 1994b, consideration A); that the social partners' extensive right in Union decision-making does bring the European social landscape closer to the citizens (European Parliament, 1994b, consideration H),[36] and thus considers that 'there is a need for Parliament to promote the social dialogue by keeping in touch with the social partners' (European Parliament, 1994d, consideration 5).

Notwithstanding the said declarations, the European Parliament requested the reinforcement of its involvement in the decision-making process in the social field. It calls for an inter-institutional agreement with the Council and the Commission which would strengthen the Parliament's right to participation in the social dialogue procedure and reserve its right of initiative if the social partners were unable to reach agreement on issues referred to them under this procedure (European Parliament, 1988b, consideration 12; 1994a, consideration 9; 1994b, consideration 11; 1996a, considerations 2 and 5; 1997a, considerations 15 and 18; 1997b, consideration 21; 1999a, consideration 25). It also suggests that all Council decisions on agreements between management and labour must be agreed in advance under its partnership with Parliament (1994a, consideration 8; 1994b, consideration 12). However, the Parliament's call for an inter-institutional agreement was never accepted by the other Union institutions.

Phase three: the Parliament's open criticism of the practical application of the social dialogue procedure

This Parliament's ambiguous position on the social partners' involvement in Union policy formation evolved into open hostility towards the greater involvement of management and labour in Union decision-making after the conclusion of the parental leave agreement. While Parliament supported the parental leave agreement, it nonetheless expressed reservations about the procedure used. Its criticism particularly concerned the sidelining of Parliament during the consultation with the social partners and the Council's implementation of the directive, which did not allow Parliament to influence the content of the agreement. In its resolution on this matter, the Parliament (1996a) did not emphasise that the social dialogue must be given a greater role in the Union social policy process as it pointed out in its previous resolutions on this issue (European Parliament, 1994a, consideration E; 1994b, considerations A and H). In the Parliament's report on parental leave, Anne-Karin Glase, the rapporteur for the Parliament's social affairs committee, apart from requesting more extensive rights of consultation and participation under the social dialogue procedure, suggested that a different procedure could have been used, allowing for input from the European Parliament (European Parliament, 1996b, p.8).

The conclusion of the part-time and fixed-time work agreements brought out the Parliament's open criticism of the social dialogue procedure. In its resolutions on those agreements, the Parliament openly criticises the social dialogue procedure as being 'too time-consuming and extremely cumbersome', and regards its rights as being curtailed by this procedure (European Parliament, 1997a, point 16 and 1999a, point 23). It concluded with the insertion that the social dialogue must not be a systematic substitute for the legislative process (European Parliament, 1997a, point 12; 1999a, point V) since it leads to the conclusion of lowest common denominator type agreements. However, the most demanding of all Parliament's requests as regards its participation in the social dialogue procedure is that it should be granted power of co-decision, analogous to that of the Council, i.e. in the form of a general right of rejection or approval (European Parliament, 1997a, consideration 17; 1997b, consideration 20; 1998a, consideration 18; 1999a, consideration 24).

Assessment of the Parliament's relations with the social partners

The European Parliament's attitude towards the greater involvement of the social partners in Union decision-making through the social dialogue procedure is driven by institutional self-interest because it is directly conditioned by distributional gains which the Parliament could obtain from cooperation with the European representatives of employers and employees. When, during the 1980s, the Parliament considered that the social partners could be mobilised in support of its cause of securing a more influential role with the Union institutional architecture, the Parliament regarded consultation with management and labour to be an indispensable precondition for achieving greater democracy within the Union. The institutionalisation of consultation with the social partners did not immediately provoke the Parliament's animosity towards the structured and compulsory involvement of management and labour in European policy formation. Rather, the Parliament's attitude in this phase could be characterised as an ambiguous one. While it regarded the institutionalisation of the social partners' decision-making powers as a step towards greater involvement of citizens in Union policy formation, the Parliament simultaneously called for its own active incorporation in the process of the adoption of the decision-implementing agreements concluded by the social partners.

However, the passage of agreements on parental leave and part-time work drew the most critical response from the Parliament. It reflected that it 'must not in any circumstances be allowed to be a systematic replacement for the normal legislative procedure' (European Parliament, 1999a, point V). It seems that EP backing for social partnership only arose in the first instance because it saw it as a way for self-enhancement. Once this concept had been operationalised through the formalisation of the social dialogue procedure, the EP did not give a wholehearted welcome to this procedure and turned into a bitter critic. Clearly, this evolution shows that the Parliament's attitude towards the social partnership concept is strictly determined by the distributional gains obtainable by it in the course of practical implication.

Conclusion

The social partners are entrusted under the Treaty on European Union with powers to define social policy. This resulted in placing constraints upon the discretion granted to the Union institutions in other areas of the European public policy process. Since the social partners are granted considerable decision-making competencies throughout the social dialogue procedure, they encroach upon the powers of all Union institutions.

The preceding discussion shows that although the involvement of the social partners in EU social policy formation resulted in significant limitation of legislative powers of both the Commission and the Parliament in this area of European decision-making, each is affected differently by these restrictions. While the Commission may gain some benefits from the formalisation of the social partners' participation in Union decision-making on social issues, the European Parliament is made redundant in this area and replaced as a co-decision-maker by the social partners. Since both the Commission and the Parliament positions towards the introduction of the social dialogue procedure are dependent upon the degree of distributional gains they can obtain through the operationalisation thereof, this helps to explain, as Boockmann (1998) emphasises, why the Commission is willing to hand over much of its agenda powers to the social partners while the Parliament requests that its prerogatives should be strengthened within the social dialogue procedure.

4
The Intergovernmental Dimension of EU Social Partnership

Hugh Compston

Introduction

The aim of this study is to determine the extent to which the development and operation of social partnership at EU level can be explained in terms of the logic of self-interest, as opposed to factors such as the influence of ideas or of cultural or ideological values. By social partnership is meant the co-determination of public policy by public authorities, management and labour. At EU level this means the procedure adopted at Maastricht in 1991 whereby the Council may translate agreements between European-level representatives of management and labour into the form of EU legislation.

The aim of this chapter is to determine the extent to which explanations of the positions and actions in relation to EU-level social partnership of Member States acting through the Council and European Council can be explained in terms of the logic of self-interest, as opposed to other factors. After a brief review of the evolution of European Council attitudes and actions in relation to social partnership, with particular reference to the concepts and arguments used in this connection, evidence is presented to demonstrate that both the adoption of the social partnership procedure at Maastricht and its subsequent use by the Council can be almost completely explained in terms of self-interest.[1]

The evolution of Member State attitudes and actions

Although prior to the 1980s Member States had taken a number of initiatives to involve business and trade unions in policy-making, including the establishment of the Economic and Social Committee by the Treaty of Rome, the introduction of the Standing Committee on Employment in 1971 and the holding of Tripartite Conferences during the 1970s, none of these initiatives institutionalised real co-determination of EU policy. Nor did the Treaty revision that preceded Maastricht, the Single European Act (SEA), although it did include a clause that raised the possibility of European-level collective bargaining in charging the Commission to 'develop the dialogue between management and labour at European level' and foreshadowed the possibility of 'relations based on agreement' (Article 118B).

During the next few years, however, the value of securing the cooperation of business and trade unions was asserted by European Council communiqués on a number of occasions. The Dutch Presidency Conclusions of the June 1986 Hague European Council suggested that dialogue with the social partners could be beneficial for employment, and advocated 'arriving at tripartite commitments by governments and the social partners' for this purpose (*Bull. EC* 6–1986, p.8). The German Presidency Conclusions of the Hanover European Council in June 1988 emphasised 'the importance of informing and consulting management and labour throughout the process of achieving the Single Market' and asked the Commission 'to step up its dialogue with management and labour, paying special attention to the provisions of Article 118B of the Treaty' (*Bull. EC* 6–1988, p.165). The Greek Presidency Conclusions of the Rhodes European Council in December 1988 stated that the European Council wished to:

> give a reminder of the increasing importance attaching to the systematic pursuit of a constructive dialogue between management and labour at Community level, in accordance with Article 118B of the Treaty. The aim of this dialogue should be the active involvement of both sides of industry in completion of the large market.
>
> (*Bull.EC* 12–1988, p. 9)

The Spanish Presidency Conclusions of the Madrid European Council in June 1989 stated that 'the internal market must be achieved in a climate of close cooperation between employers and workers so that economic and technical changes take place in a socially acceptable manner' (*Bull.EC* 6–1989, p.10).

In December 1989, eleven of the twelve Member States adopted the Community Charter of the Fundamental Social Rights of Workers (*Social Europe* 1/92, pp.7–11), with Britain dissenting. One aim of this was 'to consolidate the progress made in the social field, through action by the Member States, the two sides of industry and the Community'. Point 12 of the Charter reiterates the view that 'the dialogue between the two sides of industry at European level which must be developed may, if the parties deem it desirable, result in contractual relations in particular at inter-occupational and sectoral level'. The Charter also asserted that 'social consensus contributes to the strengthening of the competitiveness of undertakings, of the economy as a whole and to the creation of employment; . . . in this respect it is an essential condition for ensuring economic development'. If we accept that social consensus requires agreement between important social groups, in particular employers and unions, and that this implies co-determination of public policy, then the implication of this point is that social partnership is economically beneficial. The problem is that this argument occurs in no other European Council document of the period. Furthermore, the Social Charter is the only European Council document examined that was based on a Commission draft (the Treaties and Presidency Conclusions were drafted by the Member States holding the Presidency). It is therefore not clear that this point expressed the real views of Member States, as distinct from being a Commission view allowed through because the Social Charter was non-binding.

Although the Commission had raised the idea of establishing a social partnership procedure in 1989, the first specific proposal by a Member State to enhance the role of the social partners was submitted to the IGC by the Belgian delegation in January 1991. This proposed that a Labour Committee consisting of equal numbers of employers' and employees' delegates appointed by the relevant representative bodies be set up to negotiate agreements that could be transmitted via the Commission for translation into Community law by Council. The Committee would also be given the right to ask the Commission to submit a proposal within the realm of the Committee's competences. In March 1991 the Commission submitted a similar text to the IGC. Although the initial Luxembourg draft Treaty of April 1991 did not contain provisions for significantly strengthening the role of the social partners, the June 1991 version contained proposals rather similar to those eventually adopted (Falkner, 1998, pp.74, 90–5).

The 31 October 1991 Agreement between UNICE, CEEP and the

ETUC on a social partnership procedure to be inserted into the revised Treaty was based on the Commission proposal (Ross, 1995a, p.183) and inserted almost unchanged by the Dutch Presidency into the revised draft Treaty of 8 November 1991 (see Appendix 1 for text). This was then accepted almost unchanged in December 1991 by the eleven governments that signed the Social Protocol, after the British government had refused to sign a weakened version offered to them by the Dutch Presidency (Falkner, 1998, pp.88, 94–5). There was little controversy: the issue appears seldom to have been mentioned in media coverage of the IGC, and there was little or no opposition on the part of Member State governments, Britain apart. However, the Social Protocol was virtually silent on the justification for the procedure apart from citing 'the promotion of dialogue between management and labour' as an objective (Article 1).

Due to delays over Treaty ratification, the Social Protocol, including the social partnership procedure, did not come into operation until November 1993. By the end of the century social partner agreements had been presented under its provisions to Council on parental leave, part-time work and fixed-term work. All three were ratified with little controversy (see Appendices 2–4 for the text of the resultant Directives).

Examination of the rhetoric used by Member States acting collectively, as expressed in the Treaty of Rome, the Single European Act, the Social Charter, the Maastricht Treaty and Social Protocol, and the Presidency Conclusions of European Council meetings between December 1985 and December 1991, reveals just two distinctive concepts: *social partners* and *dialogue/social dialogue*. The term *social partners* refers to employer organisations and trade unions and connotes a cooperative relationship in which interests can be harmonised. *Dialogue/social dialogue* between the social partners is considered to be a means by which this cooperation and, possibly, joint action can be obtained. However, the term *social partnership* is never used.

The arguments in these documents in relation to our conception of social partnership as co-determination of EU policy were generally rather sketchy. The most common was merely a statement of value, namely that there is a need to promote dialogue between management and labour (SEA, The Hague 1986, London 1986, Hanover 1988, Rhodes 1988, Social Charter, Social Protocol). Similarly, the 1988 Rhodes European Council stated that there is a need to involve both sides of industry in the completion of the Single Market.

However, it is not always clear what the purpose of this involvement is supposed to be. Although the Social Charter adopted by eleven of the twelve Member States in 1989 does state that social consensus contributes to the competitiveness of undertakings and the whole economy as well as aiding employment creation, it is not clear that this expresses the real views of Member State governments. On the other hand, both the Social Charter and the Presidency Conclusions of the 1989 Madrid European Council asserted that the Single Market must be achieved in a climate of close cooperation between employers and workers so that economic and technical changes take place in a socially acceptable manner. This implies a concern for social peace, possibly with an eye to the electoral implications of conflict as well as the possibility that completion of the Single Market might be endangered if its implementation caused conflict.

Explaining the adoption of the social partnership procedure at Maastricht

To what extent can the adoption of the social partnership procedure at Maastricht be explained in terms of self-interest alone? To answer this question it is first necessary clearly to define what is meant by self-interest in this context. The second part of the section examines the actual decision to adopt the social partnership procedure at Maastricht. One of the reasons for this decision was that the 31 October 1991 Agreement between UNICE, CEEP and ETUC signalled that for the first time business was willing to conclude binding agreements with trade unions at EU level. The chapter by Branch and Greenwood in this volume shows that this change of heart was due to the expectation of UNICE that Member States would agree at Maastricht to extend Qualified Majority Voting (QMV) to new areas of social policy. For this reason the third part of this section on the role of Member States in the development of social partnership at EU level examines the extent to which the positive attitude of Member States at this stage to extending QMV can be explained in terms of self-interest.

Political self-interest defined

The use of the concept of self-interest as an explanatory tool has a number of advantages. Our experience of life demonstrates beyond question that self-interest is active in human motivation. Its use enables sophisticated theoretical networks of cause and effect to be constructed on the basis of a clear logic of motivation. And it has proved successful in accounting for many political phenomena in the past. It is for these reasons that our explanatory strategy in this study is to determine first the extent to which our dependent variable can be explained in terms of self-interest alone, and to turn to other types of explanation only where self-interest alone cannot provide an adequate account.

In analyses of collective decision-making by EU Member States, self-interest is often construed as national interest. In the case of social policy, this is often further narrowed down to economic interests, in particular international competitiveness (e.g. Lange, 1993). But such a definition is inadequate. EU decision-making at European Council/IGC level is a political business, and when one considers exactly who signs the relevant documents it is immediately evident that the relevant locus of self-interest is not individual countries but individual heads of government. It is their political self-interest that the self-interest theory would predict to be the determining factor, and one cannot assume in advance that this is necessarily coincident with perceived national economic interests (for a similar view see Pierson and Leibfried, 1995, p.443).

At least two foci of the political self-interest of heads of government can be identified, in descending order of immediacy for the individuals concerned.

First, *leadership interests:* heads of government would be expected to avoid any moves that endangered their leadership of their government, for instance decisions that prompt party colleagues to mount a leadership challenge or coalition partners to leave the government and thereby cause its fall. Pressure from other members of national delegations is relevant here, as well as that exerted by Ministers, party opinion, the views of coalition parties (if any) and, where governments do not command a legislative majority, the views of opposition parties. The desire of heads of government to remain heads of government sets up a system of constraints on their actions at EU level that the self-interest theory would lead us to expect to be absolute.

Second, *specific EU-related electoral interests:* heads of government would be expected to avoid action at EU level that endangered the electoral prospects of their parties, especially when an election is imminent, and to embrace positions and initiatives that advantage their parties electorally. Here public opinion on EU issues and EU-related issues is king. This in turn gives leverage to political actors whose actions in relation to government positions on EU issues can influence the electoral standing of the government. For example, actions at EU level that cause party splits would be expected to be avoided even where the personal position of the head of government remained secure. Actions that lead to adverse media reactions, adverse market reactions or social unrest would also be expected to be avoided where possible. Through the lens of political self-interest it is via the electoral significance of perceived economic reality and forecast economic prospects that perceived 'national economic interests' become relevant to the decisions of heads of government. That is, perceived economic interests are an important component of political self-interest but not the only component.

Putting this together, the self-interest theory posits that political self-interest as defined above constructs a set of parameters that constrain the scope of possible policy choices for heads of government. We avoid defining self-interest in terms of whatever a person wants because this would bring all motives within the category of self-interest and render it tautologous to assert that someone acted out of self-interest. Instead we prefer to distinguish the interests that a person has by virtue of the position they hold from other motivations they may have, and in this way contrast the influence of this position-based self-interest with the influence of other motivations.

It should be noted here that political self-interest thus defined sets parameters for action rather than determining it completely, so there remains latitude for choice on the part of heads of government within these constraints. Insofar as the political self-interest of heads of government is not affected one way or the other by which choices are made, other motivations must become relevant. That is, the political self-interest theory as expounded here posits not that self-interest is the *only* motivation in politics, but rather that it is the *dominant* motivation: other motivations do exist, but self-interest prevails in cases of conflict.

From these considerations can be deduced many of the explicit and implicit self-interest assumptions characteristic of much analysis of the EU. In particular, political self-interest implies that heads of government try to maximise both the autonomy and influence of their own country in Council (and European Council) and the power and influence of Council vis-a-vis other EU institutions, in particular the Commission and the European Parliament, as this maximises the degree to which the fortunes of these heads of government remain in their own hands. At the same time, however, it is important to note that these preferences are not absolute: if political self-interest is perceived to be better served by ceding national power, for example, then this is what the self-interest theory would expect heads of government to do.

Adoption of the social partnership procedure at Maastricht

The adoption of the social partnership procedure at Maastricht can be explained almost entirely in terms of the political self-interest of heads of government. First, there are significant political benefits for governments at both national and EU level in having employment and social policy co-determined by employers and trade unions. Second, the procedure does not constrain the power and autonomy of Member States relative to the 'normal' legislative procedure. Third, the two major barriers to its earlier introduction were removed in late 1991. Only the attitudes and actions of the British government cannot be fully understood without reference to an additional explanatory variable, namely ideology.

The social partnership procedure adopted at Maastricht covers all the social policy areas specified by the Social Protocol as being subject to decision at EU level: health and safety, working conditions, information and consultation of workers, equal labour market treatment of men and women, integration of persons excluded from the labour market, social security and social protection of workers, protection of workers where their employment contract is terminated, employment conditions for third-country nationals, subsidies for employment and job creation, and the representation and collective defence of the interests of workers and employers, including co-determination (at firm level) but excluding the sensitive areas of pay, the right of association, the right to strike and the right to impose lockouts (Articles 2 and 4, later to become Articles 137 and 139 of the Treaty of Amsterdam). It is noticeable that all these policy areas are directly related to employment, so might be more precisely termed 'employment policy' rather than 'social policy', which is often understood to be a broader category. To highlight the connection with employment, while still retaining the EU terminology, it is perhaps best to refer to the area as 'employment and social policy'.

If we look at the national level, we find that it is in the area of employment and social policy alone that social partnership is the norm in Western Europe. A recent study that covered eight of the twelve signatory Member States at Maastricht found that during the 1990s employment and social policy was subject to co-determination by governments, employers and trade unions in seven of the eight, the exception being Britain. It was also standard practice in the two non-EU West European countries examined. In only three of the ten countries – Austria, Ireland and Italy – was social partnership important in a significantly wider range of public policy (Berger and Compston, forthcoming). In other words, the adoption of the social partnership procedure at Maastricht for employment and social policy simply translates standard operating procedure at national level to EU level. The reason for this is that social partnership at national level can be explained in terms of political self-interest, and that almost all of the self-interested considerations that apply at national level also apply at EU level.

At national level, employment and social policy has been a focus of conflict between employers and trade unions ever since unions were formed late in the nineteenth century, as regulation for the benefit of employees generally involves costs for employers. Disputes over employment conditions such as working hours have been a frequent cause of economically disruptive industrial disputes. However, efforts by governments to regulate employment conditions are often resented by one or both sides, and may threaten the political self-interest of heads of government by attracting the hostility of one or both sides. Industrial action in opposition to government 'interference' may not only impede or block the implementation of government measures but may also be economically damaging in itself, thus threatening the government's reputation for economic management. It is therefore not surprising that governments often prefer to leave employment regulation to employers and unions, and that over the years employment relations have come to be largely regulated by agreements struck between them rather than by law, although regulation by law is also important (see, for example, Compston, forthcoming, Appendix 1).

In other words, unilateral government action in this area may maximise the influence of government on the content of regulation in this area, which in many cases would be expected to promote the political self-interest of heads of government, but at the cost of arousing opposition that not only threatens the electoral standing of governments but also impedes or prevents effective implementation of the relevant measures themselves. Conversely, allowing employers and trade unions to regulate their relations themselves minimises political opposition and maximises the chance that employment regulation will be effective, but at the cost of loss of influence for the government. In addition, employers and unions may be unable to reach agreement between themselves, thus leaving the original problem unresolved.

In such circumstances, regulating employment by means of agreements struck between the government, employers and trade unions has a number of advantages. First, once the agreement is struck, political opposition is minimised. Second, the willing acceptance of agreed measures by both sides means that implementation is likely to be more successful than when measures are imposed by the government. Third, the resources of government may enable it to facilitate agreement, where otherwise it would not be reached, by including in the agreement provisions that employers and unions by themselves cannot provide. One such provision is implementation of social partner agreements by legislation, which means that the contents of such agreements apply to everyone rather than merely those covered by the relevant collective agreement. Fourth, participation in the negotiations, either officially or unofficially, enables governments to exert more influence on the contents of employment regulation than when these are decided entirely by collective agreement, although dependence on the consent of employers and unions does constrain policy options compared with the freedom provided by unilateral action. Finally, country studies in this area commonly find that national governments often do seek agreement with interest groups to minimise conflict, facilitate implementation and maintain or improve their electoral standing (see, for example, Edinger, 1993, pp.179–84; Hall, 1993, pp.162–71; Heclo and Madsen, 1987, p.15; Martinez Lucio, forthcoming; Miller, 1993, pp.93–7; Slomp, forthcoming; Wright, 1992, pp.272–91).

The example of Britain, however, demonstrates that governments do not necessarily follow the logic of self-interest outlined above: the Thatcher/Major Conservative government took the view that economic prosperity, which is clearly linked to electoral self-interest, depended on confronting the trade unions (Dorey, forthcoming; Blair, 1999, pp.98, 103). While this is still a form of self-interest argument, its direction is crucially altered by the distinctive Conservative belief that trade unions and collective bargaining are economically damaging. As Weber put it, 'Not ideas, but material and ideal interests, directly govern men's conduct. Yet very frequently the "world images" that have been created by "ideas" have, like switchmen, defined the tracks along which action has been pushed by the dynamics of interests' (Weber, 1948, p.280, cited in John, 1998, p.144).

For other Member States, where social partnership in employment and social policy exists at national level and is motivated by the above logic of self-interest, this logic still applies when regulation of these policy areas is transferred to the EU level. The EU social partnership procedure is a mechanism using which European-level collective agreements on employment regulation can be implemented using EU law, but represents co-determination in that Council has to explicitly agree before this can occur. This means that the social partners have to take into account the likely reaction of Member State governments when they negotiate agreements among themselves. For this reason communication between the social partners and Member State governments is very likely to take place behind the scenes, making national governments shadow participants in the overtly bipartite negotiations. In this way social partnership at EU level is similar to social partnership at national level. Directives that result from the social partnership procedure are implemented at national level by national governments, just as if they were national measures, so the advantages relative to unilateral action for national governments are similar to those at the national level: political opposition to the measures is limited and implementation is facilitated. This gives national governments at the EU level a positive incentive to seek co-determination of employment and social policy at EU level as well as at national level, rather than relying on unilateral legislative action alone.

Furthermore, while the powers of Member States over agreements presented to the Council by the Commission on behalf of the social partners are slightly weaker than they can exert over draft legislation using the 'normal' legislative route, the difference is not very significant, and Council can still resort to the 'normal' legislative procedure if it wishes.

The Social Protocol provided for a 'normal' legislative procedure involving the European Parliament in which Council would use QMV to adopt proposals in the areas of health and safety, working conditions, information and consultation of workers, equal labour market treatment of men and women, and integration of persons excluded from the labour market. Unanimity was required to amend proposals and to adopt proposals rejected by the European Parliament. The other areas of employment/social policy within the EU's remit remained subject to unanimity voting.

The same voting procedures apply to adoption of social partner agreements, with the single exception that there is a convention that Council may not amend agreements presented to it even though the one significant alteration made when the Dutch Presidency adopted the social partner agreement of 31 October 1991 was the removal of the explicit prohibition on Council amendments (Falkner, 1998, pp.94–5). However, it is important to note that Council may reject the agreement altogether and request the Commission to bring forward a more suitable proposal using the 'normal' legislative route, although this would delay decision and risk amendment by the European Parliament. Ultimately, therefore, the existence of the social partnership procedure does not restrict Council powers at all.

A further consideration is that although the outcomes of the social partnership procedure unequivocally constitute public policy, having the force of law, the procedure can also be viewed as being merely a means through which EU institutions assist employers and trade unions to regulate the labour market via free collective bargaining. From this perspective, introduction of the procedure does not represent the ceding of power by national governments to employers and trade unions.

So far we have seen that from the point of view of the political self-interest of heads of government the social partnership procedure has advantages and does not constrain their powers relative to the 'normal' legislative procedure. But while these observations explain why the political self-interest of heads of government might lead them to favour social partnership, they do not explain why a social partnership procedure was adopted in 1991 but not before. To explain change we need to refer to explanatory factors that also change. Two such variables can be identified. Both involve the overcoming of barriers to the earlier introduction of the procedure.

The first barrier was removed on 31 October 1991 when UNICE agreed the text of what became the social partnership procedure with the ETUC and CEEP. Prior to this, UNICE had always refused to become involved in binding agreements with the ETUC, which rendered any social partnership procedure redundant and meant that any moves to establish one would attract criticism from business. The ending of UNICE's opposition to social partnership meant that for the first time there was a reasonable prospect that such a procedure would be used. It also reduced the political cost of introducing a social partnership procedure by discouraging attacks not only by business but also by political parties aligned with business. Finally, it provided a politically viable text for the Dutch Presidency to incorporate into the draft Treaty.

Second, a British veto was avoided due to the fact that Britain 'opted out' of the Social Protocol. In 1985 social policy remained an integral part of the Treaty, rendering any proposal for a social partnership procedure vulnerable to a British veto. The British opt-out in 1991 meant that no British veto was possible. This opt-out can be explained in the first instance as a consequence of Prime Minister John Major's interest in keeping his position as leader of the Conservative Party and Prime Minister, as it seems clear that his position would have been threatened if he had signed, plus his desire to keep the Conservative Party together in the face of an impending election (Blair, 1999, Chapter 5). However, it is also clear that the opposition to EU-level social policy within the Conservative Party that threatened Major's position was at least in part based on ideology, namely the belief that union involvement in policy-making is economically damaging and that deregulation is the road to economic success, which as well as being significant in itself helped to structure perceived electoral self-interest for the Conservative Party (Dorey, forthcoming). Ironically, however, the strength of this ideological opposition, by forcing Major not to sign even a weak version of the Social Protocol, led to a very similar outcome to that which would have occurred without the influence of these ideological convictions, namely the adoption of extended powers by the EU over social policy. The only difference was that legislation passed using these powers did not apply to Britain, and even this difference vanished once the new Labour government agreed to the incorporation of the Social Protocol into the Treaty of Amsterdam in 1997.

To sum up, the decision at Maastricht to adopt a social partnership procedure can be explained almost entirely in terms of the political self-interest of heads of government. Most heads of government already knew from experience at national level that social partnership can help to ensure that public policy is acceptable and effective. The powers of Member States were not significantly less than under the 'normal' legislative procedure, to which they could still resort if they chose. The social partner agreement of 31 October 1991 signalled the end of business opposition to binding agreements with trade unions at EU level. However, the British opt-out from the Social Protocol, which meant that the inclusion of the procedure could not be vetoed by Britain, cannot be understood without reference to the strength in the Conservative Party of free market ideas, including the view that union involvement in policy-making is economically damaging. This indicates that ideology as well as self-interest played a role in determining the outcome at Maastricht.

Explaining Member State attitudes to extending QMV in social policy

We have seen that one of the crucial reasons for the adoption of the social partnership procedure at Maastricht was the decision of UNICE to drop its opposition to the idea and sign the 31 October 1991 Agreement with CEEP and ETUC that formed the basis for the text included in the Social Protocol. Branch and Greenwood in this volume show that this decision by UNICE was a consequence of its expectation that the Maastricht IGC would extend QMV to new areas of social policy. Under the regime of unanimous voting, UNICE, which generally opposes social legislation as being costly for business, only needed the support of a single Member State to block legislation. In such circumstances negotiations with unions over social policy could only increase the pressure to improve social provision in the EU. Under QMV, UNICE would need the support of several Member States before social legislation could be blocked. In these changed circumstances, negotiations over social policy as an alternative to direct legislation might give UNICE an additional means of weakening social legislation, since its agreement would be required for any proposal to be put to Council for translation into law. This means that a full explanation of the role of Member States in the adoption of the social partnership procedure at Maastricht must include an explanation of their positions on QMV at the time UNICE made its judgement that QMV would probably be extended, as this was a crucial link in the chain of causation leading to adoption of the procedure. This involves examination of the attitudes of heads of government to the extension of EU-level social policy in general as well as to QMV in particular, as the main political significance of QMV is that it facilitates the passage of legislation.

There are four steps in the analysis of the extent to which self-interest alone can explain the positions of heads of government on the issue of extending QMV to new areas of social policy. First, the evolution of the positions of Member States in relation to extending

EU social policy is described. Second, the explanatory utility of each of three possible self-interest based explanations is evaluated using the available empirical evidence. Third, the analysis is illuminated by a short case study of Ireland. Finally, the findings of the analysis are summarised and conclusions drawn.

The evolution of Member State positions on social policy 1985–91

The original rationale of EU involvement in social policy, and one that continues to be restated, is that there is a need to improve working conditions through Community action as well as via completion of the Common/Single Market (Treaty of Rome, SEA, Social Charter, Social Protocol). Similarly, since the passage of the SEA it has been argued in European Council Presidency Conclusions and other documents that there is a need for the Single Market to benefit/offer improvements to all people via improvements to health and safety and to working conditions (Hanover 1988, Rhodes 1988, Social Charter, Dublin 1990). The implication here is that to obtain these benefits, market liberalisation needs to be supplemented by legislative action at EU level. A slightly different argument is that social aspects should be considered as important as economic aspects in the process of completing the Single Market (Madrid 1989, Rome 1990). Finally, the Social Charter expresses the view that there is a need for the Single Market to ensure the development of social rights for workers.

Prior to Maastricht the only area of social policy subject to QMV was health and safety, for which it had been introduced in the SEA. The four areas made subject to QMV in the Social Protocol were working conditions, information and consultation of workers, equal labour market treatment of men and women, and integration of persons excluded from the labour market. Within EU competences but subject to unanimity voting were social security and social protection of workers; protection of workers where their employment contract is terminated; employment conditions for third-country nationals; subsidies for employment and job creation; and the representation and collective defence of the interests of workers and employers, including co-determination but excluding pay, the right of association, the right to strike and the right to impose lockouts, which remained outside the purview of EU lawmaking.

By the time the SEA was agreed in 1985–6 at least three countries were already in favour of extending EC power in social policy, namely France, Belgium and Denmark. France had formally proposed majority voting in social policy as early as 1981. The introduction of QMV on health and safety into the SEA was proposed by Denmark, with contributions from France, despite the fact that at this stage Denmark opposed majority voting on principle. This provision was agreed by Member States due to a general consensus that businesses should not compete on the basis of minimising the costs of health and safety. Denmark wanted to go further in harmonising social policy, but was rebuffed. Germany, Ireland and the Netherlands had initially opposed majority voting on health and safety but, with Greece, dropped their opposition at an early stage in the negotiations. Britain was the last to agree and only accepted QMV on health and safety on condition that directives must not impose constraints on the creation or development of small business. Spain and Portugal were not yet members of the European Union (De Ruyt, 1987, pp.73–89; Kirchner, 1992, p.45; Laursen, 1992, p.67; Ross, 1995a, pp.33, 47; Teague, 1989b, p.76; Wise and Gibb, 1993, p.183).

From 1987, and possibly earlier, the governments of Italy, Spain and Greece also consistently expressed support for extending EC social policy. The idea of the Social Charter was introduced by Belgium in 1987 and strongly supported by Italy, Spain, Ireland and Greece as well as France, Germany, Belgium and Denmark. However, it is important to note here that the Social Charter was not binding, which means that its signing was proof only of rhetorical support for the extension of EC social policy. During the negotiations in the Social Affairs Council in October 1989, Ministers from the eleven Member States that supported the Social Charter weakened its provisions to try to make it more acceptable to Britain. When this move failed, they then voted to approve the weakened version rather than the one they had brought to the meeting. This led many observers to conclude that Ministers from Member States such as Germany and Spain were using British intransigence as an opportunity to dilute the Social Charter while avoiding the political consequences of more direct opposition to it (Silvia, 1991, p.638; Lange, 1991, pp.242–4, 250–1).

In 1990, as the run-up to Maastricht was gathering pace, Denmark, Greece and Portugal all presented Memorandums that recommended extending the scope of EC social policy and extending QMV in social policy (Danish Government, 1992, p.295; Greek Government, 1992, pp.278–80; Portuguese Ministry of Foreign Affairs, 1992, pp.305–6). In December 1990 a joint letter from Kohl and Mitterand to Andreotti, the Prime Minister of the Member State holding the

EU Presidency, also advocated the deepening and enlarging of Community social policy and asserted that qualified majority voting should be the rule apart from a restricted number of sectors and cases (Kohl and Mitterand, 1992, pp.313–14). Although in February 1991 Spain proposed that harmonisation of social policy should proceed but favoured the retention of unanimous voting for the adoption of social action programmes, all the other delegations that presented reform proposals during 1991 (Belgium, Portugal, Luxembourg, the Netherlands, Italy, Spain, Denmark and France) supported strengthening both competences and QMV in this area (Falkner, 1998, p.87).

By December 1991, then, the specific proposal to extend QMV to additional areas of social policy was strongly supported by France, Belgium, Denmark, Italy, the Netherlands and Luxembourg, while Germany supported a modified form of QMV and perhaps unanimity (Ross, 1995a, pp.103, 150; Kirchner, 1992, p.131). France, Italy and Belgium were especially keen to have a strong Social Chapter. Britain and Spain, quietly backed by Ireland and Portugal, opposed a strong social policy. Some sources depict Greece as being strongly in favour of strengthening EU social policy, while others report it as being one of the Member States working to dilute it. Nevertheless, in the end all of these countries apart from Britain signed the Social Protocol with its provisions on QMV (Blair, 1999, p.104; Kirchner, 1992, p.131; Dinan, 1994, p.177; Moravcsik, 1998, pp.452–3; *Irish Times*, 4 December 1991, p.10; 9 December 1991, p.6). This is in line with the expectations of UNICE in 1991. Even the British opt-out was foreseeable, as this had happened already with the Social Charter, although the rather bizarre legal form according to which eleven of the twelve opted out – 'fog in Channel, Europe isolated' – may not have been anticipated (*Economist*, 14 December 1991). The fact that Britain was unable to veto the extension of EU social policy appears to have been due at least in part to the determination of French President François Mitterand, strongly supported not only by Italy and Belgium but also by Spain (*Irish Times*, 10 December 1991, p.6). It is reported that at one point Mitterand banged his fist on the table and threatened not to sign a Treaty without strong social provisions (*Irish Times*, 12 December 1991, p.8), and that following Major's rejection of the Dutch compromise he was ready to leave, with a car waiting to take him to the airport (Blair, 1999, p.94).

There are at least three possible self-interest explanations for the positive attitude of most heads of government to extending QMV to new areas of social policy. The first is that QMV was seen as a means of legitimising the Single Market and EMU. The second is that it was seen as a means of preventing social dumping. The third is that the richer Member States were prepared to trade financial transfers for the agreement of the poorer Member States.

The legitimacy argument

The legitimacy argument posits that having agreed to complete the Single Market, and anticipating a decision to opt for EMU, heads of government collectively were keen to obtain as broad a basis of support as possible for these objectives in order to ensure that they were achieved, especially since the EMU convergence criteria were anticipated as creating pressures to cut social expenditure and therefore social protection. For this reason heads of government would be expected to take steps to secure popular support for the Single Market and EMU. They would also be expected to seek the cooperation of labour as well as capital. Falkner expresses this idea as a 'systemic requirement' to assemble consensus behind 'ever closer Union' and especially economic and monetary union (1998, pp.177–9). Since European trade unions, represented by the ETUC, were pressing for more action on social policy at EU level, this legitimacy argument posits that one way of persuading them to support Single Market completion and EMU was to make it easier to approve social measures at EU level by adopting QMV. Member States previously opposed to QMV on social policy are posited as having changed their minds because they were concerned that otherwise completion of the Single Market and/or EMU would be threatened by political opposition.

However, this argument appears to have been more important for government rhetoric than for their real positions. It is clear that some political actors had doubts about the Single Market and/ or EMU and desired the extension of EU activity in social policy. Foremost among these were trade unions, although Greens and certain left parties also took this position. Trade union doubts about the Single Market stemmed from a fear that creation of a uniform set of financial, tax and technical conditions within a largely unregulated internal market in which a variety of national systems of social regulation were left intact would open the way for competitive social dumping in the form of a contest among Member States to gain an economic edge by offering businesses low wage costs, weak labour laws and minimal government regulation, resulting in a downward spiral in the level of wages, benefits and workers' rights. Since the mid-1980s at least, European trade unions have advocated greater EC powers on social policy as a means of avoiding this scenario (Silvia, 1991, pp.626–33).

However, there is little evidence that union pressure had much effect. Although the formulation of the ETUC's Social Charter in 1988 was followed by the adoption of a Social Charter for the EC just a year later, the content of the EC Charter was considerably weaker than that of the ETUC document, which indicates that union movements in EC countries were not strong enough to impose their preferred version on national governments despite their links not only with social democratic parties but also, in some countries, with Christian Democratic parties. Even the two largest trade union confederations, the British TUC and German DGB, were unable significantly to influence the positions of their national governments despite intensive campaigns on the issue (Lange, 1993, pp.19–21; Silvia, 1991, pp.633–8). We have also seen that the positions of the governments of Germany, the Netherlands, Spain, Portugal, Ireland and Greece did not solidify in favour of extending QMV in social policy until the 1991 IGC was under way. This suggests that the reasons for these countries' agreement to extend QMV had more to do with the negotiations themselves than with the union pressure that they had already successfully resisted for a number of years.

The social dumping argument

The social dumping argument holds that governments changed their attitude towards EC social policy because they were concerned about the political consequences for themselves of the regime competition described above: a contest among Member States to gain an economic edge by offering businesses low wage costs, weak labour laws and minimal government regulation. In particular, it posits that heads of government were concerned about the electoral consequences of allowing the financing of social protection at national level, and therefore ultimately the level of social protection itself, to be undermined by letting international competition for investment force down the costs for employers of social protection (Silvia, 1991, p.626). The issue was the possibility of future social dumping, not past or current experiences of it, as there was little evidence that social dumping actually took place during the late 1980s or early 1990s (Commission of the European Communities, 1990; Mosley, 1990; Tsoukalis, 1997, pp.134–6).

The introduction of QMV for working conditions in particular is consistent with this theory, as this would potentially inhibit competitive downward bidding of employment conditions. It is also clear that Belgium, France and Germany feared that the accession of Spain and Portugal in 1986 would lead to wider inequalities in social provision among Member States, encouraging firms to chase lower social costs, and advocated Community-wide social provisions as a means of preventing this (Blair, 1999, p.97; Moravcsik, 1998, p.366; Teague, 1989b, p.79). Furthermore, it was evident that the growing internationalisation of business facilitated by liberalisation of the Single Market made business investment decisions more likely to be influenced by differences between national standards. Finally, promotion of the Single Market drew concerns about social dumping into the public arena (Teague, 1989b, p.79; Wise and Gibb, 1993, p.153). Thus during the 1980s Denmark's centre-right government consistently argued for a minimum level of social regulation to be established at the European level in order to avoid the dangers of social dumping (Bislev, 1992, p.219; Johnson, 1996, p.191), and in Germany there was an intensive public debate about the risk of industrial investment moving elsewhere in search of lower labour costs and more flexible labour legislation (Tsoukalis, 1997, p.124).

The problem with the social dumping argument, however, as Lange points out, is that it cannot explain the agreement to extended QMV of poorer Member States, as these countries would be expected to oppose raising EU social standards for economic reasons. This is because some of the proposed Directives that were blocked under unanimous voting but which would be expected to be passed under QMV, in particular the establishment of minimum workplace standards, would be expected to raise costs for employers and/or limit their ability to utilise certain sorts of work practices in countries where existing national standards were inferior to the new EC standards. Given that social standards are generally lowest in the poorer Member States, Lange suggests that Portugal, Greece, Ireland and perhaps Spain would stand to lose competitiveness under the new regime. Lange also points out that the agreement of these countries cannot be attributed to the influence of leftist ideology because by December 1991 both Portugal and Greece were governed by right-wing parties. Nor, given our theoretical emphasis on political self-interest, can their agreement be attributed to these countries setting aside short-term political self-interest in favour of a long-term developmentalist strategy based on the assumption that a gradual raising of social standards to be met by firms would stimulate them

to improve their technology and work organisation, thereby transforming the existing labour-intensive, low-skill, low-quality production
economy into a higher-skill, higher-quality production economy
(Lange, 1993, pp.10–22).

If Lange is right, one would expect the extension of QMV in
social policy to be supported by the richer countries (France, Germany,
Italy, Denmark, Belgium, the Netherlands and Luxembourg) and
opposed by the poorer countries (Spain, Portugal, Ireland, Greece
and, possibly, Britain). The historical survey presented earlier revealed that when the 1991 IGC began, the application of QMV to
additional areas of social policy was supported by France, Italy,
Denmark, Belgium and Luxembourg, and opposed openly by Britain
and covertly by Germany, the Netherlands, Spain, Portugal, Ireland
and (possibly) Greece. Only Germany and the Netherlands fail to
fit the pattern predicted by Lange, and even here it is clear that
the German government considered that there could not be a real
Single Market unless there was an even playing field in relation
not only to health and safety but also in relation to working hours
and overall employer costs (*Irish Times*, 12 December 1991, p.8).

This implies that concern about social dumping does explain why
France, Italy, Denmark, Belgium and Luxembourg supported extending
QMV. Admittedly Germany and the Netherlands as rich countries
would have been expected to have been more supportive than they
were, but they did sign in the end, so the actions of these countries
too can be explained in terms of self-interest by the social dumping theory. In fact it was Chancellor Kohl who placed the stronger
version of the Social Protocol on the table after Britain had refused
to sign the weaker version offered to them by the Dutch Presidency
(Ross, 1995a, p.191). However, the theory fails to explain why Spain,
Portugal, Ireland and Greece were prepared to sign, so cannot by
itself explain why in October 1991 UNICE judged that there was a
good possibility that the scope of QMV in social policy would be
extended at Maastricht.

At the same time it should be noted that conceding QMV in the
nominated areas of social policy may not be as great a concession
on the part of the poorer countries as Lange implies. First, of the
social standards that are most vulnerable to social dumping, only
working conditions are designated in the Social Protocol as being
subject to QMV. This limits the potential impact on competitiveness
of the shift to QMV. Second, the emphasis on minimum standards,
as opposed to harmonisation, would also limit any loss of com-

petitiveness for poorer Member States overruled by QMV. Third, Article 2 of the Social Protocol states that 'such directives shall avoid imposing administrative, financial and legal constraints in a way which would hold back the creation and development of small and medium-sized undertakings'. This would appear to open the way for poorer Member States to mount legal challenges to any directives that significantly impaired their competitiveness. Fourth, electoral considerations would be expected to impede the governments of poorer Member States from opposing measures to strengthen EU social policy, given the popular aspiration one day to approximate the social standards enjoyed in the richer Member States. Finally, the ideal position for the poorer Member States in relation to social dumping would be one in which their lower labour costs poached a certain amount of investment from the richer countries but not enough to prompt these countries to take steps to reduce social protection, because if this happened it would erode the relative competitiveness of the poorer countries themselves and thereby create pressures for these countries to depress already low standards even further, which would result in the same political problems faced by the richer countries. Taking these factors into account, the optimal strategy for poorer countries would seem to be to give ground if there is a danger of wholesale social dumping, but not too much ground. From this perspective, agreement to the Social Protocol might not look too disastrous even within the logic of Lange's argument. This consideration does not explain precisely why they signed, but it may help to explain why in October 1991 UNICE judged that the poorer Member States would not block the extension of QMV in social policy at Maastricht.

The political exchange argument

A further explanation for the QMV decision at Maastricht, and one that could be anticipated in advance by UNICE and others, is that it was accepted by hitherto opposed heads of government in the course of political exchange as a tradeoff for gaining the agreement of other Member States on other provisions. In particular, it is argued that while concern about social dumping led the richer countries with higher social standards to support the strengthening of EU social policy, the poorer countries were bought off by the promise of more money for economic and social cohesion (Lange, 1993, pp.22–5). In this way the richer countries became better able to resist social dumping in exchange for using financial transfers to soften any negative impact of additional social regulation on the poorer countries.

Lange argues that the Social Protocol of 1991 was accepted by the poorer countries as part of accepting the entire set of Maastricht reforms, for which they were compensated financially in the form of increases in cohesion funds. The idea that these side payments were agreed as specific compensation for accepting the Social Protocol in particular is rejected on the grounds that the planned increase in funding was larger than would be warranted either by the expected costs to the poorer countries of accepting the social dimension or the expected benefits to the richer countries of gaining this agreement (Lange, 1993, pp.22–5).

The available evidence suggests that to some extent this buyout did take place. First, at an early stage Spain tied its possible support for decision-rule changes to additional financial support from the richer Member States, a position that won support from the other poorer Member States (Lange, 1991, p.251). Second, a month before the Maastricht summit, Commission President Jacques Delors met with Greek, Irish, Portuguese and Spanish foreign ministers and promised them large increases in structural funding if they signed the Maastricht Treaty, which Moravcsik argues would have been impossible without prior coordination with donor countries (Moravcsik, 1998, p.446). Finally, when Britain opted out and these countries were faced with a stronger social policy than expected and pressure to conclude the summit rapidly, Delors reportedly won over the poorer countries with promises of more substantial structural funding (plus, in the case of Spain, apparently with an appeal to Socialist solidarity) (Moravcsik, 1998, pp.452–3).

It seems clear that the potential for such a tradeoff would have been evident in October 1991, when UNICE made its decision to drop its opposition to social partnership at European level. After all, this had happened before, for instance in the negotiations for the SEA in 1985, when expansion of the structural funds was the political price of support for economic liberalisation from Greece, Ireland and Italy, and later Spain and Portugal (Moravcsik, 1998, p.367). Although no one could be certain that a similar exchange would take place at Maastricht, the possibility of political exchange would have provided a reasonable basis for a judgement by UNICE that agreement at Maastricht on QMV in new areas of social policy could not be ruled out.

The case of Ireland

Looking more closely at the case of Ireland further illuminates why the poorer countries agreed to extend QMV to new areas of social policy despite concerns about competitiveness.[2]

The position of the Irish government was that although it was concerned about the effect of specific social policy provisions on competitiveness and employment, in principle it favoured the extension of social policy and was never prepared to try to veto the Social Protocol package.

One reason for this positive attitude was that in Ireland there existed a widespread pro-European sentiment based on the view that the country had been well served by EU membership. For instance, Ireland had benefited from significant financial transfers from the EU – a clear case of motivation by self-interest – and in respect of social policy there was a view that EU legislation had accelerated modernisation in areas such as equal pay. To this was added a widely shared perception that the EU was never meant to be exclusively economic, which implied that it was time to build up integration in social policy to balance integration in economic policy. In contrast to Britain, therefore, there was little if any ideological opposition to the extension of social policy (*Irish Times*, 4 December 1991, p.6). In addition, Irish business was not greatly concerned by the prospect of more EU social policy until the British opt-out occurred, which led to fears that Ireland would lose competitiveness in relation to its biggest trading partner (*Irish Times*, 11 December 1991, p.6).

There was, however, official concern in Ireland about the implications of specific social policy provisions for Irish competitiveness and employment. This follows the logic of the social dumping argument corollary according to which prevention of social dumping via harmonisation of social policy leads to competitive disadvantage for poorer countries with lower social standards. In particular, the Irish government opposed the extension of QMV to working conditions, fearing that this would open the way for majority voting across wide areas of social policy. The Prime Minister, Charles Haughey, acknowledged the consequent similarity in practice between the Irish and British positions on social policy (*Irish Times*, 4 December 1991, pp.4, 6). It is therefore not surprising that Ireland, along with Germany, Spain and Portugal, worked over the year leading up to Maastricht to water down the draft Social Chapter (*Irish Times*, 13 December 1991, p.8).

However, there was never any question of the Irish government vetoing the Maastricht package in December 1991 even though its opposition to extending QMV to working conditions had not prevented its inclusion in what became the Social Protocol. Haughey was always prepared to compromise on social policy in order to get an overall agreement, his main concern being to secure binding agreement on wealth transfers (*Irish Times*, 9 December 1991, p.1). Furthermore, it has already been noted that the provisions of the Social Protocol on QMV were hardly draconian, and Irish (and Portuguese) agreement was facilitated by the insertion by the Dutch Presidency of provisions on employment and investment (*Irish Times*, 12 December 1991, p.8). In addition, rejection of the social package would have brought Haughey into conflict with the widely shared desire in Ireland not to be relegated to the periphery of Europe, especially as this would have resulted in Ireland becoming associated with the anti-European British Conservative government. For this reason, rejection of the Social Protocol would have endangered the electoral interests of the governing party, Fianna Fail, and, arguably, Haughey's own efforts to keep the leadership of his party. Finally, rejection of an extension of EU social policy would have endangered the Irish social partnership, which had been born in 1987 but was still fragile, because Irish trade unions were strongly committed both to Europe and to social policy. A breakdown in the Irish social partnership would have threatened both the electoral position of Fianna Fail and the leadership of Charles Haughey.

After the IGC was over, Haughey argued that although the definition of working conditions was not as clear as Ireland would have wanted, there was no scope for seeking a permanent derogation given Ireland's refusal to accept a two-tier Community:

> I cannot understand how anyone who claims the interests of workers at heart should advocate forcing a complete breakdown . . . It was unthinkable that Ireland should refuse to join in a major step forward in the Community in an area to which Member States attach a very high priority.
>
> (*Irish Times*, 13 December 1991, p.4)

This short case study highlights the fact that after a certain point in negotiations the issue changes from consideration of specific provisions, such as the extension of QMV in social policy, to whether or not individual Member States are prepared to veto the entire package on account of objections to specific provisions. Although several countries opposed the extension of QMV to social policy, only Britain was prepared to veto a package that included this. In addition, the experience of Denmark and its post-Maastricht refer- endums suggests that in reality smaller countries are not allowed to veto agreements. Given that this implies that none of the poorer countries were going to veto the Maastricht package on account of their opposition to specific aspects of its social provisions, plus the possibility of a British opt-out even if Britain attempted to veto the package, it is not surprising that in October 1991 UNICE judged that an extension of QMV in social policy was likely, and hence signed the 31 October 1991 Agreement with the ETUC and CEEP that made social partnership at EU level a viable proposition.

Self-interest and the extension of QMV in social policy

Three possible explanations based on the logic of political self-interest have been examined in order to evaluate the extent to which they can account for the extension of QMV to new areas of social policy at Maastricht. It was found that although the concern to legitimise the Single Market and EMU does not appear to explain the decision, the positions taken by nearly all the Member States in 1991 can be substantially explained by the concern of the richer countries to prevent social dumping, promises to expand financial transfers to the poorer countries, the limited nature of the extension of QMV and the unwillingness (or inability) of the poorer countries to veto the entire Maastricht package. The only head of government whose actions cannot be completely explained in terms of self-interest was British Prime Minister John Major, whose position was threatened by the strength of free market ideas in his Conservative Party. In this way the divergent ideological beliefs of the British Conserva- tive Party, compared to those held elsewhere in Europe, affected the outcome at Maastricht.

From the perspective of UNICE considering its position in October 1991 and earlier, of course, the specific events at Maastricht were not foreseeable in detail. Nevertheless, it was clear that only the British were (possibly) prepared to veto the entire Treaty revision in order to block the extension of QMV in social policy, and the example of the Social Charter in 1989 demonstrated that a British opt-out was a possibility. In short, there were strong reasons for UNICE to believe that QMV would in fact be extended at Maastricht, and certainly reason enough to sign the agreement with the ETUC and CEEP as insurance against this eventuality. After all, if QMV were not extended, UNICE could always refuse to use the social partnership procedure.

Council ratification of social partner agreements 1993–9

Between 1993, when the Social Protocol finally came into force, and 1999 social partner agreements were presented under its provisions to Council on parental leave, part-time work and fixed-term work. All three were ratified with little controversy. This ready acceptance of social partner agreements can be explained very simply in terms of the self-interest theory as being attributable to the fact that the political dynamics of negotiations between the social partners tend to produce provisions that are very similar to those preferred by Council.

The chapters on employers and unions in this study show that the ETUC pursues high social standards in order to produce benefits for its constituents and prevent social dumping, while UNICE opposes raising standards on grounds of cost. Given that social legislation can also be passed via the 'normal' legislative procedure involving the European Parliament, each social partner has an interest in trying to ensure that any agreements they strike on social policy do not contain provisions that are less favourable to them than what they believe Council would pass using the 'normal' legislative procedure if they did not reach agreement. It follows that UNICE will not accept an agreement if it includes more stringent social policy than it considers the Council would pass anyway, while the ETUC will not accept an agreement that includes lower social standards than it considers the Council would pass anyway. The consequence is that the process of negotiation produces a text that converges on what the social partners think that Council would pass using the 'normal' legislative procedure. Assuming that the perceptions of the social partners are accurate, the result is that Council ratifies these agreements. Individual Member States may quibble about specifics, but the package, which by convention may not be amended, will be accepted rather than rejected. A corollary of this convergence on Council preferences is that social partnership of the EU variety does not imply much social partner influence on public policy, as the results of the normal legislative path and the social partnership procedure are likely to be rather similar.

This argument explains why Council accepted the three social partner agreements presented to it during the 1990s, but it is difficult to test it against independent evidence about actual Council preferences on the relevant issues, and impossible to determine exactly what sort of legislation would have been passed if the social partners had failed to reach agreement. This uncertainty is not only a problem for researchers but also for UNICE and ETUC leaders trying to determine whether they would get a better deal by compromising or by standing firm and risking the breakdown of negotiations and the passage of legislation via the 'normal' legislative route. Ideally one would ascertain the self-interested preferences of each labour/social minister in relation to parental leave, part-time work and fixed-term work, then contrast these with their actual positions on these issues in order to determine the extent to which self-interest can explain these positions, but such an analysis would require a detailed study of the politics of employment and social policy that is well beyond the scope of this chapter.

Nevertheless, there are least two types of evidence that can be brought to bear on the question of whether the social partner agreements were in fact close to Council preferences.

First, if the content of agreements presented to Council were not very close to Council preferences, we would expect extensive discussion if not controversy in the relevant Council meeting(s) and the passage of such agreements by QMV rather than unanimity. In fact the Directives on parental leave, part-time work and fixed-term work were all passed unanimously and with little discussion, minor reservations of particular Member States notwithstanding (Falkner, 1998, p.119; Labour and Social Affairs Council, 15 December 1997 and 25 May 1999; Culture/Audiovisual Council, 28 June 1999.)[3] This suggests that the contents of the agreements on which they were based were reasonably close to Council preferences.

Second, if the contents of agreements presented to Council were close to Council preferences, we might expect them to be similar to the contents of similar proposals discussed already in Council. In fact we find that the provisions of both the parental leave and part-time work agreements were somewhat more stringent than those of previous texts discussed in Council. The explanation for this appears to be that the earlier versions of both texts had been watered down to avoid a British veto (Falkner, 1998, pp.123, 131–2, 135). This implies that the eleven Member States making the decision under the Social Protocol, and the twelve once Labour came to power in Britain and signed up to EU social policy, preferred stronger documents similar to the social partner agreements presented to them. Again this suggests that the contents of the social partner agreements were reasonably close to Council preferences.

This evidence is suggestive rather than conclusive, but none of it contradicts the proposition that the contents of the social partner agreements were fairly close to the preferences of Council, consistent with the argument that the contents of these agreements tend to converge on Council preferences. This implies that we can expect Council to continue to ratify social partner agreements unless one or both social partners makes a serious error in evaluating Council preferences, or they find an issue on which employer and union preferences do not conflict with each other but do conflict with the preferences of national governments, for example by transferring costs from social partners to governments.

Conclusions

The purpose of this chapter was to determine the extent to which the attitudes and actions of EU Member States in relation to the development and operation of EU-level social partnership can be explained in terms of political self-interest, defined in relation to the Maastricht IGC in particular as the leadership interests and electoral interests of the heads of government of Member States.

It has been found that the decision at Maastricht to adopt a social partnership procedure can be explained almost entirely in terms of the political self-interest of heads of government. Most heads of government already knew from experience at national level that making employment and social policy by agreement with employers and trade unions facilitates the implementation of measures in this area and minimises political threats to the government arising from employer and/or trade union opposition to such measures.

Furthermore, under the social partnership procedure the powers of Member States are not significantly less than those they hold under the 'normal' legislative procedure, to which Council can still resort if it wishes. The fact that the social partnership procedure was adopted at Maastricht but not earlier can be explained by the removal of two major barriers in 1991. First, the social partner agreement of 31 October 1991 signalled the end of business opposition to binding agreements with trade unions at EU level. This meant that the social partnership procedure would not be a dead letter and minimised political attacks on this issue by business and allied political parties. Second, the British opt-out from the Social Protocol meant that inclusion of the social partnership procedure in the Protocol could not be vetoed by Britain. This opt-out was the result of Prime Minister Major acting in accord with his political interests in protecting his leadership and avoiding a party split, but the pressure on him not to sign is partly attributable to the strength in his Conservative Party of the belief that trade union involvement in policy-making is economically damaging. To this extent a full explanation of the adoption of the social partnership procedure at Maastricht must include reference to ideology as well as self-interest.

The positive positions of Member States on extending QMV in social policy during the lead-up to Maastricht, which need to be explained because it was on the basis of its perception of these that UNICE made its crucial decision to sign the 31 October Agreement with CEEP and ETUC, can also be explained almost entirely in terms of self-interest. The richer countries wished to harmonise social policy to prevent investment being lost to other countries with lower social standards. The poorer countries, which had lower social standards and therefore stood to lose competitiveness if minimum EU social standards were raised against their will using QMV in Council, agreed because they believed that potential losses would be limited due to the limited scope of the extension of QMV plus receipt of increased cohesion funding. In addition, the substantial financial benefits already being received by the poorer countries from the EU made it unlikely that their heads of government would take the political risk of trying to veto the entire Maastricht package due to their objections to certain aspects of the Social Protocol. Britain, of course, opted out due to Conservative Party opposition to social regulation. All these dynamics were foreseeable as possibilities in October 1991, when UNICE made its judgement that extension of QMV on social policy was likely.

Council ratification of social partner agreements presented to it so far can be explained by the tendency of the content of these to converge on pre-existent Council preferences due to the concern of employers not to agree to a text with stronger provisions than Council would pass using the 'normal' legislative procedure interacting with the concern of the ETUC not to agree to a text with weaker provisions than the Council would otherwise pass.

Together these findings indicate that while the actions of Member States in relation to the development and operation of social partnership at EU level can be largely explained in terms of self-interest, self-interest alone does not provide a complete explanation. Instead, two other factors need to be brought in as well.

The first is ideology. Although Major's decision not to sign the Social Protocol was due to self-interest, the pressure that led him to act in this way was in part due to the strong belief within his Conservative Party that trade unions and social regulation are economically damaging.

The second factor is contingency. For instance, if Michael Howard had not been Minister for Employment in Britain in December 1991, he might not have been able to exert so much pressure on Major not to sign (Blair, 1999, Chapter 5), which in turn might have led Major to sign the weak Dutch version of the draft Social Chapter that did not include a social partnership procedure. The apparent preparedness of French President Mitterand to refuse to sign a Treaty revision if social policy was *not* strengthened is another case in point. The picture that emerges in relation to the intergovernmental dimension of EU social partnership, therefore, is one in which the main causal dynamics are laid down by the positional self-interest of the relevant decision-makers but inflected by ideological beliefs and, at the point of decision, by the specific circumstances in which the relevant decisions are made.

5

The European Sectoral Social Dialogue

Tina Weber

Introduction

Approximately 70 million workers in the European Union are covered by the European sectoral social dialogue (Commission of the European Communities, 1996a). Despite this breadth of coverage, it is a little publicised and researched process. Very little is commonly known about the actors involved, its outcomes and even less about the impact of discussions and actions at Member State level. Despite the adoption in 1997 by the social partners in the maritime transport sector of a proposal for a Directive on the regulation of working time (EIRO, February 1998), which Council agreed to implement as Community law on 25 May 1999 (EIRO, June 1999), the sectoral social dialogue process is generally hidden in the shadow of its 'bigger brother', the European intersectoral social dialogue between ETUC (European Trade Union Confederation), UNICE (the European employers' organisation), CEEP (the European Centre for Enterprises with Public Participation), and, from 1999, UEAPME, which represents small business at European level. It has also been overtaken in the publicity stakes by company-level European Works Councils agreements and the emergence of consultation at this level. On the whole, the European sectoral social dialogue has so far failed to fulfil the original goal set by the European Commission, namely that it contribute to the development of a European system of industrial relations and the formulation of European collective agreements at sectoral level.

This chapter seeks to assess the rationale for the emphasis placed by the European Commission on the sectoral social dialogue, the approach taken by different social partner organisations to this process, and the extent to which it has produced any tangible outcomes. In doing so, it will also address the question of whether there has been a significant shift in the perception and operation of social partnership at the sectoral level as a result of the Single European Act, the Maastricht Agreement on Social Policy and its recent incorporation into the Amsterdam Treaty, and the introduction of the single currency, or whether the sectoral social dialogue merely represents 'old wine in new bottles' (Keller and Sörries, 1999). The analysis also assesses the extent to which economic self-interest lies at the heart of the actions of social partner organisations at the sectoral level, as opposed to other motivations. This is done using case study examples of the sectoral social dialogue in the road transport and maritime sectors, as well as in the private security industry. The road transport and maritime sectors are considered of interest not only because the social dialogue in the maritime sector has yielded the first sectoral agreement based on Articles 138–9 of the Amsterdam Treaty, which provide for the translation of agreements reached by the social partners into Community law (the social partnership procedure), but also because they demonstrate the importance of positive interactions between personalities in the negotiating teams, as well as the historical background of social partner relations in a given sector. The private security sector is of interest because it provides an example of a sector in which common self-interest has provided a strong driving force for joint actions.

The chapter seeks to argue that while in recent years the sectoral social dialogue has become qualitatively different in its outcomes, its dynamics and the social partners' perception of its role remain entrenched. Although there has been a significant increase in the spirit of cooperation between a number of sectoral social partner organisations, negotiations leading to binding legislation remain limited to areas in which there is a 'threat' of the Community taking legislative action. Where such legislative actions – but also other joint initiatives – have been successful, they have been strongly influenced by economic self-interest. Significantly, in many cases the employer and trade union sides shared a common economic interest. Other important factors include the influence of key individuals and the establishment of positive interactions between certain institutional actors. There also remains a strong guiding influence on the part of the Commission as the initiator of policy and legislation in the social field.

The content of this chapter is based mainly on research carried out in the course of my duties as EU-level correspondent for the European Industrial Relations Observatory (EIRO[1]) between 1996 and 1999. Information is also drawn from my work providing research and consultancy advice to European social partner organisations in a number of sectors between 1993 and 2000, as well as research undertaken for a paper presented at a conference on the European Social Dimension in 1997[2] and interviews with social partner representatives carried out for the purposes of this project.

The historical development of the sectoral social dialogue

Industrial relations systems in many, although by no means all, Member States display elements of collective bargaining at sectoral level with a framework for wages and/or working conditions being set for an entire industry by sectoral social partner organisations (with a variety of modifications possible at company level). Whatever the ambitions of the creators of the European Communities, the formulation of such standards at European level always appeared unlikely in light of differences in economic situation and industrial relations systems between the different Member States (Ferner and Hyman, 1992). Such a 'Europeanisation' of bargaining seemed even less likely in the context of the trend towards the decentralisation of collective bargaining, employer resistance, and the lack of a mandate among European sectoral social partner organisations for collective bargaining (Carley, 1993). However, in recent years there have been a number of initiatives aimed at greater coordination of bargaining goals at transnational level, particularly in cross-border regions. The most widely publicised was the agreement reached between national confederations and large sectoral unions at Doorn in the Netherlands in 1998 establishing a set of joint bargaining guidelines (EIRO, October 1998). In September 1999, the European Trade Union Federation-Textiles Clothing and Leather (ETUF-TCL) adopted guidelines on collective bargaining coordination in the form of an internal sectoral protocol (EIRO, October 1999). Despite these initiatives and the call for a greater Europeanisation of collective bargaining issued by ETUC at its Statutory Congress in Helsinki in July 1999, experience in this area remains limited and is often hampered by cross-country competition for jobs between European sites.

Since the inception of the European Coal and Steel Community, the European Commission has considered consultations with representatives of management and labour to be vital to increase the support and legitimisation of its policies and to benefit from the national expertise of these organisations. The European social dialogue process takes place at several different levels: inter-sectoral level, sectoral level, within the fora of the Economic and Social Committee and the Standing Committee on Employment, and in interprofessional advisory committees. Article 118b of the Single European Act called upon the European Commission to 'endeavour to develop the dialogue between management and labour at European level which could, if the two sides consider it desirable, lead to relations based on agreement' (Commission of the European Communities, 1996d, p.10). Following the adoption of the new decision-making procedure in the Maastricht Treaty, which requires social partner organisations to be consulted on all social policy proposals (see below), the inter-sectoral social dialogue has become increasingly widely publicised, especially following the conclusion of framework agreements on parental leave, part-time work and fixed-term contract work.

Amidst the attention accorded to the inter-sectoral social dialogue process, it is often forgotten that the sectoral social dialogue process in fact predates its 'big brother' by several decades. The first sectoral Committee was the European Coal and Steel Community's tripartite Consultative Committee, which was established in 1955 to ensure the consultation and involvement of the social partners on social and other policies with likely repercussions on employment in the sector (Carley, 1993). The development of the early sectoral social dialogue was very much determined by the policy focus of EU institutions and the existence of European initiatives affecting different sectors. The predominance of the Common Agricultural Policy (CAP) saw the establishment in 1963 of the Joint Advisory Group on the Social Problems Affecting Agricultural Workers, which was succeeded in 1974 by a Joint Committee. To this day, the sectoral social dialogue in agriculture remains among the most structured and active at European level. Similarly, the impact of EC policies on their sectors led to the establishment of Joint Committees in the areas of road transport, transport by inland waterways, sea fishing and rail transport.

Table 5.1 presents a full list of Joint Committees in place prior to January 1999. Each of these was composed of equal numbers of representatives from employer and employee organisations appointed by the Commission on the recommendation of the social partners.

Table 5.1 European Sectoral Social Dialogue: Sectors with Joint Committees

Sector	Year	Employer side	Trade union side
Agriculture	1963*	GEOPA-COPA (Employers Group of Agricultural Organisations in the European Community)	EFA (European Federation of Agricultural Workers Unions)
Road transport	1965	IRU (International Road Transport Union)	FST(European Transport Workers Union)
Inland navigation	1967**	IUIN (International Union for Inland Navigation)	FST (European Transport Workers Union)
		ESO (European Shippers Organisation)	
Railways	1972	CCFE (Community of European Railways)	FST (European Transport Workers Union)
Maritime transport	1987	ECSA (European Community Shipowners Association)	FST (European Transport Workers Union)
Civil aviation	1990	AEA (Association of European Airlines)	FST (European Transport Workers Union)
		ERA (European Regional Airlines Association)	
		ACE (Independent Air Carriers of the EC)	
		ACCA (Air Carriers of the EC)	
		ACI (Airports Council International)	
Sea fishing	1974	Europêche (Association of National Organisations of Fishing Enterprises in the EU)	FST (European Transport Workers Union)
		Cogeca (General Committee for Agricultural Co-operation in the EU – fishing sector)	
Telecoms	1990	Representatives of public and private sector operators	PTTI (Postal, Telegraph and Telephone International)
			Eurofedop (European Organisation of the International Federation of the Public Services)
Postal services	1994	see telecommunications	see telecommunications

Source: Commission of the European Communities, 1996a, 1997b.
* Joint Advisory Committee on the Social Problems of Paid Agricultural Workers; Joint Committee since 1974.
** Joint Advisory Committee; Joint Committee since 1980.

The administration of the Committees was carried out by the European Commission Directorate-General for Employment and Social Affairs. The establishment of the Joint Committees was seen by the Commission as a contribution to the establishment of a European system of industrial relations and was designed to foster free collective bargaining at the European level (Commission of the European Communities, 1996a). However it soon became apparent that despite the formulation of joint opinions and recommendations on issues such as health and safety, working conditions and employment, the aim of achieving European sectoral collective bargaining remained unrealistic in the 1960s, 1970s and 1980s. This was the result of a number of interrelated factors:

- the lack of standing of any such agreements or recommendations in Community law;
- the fact that in EU policy-making economic issues were generally considered in isolation from social issues at both sectoral and inter-sectoral levels;
- the lack of representative employer organisations willing to enter into a social dialogue process at sectoral level;
- the fact that European sectoral social partner organisations had not been given a mandate for collective bargaining by their national constituents;
- problems with the representativeness of social partner bodies;
- tensions between the Commission and the social partners; and
- differences between the views of national member organisations of European social partner bodies as a result of different national social, legislative and economic parameters and a lack of understanding of the industrial relations systems of other Member States.

In light of these difficulties, the Commission began to view the sectoral Joint Committees primarily as consultative bodies which could assist in the drawing up of social policy and other legislative proposals of relevance to specific sectors. At the same time, the Joint Committees had the ability to initiate their own research and opinions and to hold seminars and conferences on specific subjects. Despite this, Community activities and Commission initiatives long remained the main impetus behind sectoral activities. This was highlighted by the revival of the sectoral social dialogue process around common EC policies and the signing, in 1987, of the Single European Act in particular. As a result of the need to assess the impact of the Single Market on different sectors, and in order to be able to have some influence over policy-making, new Joint Committees were formed towards the end of the 1980s after a long period of stagnation. The year 1990 also witnessed the setting up of a dedicated sectoral social dialogue unit in DG Employment and Social Affairs to concentrate the efforts of the Commission in this area.

Because of the problems facing the Joint Committees in the 1980s, the Commission began to favour a less formal approach to the sectoral social dialogue and supported the setting up of informal working parties and non-structured discussion groups. Table 5.2 sets out a full list of Informal Working Groups in place prior to January 1999. A far cry from the aim of fostering European-level collective bargaining, these informal groups were intended to 'create a climate of confidence between employers and workers' and to enable them to analyse the problems of their sector together (Commission of the European Communities, 1996a). They received similar treatment to the Joint Committees in the sense that they were consulted by the Commission on social policy proposals as a matter of course and had the ability to initiate their own studies and activities. However, the lack of representative employer bodies, and their unwillingness to enter into any negotiations, and in some cases even consultations, remained a problem.

While the employee representatives on Joint Committees, informal working parties and non-structured discussion groups were mainly drawn from one of the 15 European Industry Committees recognised by ETUC, the identification of sectoral social partners on the employer side has always proved more difficult. UNICE has no sectoral structure, and many European industrial/trade associations do not see themselves as employer organisations as such. A survey of European Industry Committees in 1991 identified this as one of the key reasons for the lack of progress in the European sectoral social dialogue process (Carley, 1993). In addition, the cross-sectoral social partner organisations have arguably remained ambivalent about the role of the sectoral social dialogue even after the adoption of the Maastricht Social Chapter.

The sectoral social dialogue post-Maastricht

Carley (1993) argues that the social dialogue process entered a qualitatively different phase post-Maastricht. While this is certainly true, the establishment of the new process was delayed while the Commission and the social partners sought to define its parameters more clearly. As a result of the deadlock reached with so many social

Table 5.2 European Sectoral Social Dialogue: Sectors with Informal Working Groups

Sector	Year	Employer side	Union side
Horeca (hotels, restaurants, cafés)	1983	Hotrec (Confederation of the National Hotel and Restaurant Associations in the European Union and the European Economic Area)	ECF-IUF (European Committee of Food, Catering and Allied Workers' Unions within the IUF)
Commerce	1985	EuroCommerce	Euro-FIET (European Regional Organisation of the International Federation of Commercial, Clerical and Technical Employees) (known as Uni Europa as from 1 January 2000)
Insurance	1987	CEA (European Insurance Committee)	Euro-FIET
		BIPAR (International Association of Insurance and Reinsurance Intermediaries)	
		ACME (Association of European Co-operative and Mutual Insurance Companies)	
Banks	1990	FB-UE (Banking Federation of the European Union)	Euro-FIET
		GECE (European Savings Banks Group)	
		GEBC (European Co-operative Banks Group)	
Footwear	1991	ECFI (European Confederation of the Footwear Industry)	ETUF-TCL (European Trade Union Federation for Textiles, Clothing and Leather)
Construction	1992	FIEC (European Construction Industry Federation)	FETBB (European Federation of Building and Woodworkers)
Cleaning	1992	EFCI (European Federation of Cleaning Industries)	Euro-FIET
Textiles and Clothing	1992	Euratex (European Textile and Clothing Organisation)	ETUF-TCL
Private Security	1993	CoESS (European Confederation of Security Services)	Euro-FIET
Woodworking	1994	CEI-Bois (European Confederation of Woodworking Industries)	FETBB (European Federation of Building and Woodworkers)
Sugar	1968	CEFS (Sugar Manufacturers)	ECF-IUF (European Committee of Food, Catering and Allied Workers' Unions within the IUF)

Source: Commission of the European Communities, 1996a, 1997a.

policy initiatives, due to the opposition of certain Member States in the 1980s, and in order to involve the social partners further in the European decision-making process, the Commission had suggested the implementation of a Belgian-style model of social partner involvement in the run-up to the 1991 Intergovernmental Conference (IGC). In the Belgian system of 'law by agreement', agreements reached between the parties in the tripartite *Conseil National du Travail* (CNT) can be made universally applicable by royal decree. The ad hoc social dialogue working group set up to prepare the social partners' input to the IGC reached agreement on 31 October 1991 on a recommendation that the new Treaty provide for the obligatory consultation of the social partners on both the principle and content of social policy directives (Hall, 1994). In the course of this process, the social partners were to have the option to jointly decide to attempt to deal with the issue by means of a Community-level framework agreement concluded between 'management and labour'. If such an agreement was reached, it could be implemented either 'in accordance with the procedures and practices specific to management and labour and the member states' or through a Council decision on the basis of qualified majority voting (in areas covered by Article 2 of the Protocol). This agreement was included in the Social Protocol attached to the Maastricht Treaty almost in its entirety (Articles 3 and 4). The Amsterdam Treaty consolidates these provisions by including them in Articles 138–9.

The introduction of this new social partnership procedure for the passage of binding measures has not been without controversy. While some authors argue that the changes implemented by the Maastricht Social Protocol (and consolidated by the Amsterdam Treaty) made European collective bargaining more likely, others continue to see prospects for such developments as being bleak, albeit differentiating between the prospects for the sectoral and the inter-sectoral social dialogue. Carley (1993) argues that progress is more likely in the area of the sectoral social dialogue than in the inter-sectoral dialogue because of the former's longer history and greater attachment to realities on the ground. Hall (1994), on the other hand, argues that the Maastricht accord is likely to render progress in the European social dimension and social dialogue less speedy and less likely because of the complex and lengthy consultation and negotiation process prescribed in the Maastricht Social Protocol. In addition, the new process has been criticised from other quarters as being undemocratic and ambiguous in its outcomes. The latter is certainly true to the extent that it long remained uncertain what the standing of agreements reached by the sectoral social partners on Community legislation would be. It was not until a precedent was set in the maritime sector that the decision was taken by the Commission services that this initiative could be based on the Maastricht Agreement on Social Policy and therefore result in the formulation of a proposal for a Council Directive. The Maastricht Agreement clearly created more impetus at the inter-sectoral than the sectoral level to reach binding agreements. This is not altogether surprising, as a sectoral approach to matters of fundamental legal rights would lead to an overly fragmented approach. This is certainly the view of the cross-sectoral social partners.

The reform of the sectoral social dialogue

More recently, the Commission has reformed the structures of the sectoral social dialogue in order to adapt them to the new post-Maastricht requirements and to inject renewed focus and dynamism into an organisational framework which was essentially established 30 years ago (EIRO, March 1999). Reform was based on a review of the social dialogue initiated by a Communication Concerning the Development of the Social Dialogue Process at Community Level (COM(96) 448 final) on 18 September 1996. This was followed by a period of intense consultation between DG Employment and Social Affairs and the social partner organisations culminating in the adoption by the Commission in May 1998 of a second Communication on Adapting and Promoting the Social Dialogue at Community level (COM(98)322).

In this latter Communication, the Commission announced a decision to set up new Sectoral Dialogue Committees to promote the dialogue between the social partners at European level. These Sectoral Committees were to replace the existing Joint Committees and Informal Working Groups. There was a view that the existing structures had become over-institutionalised and that a new structure would inject new focus and dynamism into the sectoral social dialogue.

The decision to abolish the existing Joint Committees was controversial, particularly among their members, who perceived the reorganisation as bringing about a loss of status. Members of the Joint Committees were previously officially nominated by their organisations as members of the Committee. The new framework of 'variable geometry' implies that different individuals may attend meetings depending on the subject matter under discussion. The number of individuals attending the meetings has also been reduced. The new Sectoral Committees are to have 15 fully funded attendees on each side, with the possibility of including another five self-funded participants in each of the delegations. The Commission decision makes provision for the new bodies to have one plenary meeting per year, with additional meetings scheduled depending on the nature of the workplan.

By 1 November 1999, the Commission had received applications to establish new Sectoral Dialogue Committees from the social partners' representatives in the following sectors:

- Agriculture
- Road transport
- Inland navigation
- Railways
- Maritime transport
- Civil aviation
- Sea fishing
- Telecommunications
- Postal services
- Hotels, catering and tourism
- Commerce
- Banks
- Insurance
- Footwear
- Construction
- Private security
- Cleaning industry
- Personal services
- Temporary work agencies
- Textiles
- Leather
- Sugar
- Woodworking
- Performing arts
- Electricity industry

Some of the above sectors represent new developments. For example, the social dialogue initiated in the hairdressing sector is to be expanded to cover all other personal services, and new formalised sectoral social dialogue initiatives are being developed in the temporary work sector and in the performing arts. In the electricity industry there has been for some time an informal dialogue between Eurelectric (the European Grouping of the Electricity Supply Industry), EMCEF (the European Mine, Chemical and Energy Workers' Federation) and EPSU (the European Public Services Union), which led to the adoption of a joint document on health and safety and training in 1996.

A number of additional sectors are widely anticipated to join the 21 listed above, including public services. The coverage of public services remains to be decided, but it appears likely that an application will be made by public sector unions together with CEMR (Council for European Municipalities and Regions).

Industrial evolution and developments in the sphere of social partner representation have led to some realignment in the social dialogue in the different sectors. This is partly associated with the liberalisation of previously publicly provided services. The possibility of a separate social dialogue in the electricity industry is a function of the increasing privatisation of electricity generation and supply, and it will be interesting to see whether similar developments occur in the gas and water industries.

Another example of a possible realignment of social partners is apparent in the postal services, where employers in certain privatised delivery services (such as door-to-door delivery and couriers) hesitate between applying for membership in this sectoral committee or the road transport committee. Another change in the postal sector is the establishment of a common employer organisation 'POSTEUROP'. Previously, each national post office was represented by its own independent representative.

The Commission has recently underlined its intention to focus the social dialogue more on the key themes outlined in the Employment Guidelines, such as equal opportunities, employability and adaptability. In particular, pressure is being applied to the social partners to negotiate agreements to modernise the organisation of work.

The changing face of the sectoral social dialogue

During the 35 years between 1960 and 1995, 90 joint opinions, recommendations, memoranda and agreements were formulated in the sectoral social dialogue. The three years between 1996 and 1999 saw the adoption of an equivalent number of such texts. Although this quantitative increase is remarkable in itself, it is not the only sign of what is arguably a shift in the nature of the sectoral social dialogue. It will be argued here that there has equally been a qualitative shift in the nature of agreements concluded and activities undertaken at this level.

In order to analyse the change in the nature of the sectoral social dialogue, it is first necessary to understand how social partnership and the social dialogue are conceptualised by the different sectoral social partner organisations at European level, as well as their rationale for participating.

Interviews with the social partners about their understanding of the concept of social partnership showed some significant agreement, but also some divergence of views between employer and trade union organisations on the meaning of the concept and its applicability to the European level (see Table 5.3). The term 'social partnership' is not used in any documentation or common parlance. The process is usually referred to as the 'social dialogue' and is primarily understood as being aimed at an exchange of ideas, the launching of joint initiatives, and the formulation of joint opinions on the part of European sectoral social partner organisations and the Commission.

While sectoral trade union organisations on the whole are strongly supportive of the sectoral social dialogue process and would like to see it develop towards being a forum for collective bargaining, they are also realistic about its limitations. Despite the fact that unions are represented at the inter-sectoral level by the ETUC in negotiations under the Maastricht Social Protocol, efforts are always made by the Commission to consult sectoral organisations as well on the impact of any proposed action on their sector. European sectoral trade union organisations are therefore partly driven by organisational self-interest on two fronts: vis-a-vis the Commission in respect of their role as a recognised social partner and vis-a-vis their membership because of the financial contributions made by each national organisation towards the operation of a Brussels base. In their actions, therefore, they have to balance these interests. Because of the limited resources of European-level trade union organisations, they welcome the budget made available by the Commission for joint actions to enhance their knowledge about working conditions and relevant policies in different countries, which can help to inform the policies of their national membership. Their actions are also driven by the economic interests of their membership in terms of protecting and improving working conditions. European sectoral

Table 5.3 Key Terms in the European Sectoral Dialogue

Term	Meaning
Social partnership	This term is rarely used
Social dialogue	Discussions on areas of joint concern, joint actions, plus the possibility of joint negotiations
Social partner (national level)	Employer or trade union organisation with representative membership and the power to bargain collectively
Social partner (European level)	European-level employer or trade union organisation mandated to represent the interests of its member organisation at European level

trade union organisations also take part in campaigning activities, such as campaigning against the war in Kosovo etc., that cannot be explained either by institutional or by economic self-interest but instead must be classified as ethically or ideologically motivated activities.

Despite union support for the sectoral dialogue, however, there are a number of large sectoral trade union organisations which are kept out of the social dialogue process at this level because of the absence of a partner on the employer side.

Among employer organisations, attitudes towards the social dialogue and motivations for taking part vary more significantly (see Table 5.4). A number of employer organisations, including in key sectors such as metalworking and the chemical industry, have so far opted not to engage in a sectoral social dialogue. These organisations tend to perceive themselves as being large and influential enough in their own right to lobby Commission services on their areas of interest without needing to participate in the sectoral social dialogue. They also see their interests in the social sphere as being represented at the inter-sectoral level by UNICE, in which they play a significant role. Among these organisations, concern is widespread that the sectoral social dialogue is a stepping stone towards European collective bargaining, a development they strongly oppose.

The next category of employer organisations can be termed 'reluctant participants'. These organisations are keen to be consulted on social policy matters and therefore seek to receive official recognition as social partner organisations by the Commission. As a result, they are required to take part in the dialogue process but

Table 5.4 European Sectoral Social Dialogue: Nature of Employer Group Participation

Nature of participation	*Sectoral employer organisations*
Informed non-participation	CEFIC (European Chemical Industry Council)
	European Employer Organisation in the Metalworking Sector
Reluctant participants	BIPAR (International Association of Insurance and Reinsurance Intermediaries)
	CEA (European Insurance Committee)
	Hotrec (Confederation of the National Hotel and Restaurant Associations in the European Union and the European Economic Area)
	FB-UE (Banking Federation of the European Union)
	GEBC (European Co-operative Banks Group)
	IRU (International Road Transport Union)
	IUIN (International Union for Inland Navigation)
	CCFE (Community of European Railways)
	AEA (Association of European Airlines)
	ERA (European Regional Airlines Association)
	ACE (Independent Air Carriers of the EC)
	ACCA (Air Carriers of the EC)
	ACI (Airports Council International)
Issue-driven participants	EuroCOMMERCE
	ECFI (European Confederation of the Footwear Industry)
	FIEC (European Construction Industry Federation)
	Euratex (European Textile and Clothing Organisation)
	CoESS (European Confederation of Security Services)
	CEFS (Sugar Manufacturers)
	GEOPA-COPA (Employers Group of Agricultural Organisations in the European Community)
	ECSA (European Community Shipowners Association)
	CEI-Bois (European Confederation of Woodworking Industries)
	GECE (European Savings Banks Group)

often expend a minimum of effort and resources in doing this. Any joint statements issued in such dialogues tend to be limited to weak declarations. This strategy has become more difficult in recent years, as the Commission has become more active in seeking to achieve results in this process, for example by requiring social partners to define annual work programmes.

Finally, there is a category of employer organisations that are keen to engage with their trade union counterparts on issues of common concern, in particular in the areas of training, employment, and health and safety. A perception of common interests is also important in policy areas in which Commission legislative action is threatened. This can be seen to have influenced the outcomes of negotiations on legislation in the area of working time in the maritime transport and road transport sectors, with the former resulting in a joint proposal for a Community Directive and the latter breaking down. These developments, as well as the experience of the social dialogue in the private security industry, are elaborated in more detail below to illustrate both areas of progress and areas in which old divisions remain entrenched.

Table 5.5 displays the arguments commonly made by social partner organisations for and against social partnership and social dialogue. This reveals both similarities and differences in views between trade union and employer organisations, and shows that the sectoral social dialogue process is generally perceived to provide a positive contribution to the European social area. While trade unions would clearly like to see the dialogue go further than it currently does, employers do not perceive it as a significant threat to managerial prerogative, as long as strong employer organisations are in place to defend the interests of business.

The social dialogue in the maritime and road transport sectors

Closer examination of the social dialogue in the maritime and road transport sectors provides a more detailed illustration of the dynamics of European social partnership at sectoral level.

Both the maritime and road transport sectors were among those excluded from the scope of the provisions of Directive 93/104 on working time. Since its passage, the Commission has published a White Paper on the sectors and activities excluded from the Directive. In the White Paper, then Commissioner Flynn termed the

Table 5.5 Arguments For and Against European Sectoral Social Partnership and Social Dialogue

Argument	For	Against
Problem-solving competence	Globalisation requires more issues to be dealt with at European level (employers, unions)	Cannot solve traditional collective bargaining issues (employers, unions)
	Initiatives at European level can improve national policy-making (employers, unions)	Principle of subsidiarity needs to be respected (employers)
Economic utility	Helps to ensure that European legislation takes business needs into account (employers)	
	Can often ensure greater flexibility than Commission-initiated legislation (employers)	
Participation	Allows social partners to shape European decisions in social sphere (employers, unions)	Favours social partners over other groups in civil society (employers, unions)
Conflict reduction		Cannot reduce national-level conflict, but may exacerbate it (employers)
Wages and working conditions	Facilitates harmonisation of wages and benefits in response to EMU making them more comparable across borders (unions)	Weakens resistance to pressure to harmonise wages and benefits created by EMU making wages and benefits more comparable across borders (employers)
	Integration without European-level regulation can lead to 'social dumping' (unions)	
Legitimacy	Enhances the legitimacy of the European Union (employers, unions)	
	Increases acceptability of EU decisions among national social partners (employers, unions)	
Democracy	Enhances democracy (employers, unions)	Sidelines European Parliament (unions)
Substitute for lobbying	Strengthens the relative position of unions, which lack resources for lobbying (unions)	Not a substitute for lobbying (employers)
	Attempts at lobbying outside the social dialogue become more transparent (unions)	Strengthens relative position of unions, which lack resources for lobbying (employers)
Brake on social policy innovation	Gives employers more influence than Commission-proposed legislation; makes outcomes more predictable (employers)	Can further stall progress in areas where employers are intransigent (unions)
	Can free up legislation blocked in Council (unions)	
Power	Unions gain influence relative to employers, who are well resourced and connected in any case (unions)	Unions gain influence relative to employers, who are well resourced and connected in any case (employers)
Collective bargaining	Facilitates Europeanisation of collective bargaining (unions)	Facilitates Europeanisation of collective bargaining (employers)
Managerial prerogative		Can restrict managerial prerogative (employers)

exclusion of these sectors an anomaly and suggested a variety of options for rectifying this. A particular preference was expressed for the sectoral social partners to reach their own agreements on working time, which could then be implemented through Community legislation. For this purpose, the Commission launched a first round of consultations with the social partners. The social partners in both the road transport and maritime transport sectors initiated negotiations on the working time issue, but while in the maritime sector agreement on a Directive on Working Time was reached between the Federation of European Transport Workers Unions (FST) and the European Community Shipowners Association (ECSA) in December 1997, negotiations in the road transport sector between FST and, on the employer side, the International Road Transport Union (IRU) broke down in September 1998.

In order to understand the different outcomes in these negotiations, it is important to understand the context of the negotiating process as well as some of the motivating factors behind different actors' decisions.

The maritime sector in the European Union has suffered a period of significant decline, and its share of the total world fleet currently accounts for no more than 10–15 per cent of world market share. There has been increasing concentration in the industry and a trend towards deregulation in order to maintain market share. There are now only approximately 153 000 employees in the sector, of whom 128 000 are Community nationals. The share of employment of Community nationals has declined significantly as more and more operators have adopted flags of convenience. At a Conference entitled 'Is the EU Seafarer an Endangered Species' held in Dublin in 1996, Commissioner Kinnock warned that the disappearance of the EU seafarer was inevitable if current trends persisted (EIRO, February 1998).

Until January 1999, the social dialogue in the European maritime sector took place within the framework of a Joint Committee set up in July 1987 to assist the Commission in formulating and implementing policy to improve living and working conditions in the sector as well as the competitive position of the sector. Attached to the Committee was a specialised working party on working time. The social dialogue in the sector has largely focused on the issues of employment, health and safety, and working time, and has so far yielded joint opinions on health and safety, VAT and duty free, training, working time, and the future of the social dialogue.

The negotiations on working time therefore took place in a framework in which both trade unions and employer organisations were perceiving common threats to the future of the EU seafaring sector and therefore wished to ensure that any provisions agreed would not render Community ships less competitive vis-a-vis their non-EU competitors. At the same time as these negotiations were taking place, ILO regulation 158 on working time aboard ships was also being renegotiated in Geneva. It so happened that strong personal links existed between the employer and trade union negotiating sides at ILO level and the EU negotiating teams, which allowed them to exchange information and combine efforts to reach a settlement at EU level that would be consistent with the global regulations of the ILO. These factors all facilitated the achievement of an agreement in this sector on working time regulations, which was translated into Community law on 25 May 1999 (EIRO, June 1999).

In the road transport sector, which is by far the largest of the transport sectors, this confluence of supporting factors was not in place. Indeed there is a long history of adversarial relations between the trade unions and employer organisations in the sector, which regularly erupt in strike action. During the final negotiating phase on working time at EU level, the International Transport Workers Federation, with the support of the FST, coordinated an International Day of Action by transport workers world-wide to highlight the dangers of long driving hours under the banner 'Fatigue Kills'.

Discussions on ending the exclusion of the sector from the Working Time Directive had dominated the activities of the Joint Committee on Road Transport during the latter part of 1997 and in 1998. In early July 1998 the partners had reached provisional agreement on a joint text in relation to working time in the industry. Subsequent discussions indicated a convergence of views on an approach similar to that taken in Germany. Under German regulations, non-driving time is taken into account in calculating pay but is not counted as working time as defined in the Directive. The draft accord was to be finalised and agreed at a meeting on 18 September 1998. However, the optimism expressed by both sides prior to the meeting that a final accord could be reached was confounded when last minute disagreements emerged over a number of general principles contained in the draft.

The area of contention was based upon the employers' objection to the wording of the text regarding the 'more favourable provisions and safeguarding clause', which is designed to protect national standards where they are higher than the standards established by the general agreement. In addition, there was disagreement concerning the employers' proposal to make it possible to derogate certain issues covered in the agreement to national level. This would, in the FST's opinion, render the agreement useless. It was also argued by the FST that by adopting a position whereby progressive national standards were not protected, steps towards reaching an agreement were going backwards rather than forwards.

Transport Commissioner Neil Kinnock and Social Affairs Commissioner Padraig Flynn expressed disappointment at the inability of the social partners to reach an agreement. In a joint statement they commented: 'A great opportunity has been missed. If there is no agreement on 30 September, the Commission will table its own proposals on working time in the excluded sectors. The specific legislation for the road sector will of course take account of the elements of convergence reached during the recent discussions' (EIRO, September 1998).

The social dialogue in the private security industry

The social dialogue in the private security industry between the European Confederation of Security Services (CoESS) on the employer side and the European Regional Organisation of the International Federation of Commercial, Clerical and Technical Employees (Euro-FIET) on the employee side is a relatively recent addition to the sectoral social dialogue process, an informal working group having been established at Community level in 1993. The initiation of a dialogue at the European level was partly a reflection of the increasing importance of the sector in providing internal security functions that had previously been provided by state authorities. The sector also featured among the 'new sources of employment' pinpointed in the 1993 Commission White Paper on Growth, Competitiveness and Employment. Between 500 000 and a million staff are currently employed in this sector to carry out tasks such as the guarding of industrial sites, shops, public buildings and money transports. There is a strong commitment among both sides of industry to make progress in the sectoral social dialogue and there are many common concerns, particularly in relation to the professionalisation of the sector and lowest price competition.

Demand for private security services is rising as a result of economic, demographic and political changes that are leading to a greater polarisation in society. At the same time as these developments are taking place, the state and public authorities are taking a declining share of the direct responsibility of ensuring public safety. In order to ensure maximum flexibility and cost effectiveness, these functions are increasingly being delegated to the private security industry.

Private security contractors have therefore become responsible for ensuring public safety and protecting public and private property in a wide variety of locations, including high risk areas such as nuclear power plants, banks, embassies and airports. They are also increasingly providing security services at public events and escorts for high risk transports, including prisoner transports, and are taking over a number of functions previously supplied by police, fire and ambulance services.

Public authorities at European, national, regional and local level are finding themselves more and more in a position of having to contract for the external provision of manned guarding services. Their 'buying power' is therefore more and more important in determining the rules and quality of the security services provided. A survey carried out by CoESS and Euro-FIET in 1998 showed that the market share of public tendering in the private security sector is rising constantly and in many Member States amounts to over 30 per cent of the market.

The increasing market share of public tendering means that the standards set by public authorities in terms of the price paid for guarding services have a significant impact on salaries, working conditions, and company infrastructure and therefore, as a result, on the quality of the service provided. Despite the sensitive nature of many of the public buildings and locations serviced, the CoESS survey showed that the majority of public authorities today select security contractors solely on the basis of the lowest price. There is increasing concern among the social partners representing employers and workers in the industry that the application of the principle of awarding contracts to the lowest bidder is leading to a gradual lowering of quality standards.

While the awarding of contracts on the basis of the lowest price is partly the result of declining public budgets, the social partners argue that it can also be attributed to a lack of available guidance to assist contracting authorities in selecting a 'best value' provider.

In 1998, CoESS and Euro-FIET therefore decided to commission a manual to help interested public authorities select a provider on the basis of quality as well as price. This joint initiative was clearly based on a common perception of the threats facing the sector, which are affecting employees and security companies alike. It is hoped that this initiative will discourage irresponsible operators and increase the level of professionalisation in the sector. It has attracted widespread attention in the Commission and in other sectors affected by public tendering, which means that it could have a widespread impact at the national level, should this approach to tendering find application among public authorities, even though it is not a legally binding initiative.

Conclusions: the dawn of a new era?

The conclusion so far of three framework agreements at the inter-sectoral level, one proposal for a Directive at the sectoral level, and an increasing number of joint projects, initiatives and joint opinions at sectoral level together constitute a qualitative change in the social dialogue. This is conditioned by a number of key factors. Some of these may have only a temporary effect, but others can be seen to be more lasting and therefore can be argued to present an indication of future developments. These key factors are as follows:

- the changed standing of framework agreements between the social partners post-Maastricht and Amsterdam;
- the changed nature of the social dimension after Britain's accession to the Social Chapter and changes in industrial relations systems in Britain as well as in other Member States;
- the consolidation of the internal organisation of DG Employment and Social Affairs and its increasing commitment to the sectoral social dialogue;
- increasing pressure from the Commission for sectoral social dialogue to achieve tangible results;
- the greater experience of the social partner organisations, which means that they now have a better understanding of the Commission and of each other, as well as greater familiarity with the systems and policies of the various Member States;
- a greater commitment to the social dialogue on the part of a number of employer organisations in certain areas of activity;
- the common emphasis on employment creation generated by Commission and Council initiatives;

- the push to achieve positive outcomes in light of the Commission Communication on the future of the social dialogue and the involvement of the social partners in the European Employment Strategy;
- the less interventionist Community stance in terms of social and labour legislation and the increased emphasis on negotiated flexibility post-Maastricht;
- common pressures affecting employer and trade union organisations as a result of globalisation, low cost competition and the underground economy.

The social partnership procedure devised in Maastricht and reaffirmed in Amsterdam, which gives social partner organisations a greater say in social policy-making, has clearly boosted the inter-sectoral and sectoral social dialogue processes, although agreements are still only forthcoming in areas where there is a 'threat' of Community legislation. In addition, recent years have seen a greater focusing of Community policy, especially on employment, which has not failed to have an impact on the social dialogue, especially in the areas specified in the Employment Guidelines, namely employability, adaptability, entrepreneurship and equal opportunities. Despite the absence of additional binding agreements, joint projects and opinions in recent years have taken a more 'practical' flavour, which makes them more likely than previously to have an impact at the national level. Such initiatives have been especially strong in sectors facing strong global and low cost competition, as well as competition from the underground economy, and in sectors seeking to encourage professionalisation. It is in these areas that we can see the strongest confluence of interests between employer organisations and trade unions, at least as far as these initiatives are concerned.

Progress at the sectoral level has also been assisted by institutional changes at DG Employment and Social Affairs and the increasing experience of the social dialogue process of the various organisations involved. DG Employment and Social Affairs, the Directorate-General responsible for the formulation of legislative and policy initiatives in the social dimension, experienced a period of intensive internal organisational and personnel restructuring in the early to mid-1990s, partly as a result of the accession of Sweden, Finland and Austria, which added substantially to the experience of the Community in the area of the social dimension and the social dialogue. Once this reorganisation was complete, and key personnel were in place, policy planning became more strategic and coordinated. Personnel were increasingly equipped with experiences from countries with long traditions of social partnership and/or strong trade union and social partner involvement in policy-making, and the emphasis of the social dialogue unit has moved on from the encouragement of employer–worker dialogue at the European level to the fostering of concrete outcomes. While the social partners had in the past criticised the excessively directive intervention of the Commission, the overall approach has now become more constructive and managerial, lending support to focused initiatives while refusing to tolerate stalling of progress. The Commission has particularly emphasised the importance for sectors of addressing issues such as work organisation and telework.

The transformation of the social dialogue was assisted by the greater focusing of Community activities on the encouragement of employment. In the light of the increasing involvement of the social partner organisations in the decision-making process in relation to the employment strategy, there is also an increasing expectation that they will contribute positively and constructively to this process. It remains to be seen whether this momentum will be sustained. The common emphasis on employment creation has led to a greater concentration of efforts and to initiatives in areas which have proved relatively uncontroversial at the level of the sectoral social dialogue, but initiatives at this level remain very much focused on the specific problems facing individual sectors, rather than looking at the 'general social dialogue issues' tackled at the inter-sectoral level. This can be attributed to the narrow view taken of the process by employer organisations and, to some extent, to the reluctance of cross-sectoral social partner organisations to support such actions at the sectoral level. The content of the sectoral social dialogue process is therefore still mainly determined by the employer side, despite the Commission's support for sectoral actions in the social sphere, and the sectoral dialogue in a number of sectors remains blocked as a result of employer reluctance to cooperate.

In addition, further progress is inhibited by the fact that the issues of representativeness and of mandates granted to social partner organisations for negotiations at European level remain problematic. In this connection, it is crucial that more resources be spent on liaison between national and transnational social partner organisations, as links here are often weak and many national organisations continue to accord little priority to European issues. This applies to both employer and trade union organisations. While employer organisations often do not accord any significant mandate to European-level organisation because of their opposition to consultation and negotiation at this level, on the basis that social and labour market issues are national or even company-level concerns, trade unions often suffer from lack of resources. Much therefore remains to be done to improve the effectiveness of the sectoral social dialogue despite recent advances.

Where a mandate is granted and information exchange, joint working, consultation and negotiation takes place, this can often be seen to be motivated by institutional self-interest, as it occurs either as the result of a perceived need to justify an organisation's privileged position as a social partner through some action or concession, or as a means of averting other less desirable outcomes, such as Commission-initiated legislation in the case of negotiations under the social partnership procedure. In a number of cases joint actions have resulted from joint self-interest due to a perception of common social or economic challenges. Opposition to certain actions and agreements on the part of national member organisations can therefore act against the interests of the European-level organisation, but remains a defining factor in its operation.

6
Social Partnership in the European Union

Hugh Compston and Justin Greenwood

Introduction

Can the behaviour of policy actors in EU-level social partnership be explained by reference to self-interest alone? By social partnership (or policy concertation) is meant the co-determination of EU policy by means of agreements struck between EU institutions, European-level employer organisations and trade union confederations. At inter-sectoral level this means the procedure using which the Council may transpose agreements struck between the peak European-level private sector employer confederation UNICE, its public sector equivalent CEEP and the peak European trade union confederation ETUC into the form of EU legislation, which we have called the social partnership procedure for short (Articles 137–9 of the Treaty of Amsterdam). We are especially interested in the extent to which the positions and actions of the organisations involved in the development and use of the social partnership procedure can be explained in terms of self-interest alone. In this concluding chapter we consider and summarise the findings of the chapters on the relevant policy actors, set them in the context of contemporary accounts of European integration, and explore the significance of EU social partnership to accounts of European integration. The chapter ends with a summary of our main conclusions.

Social partnership and self-interest

The ETUC and the Commission have long been in favour of involving the social partners in the co-determination of EU policy, while UNICE was opposed to the idea until late 1991, when it reversed its position, CEEP has raised no objections of principle, and Member States were broadly favourable too, apart from Britain. The key events in the process that led to the adoption of the social partnership procedure were therefore the social partners' agreement of 31 October 1991, and Britain's 'opt-out' from the Social Protocol agreed by the other eleven Member States at Maastricht. To what extent can these positions and actions be explained in terms of self-interest alone?

In conceptualising self-interest we focus on both the actual people who made the critical decisions and the heterogeneous organisations in which they operate. We consider the interest-based incentives affecting them as decision-makers and leaders, in particular their interest in retaining their position and maximising their power. Among other things, this depends on the degree to which decision-makers are successful in expanding the autonomy and influence of their organisations and in furthering organisational goals. In this way the individual self-interest of decision-makers is linked to organisational interests, to the extent that separating out individual interests from organisational interests can be difficult if not impossible. At the same time, all of the organisations which we examine contain considerable diversity, and coming to a clear sense of identifying how an organisation interprets its self-interest can be problematic. For example, the institutional self-interest in enhancing the status of their organisations in the EU policy-making process may lead them to support deepening arrangements for social partnership, while their interest in furthering the perceived interests of their members may imply opposition to EU-wide social legislation. This view of individuals and organisations as calculating utility maximisers can be contrasted with 'autopilot' behavior based on learnt convictions derived from rules, norms, felt identities, and standard operating procedures: the 'logic of appropriateness' (March and Olsen, 1989).

In analysing the extent to which the development and operation of the social partnership procedure can be explained in terms of self-interest we also pay particular attention to the role of ideas. Ideas affect public policy in the immediate sense of being the medium of policy-making: policy proposals, argumentation and negotiation all consist of linked ideas expressed in words. Policies are designed to achieve certain goals, which express values held by policy-makers that may be self-interested or not, and are built on statements of causality based on the use of technical expertise. Values may derive from a number of sources, including organisational culture, ideology and political culture. Policy change can be attributed to changes in values and in causal belief systems over time resulting from 'policy oriented learning', such as iterative interaction with a rival belief system, or learning to live with compromises imposed by the policy process (Sabatier and Jenkins Smith, 1988).

ETUC

We interpret the self-interest of trade union leaders as being survival and power. For union leaders to remain union leaders they need to retain the confidence of their constituents by being seen to protect and/or advance the interests of union members (mainly in relation to jobs, wages and working conditions) and, in the case of leaders of peak confederations, by confining their actions to those approved by the lower-level trade union leaders to whom they owe their positions. Their power is enhanced to the extent that they succeed in protecting and advancing the interests of union members, broadening the range of issues over which they make decisions, and gaining decision-making autonomy vis-a-vis lower-level trade unions.

From this perspective, the positive attitude of the ETUC towards the idea of making public policy by agreement with employers and the Council, which is the principle of the social partnership procedure, can be understood in terms of self-interest alone. However, self-interest cannot fully explain its negotiating positions on the specific issues addressed using the social partnership procedure once it came into force in 1993. For instance, as Branch and Greenwood suggest, its enthusiasm to further the long-term cause of social partnership has led the ETUC to sign agreements which have been of dubious value to the trade union movement, such as that on part-time work. In addition, its dependence upon the Commission to achieve its goals has led it to accept broader economic ideas, such as monetarist economic policy, which do not appear to be consistent with the interests of trade union members.

Wage-setting is outside the bounds of EU competencies, so the relevant economic interests of the ETUC are the reduction of unemployment and the protection and advancement of working conditions along with securing the organisational capacity of trade unions to obtain reasonable wages and working conditions via the rights to organise, bargain collectively and strike. European-level social legislation is seen as desirable due to union fear that creation by the Single Market process and EMU of a uniform set of financial, tax and technical conditions within a largely unregulated internal market, while leaving a variety of national systems of social regulation intact, would open the way for competitive social dumping in the form of a contest among Member States to gain an economic edge by offering businesses low wage costs, weak labour laws and minimal government regulation, resulting in a 'race to the bottom' in the level of wages, benefits and workers' rights. Since the mid-1980s at least, European trade unions have advocated greater EC powers on social policy (Silvia, 1991, pp.626–33; Dølvik, 1997, pp.5–6, 17; Ross and Martin, 1998, p.31). The actions of ETUC leaders would be expected to be constrained by the views of their affiliated constituent national trade union confederations and sectoral European Industry Federations, but they would be expected to push for greater decision-making powers for the ETUC at European level vis-a-vis their affiliates. A situation whereby ETUC leaders co-determine EU policy by means of negotiations with their employer counterparts (and, less openly, in conjunction with the Commission and Council) is therefore clearly in the interests of these leaders.

Once a social partnership procedure was in place, we would expect ETUC leaders to refuse to agree to any provisions that were weaker than what they would expect Council to pass using the 'normal' legislative procedure. However, while in general the evidence is consistent with this prediction, there is also evidence that at times the ETUC has agreed to weaker social standards than this logic would predict. Dølvik and Visser (this volume, Chapter 1) remark that:

> The internally contested process of ETUC integration and support for EU social partnership reflects an interplay between common European and competing national, both economic and institutional *interests,* and *values, ideas and identities* of even more diverse character, varying across national boundaries and between actors at national and European levels. This process is mediated by the *institutional* dynamics at the European level that have tended to influence and re-shape notions of interests and ideas. EU-level institution-building has changed the preferences, interests and ideas among ETUC players *and* – more limited and in recent years – among national union leaders, drawing them into what may broadly be called the European social policy community.

The ETUC's identity has become closely intertwined with sections of the European Commission, to the point that it has become over-dependent upon the Commission to achieve its goals. Its principal hope of adding 'social Europe' through social partnership rests considerably on the ability of the Commission to draft alternative social legislation that might be unacceptable to employers. The construction of 'self-interest' is dosed in this case with a strong sense of the values, ideas and identities of the institutional patron.

Employers

We interpret the self-interest of employer leaders, like trade union leaders, as being survival and power, which includes enhancing the influence of the organisations they lead. For the leaders of private sector employer associations, survival means retaining the confidence of their constituents by being seen to protect and/or advance the interests of employers by maximising the conditions for profit protection and enhancement and, in the case of peak employer confederations, by confining their actions to those approved by the lower-level employer associations to which they owe their positions. The power of employer leaders is enhanced to the extent that they are successful in securing and advancing the opportunities for employers to make profits, broadening the range of issues over which they make decisions, and gaining decision-making autonomy from lower-level employer associations. In relation to public policy this implies, among other things, opposition to legislation that imposes extra costs on employers.

Yet it is possible that these objectives can conflict, such that members take measures to prevent their organisation having too much autonomy to agree to measures that might not be in the best interests of employers but which enhance the influence of the representative organisation. This possibility looms large in the constitutional arrangements governing the positions employer organisations may adopt in social partnership. That is, both UNICE and CEEP are on relatively 'short leads' held by their members. In the case of UNICE, despite somewhat heterogeneous member views, this makes their position in social partnership relatively uncomplicated. As the chapter on European-level employers by Branch and Greenwood shows, the positions and actions of UNICE in relation to social partnership at EU level, including the reversal of its opposition in October 1991, can be readily understood in terms of the pragmatic self-interest of business in seeking to make and protect profits. In line with the self-interest theory, UNICE has consistently opposed EU-level social legislation or, when it was unable to prevent it, has engaged in damage limitation. Until 1991 UNICE could block such legislation by persuading just one Member State to oppose it, since social policy was covered by unanimity voting. As the prospect of social legislation becoming subject to Qualified Majority Voting (QMV) approached in 1991, however, the likelihood of such legislation being passed increased, so the idea of a social partnership procedure became more attractive as a means of keeping matters out of the hands of the legislator. Making EU legislation contingent on agreement between the social partners would give UNICE a veto on the contents of legislation passed this way, which UNICE does not have in relation to social legislation passed the 'normal' way, and ensures a bypass of the European Parliament. It is therefore not surprising that, as the Maastricht meeting approached, UNICE agreed to the proposal to adopt a social partnership procedure.

The self-interested concern to minimise the impact of social regulation also explains why since 1991 UNICE has refused to negotiate on social proposals unless social legislation that it sees as undesirable seems inevitable, as Branch and Greenwood point out, and, where negotiation is unavoidable, refuses to agree to any provisions that are more costly for business than what they would expect Council to pass using the 'normal' legislative procedure (see also Falkner, 1998, Chapter 4). There have been clear points in UNICE's involvement in social partnership in which it is possible to interpret positions and behaviour as evidence of 'institutional self-interest' and 'the role of ideas', but neither of these seem to detract from the pursuit of pragmatic employer self-interest in seeking to protect and enhance the conditions for profit maximisation.

The position of CEEP leaders is slightly different from that of UNICE leaders. While state-owned enterprises, like private sector firms, aim to make a profit (or at least to minimise losses), Branch and Greenwood point out that they often have other objectives as well, deriving from their ownership by the state. In relation to EU social policy this means that cost considerations would not be expected to be of such overriding importance as they are for private sector employers, so EU-level social legislation is not quite as threatening. In addition, Branch and Greenwood point out that institutional self-interest provides incentives for CEEP to support social partnership because involvement in discussion and negotiation at EU level is the principal factor sustaining CEEP at its present scale of activity and organisation. Indeed, social partnership has acted as a 'recruiting sergeant' for CEEP. This characterisation of CEEP self-interest implies that it would be expected to be less negative towards the social partnership procedure than UNICE. It also implies that any CEEP reservations about participating in the co-determination of EU policy that it held prior to striking the agreement of 31 October 1991 with UNICE and the ETUC would be obscured by the fact that it could rely upon UNICE to take a stand, while CEEP remained in the background to benefit from UNICE's veto while still appearing reasonable and cooperative by comparison. Furthermore, the less negative stance of CEEP in relation to social partnership, at least in public, implies that once UNICE reversed its position in 1991 CEEP would not object. All these predictions of the self-interest theory are consistent with the findings of Branch and Greenwood in relation to CEEP's conduct.

The Commission

Although the Commission was not a signatory to either the 31 October Agreement (social partners) or the Social Protocol (Member States), it is hard to imagine that the 31 October Agreement would have been struck without the groundwork laid by the Commission under Jacques Delors. Delors had launched the social dialogue in 1985 and relaunched it in 1989. The Commission had given substantial financial and logistical support to the dialogue, especially to the ETUC, had applied pressure on UNICE to negotiate by bringing forward proposals for social legislation, and was the first to propose a social partnership procedure in 1989. Furthermore, its proposal of early 1991 formed the basis of the text of the 31 October Agreement, which it brokered (Dølvik, 1997, p.18; Falkner, 1998, pp.74, 170; Ross, 1995a, p.183; Ross and Martin, 1998, pp.11–12, 16). Counterfactuals are difficult to evaluate, but it seems unlikely that UNICE would have signed on 31 October 1991 without having had extensive experience of discussing employment and social policy with the ETUC. This, in turn, was a consequence of the intensified series of meetings encouraged and largely financed by the Commission, the threat of impending social legislation proposed by the Commission, and the Commission's own social partnership proposals put forward as a starting point for negotiations (see, for example,

Tyszkiewicz, 1999). For this reason it seems reasonable to conclude that the Commission's support was crucial to the adoption of the social partnership procedure at Maastricht. In addition, the operation of the social partnership procedure since Maastricht has been largely dependent on the Commission's power to initiate alternative legislation in the event of failed or refused negotiations.

The interests of any President of the Commission can be summarised, as for the leaders of the other organisations, as survival and power. The survival constraint means not departing too far from the wishes of the heads of government on whom the President is dependent for reappointment. Hugh Compston's chapter on Member States shows that the great majority of governments were sympathetic to the Commission's pro-social partnership stance, which never put the reappointment of then-President Jacques Delors in question. Maximising the power of the President of the Commission implies three things: maximising the range of policy areas subject to decision-making at EU level, which means pushing European integration as far as possible in accord with the acknowledged role of the Commission as the motor of integration; maximising the influence of the Commission on legislative proposals vis-a-vis Council and the European Parliament; and maximising the effectiveness of EU policy by ensuring that decisions are technically sound and fully implemented.

Adoption of the social partnership procedure did not in itself increase the range of policy areas subject to decision-making at EU level, as the range of areas in employment and social policy covered by the procedure is no greater than that covered by the 'normal' legislative procedure, but its adoption can be said to contribute to the Commission's long-term strategy of deepening European integration (integrating more policy areas). In terms of democratic support, social partnership helps by keeping the European trade union movement broadly supportive of the integration process despite concerns about the effect on workers of the Single Market and EMU (Falkner, 1998, pp.187–9). There is also the possibility of social partnership influencing employer perceptions in the longer term, resulting in increasing numbers of agreements, while in general the procedure constitutes an additional route to legislation that deepens European integration.

The chapter by Daniela Obradovic demonstrates that the existence of the social partnership procedure improves the power position of the Commission relative to other EU institutions when compared to its position in the 'normal' legislative procedure. First, the entry of the social partners into the decision-making process is balanced by the exclusion of the European Parliament. Second, only the Commission may present a social partner agreement to Council, and although the Commission may not refuse to do this on account of its contents, it does have the right to decide whether to present it to Council on the basis of its assessment of the representativeness of the parties, their mandate, the legality of each clause and its provisions in relation to small and medium business. Third, while social legislation passed the 'normal' way is subject to amendment by Council, which almost always avails itself of this option, the accepted convention is that Council may not amend social partner agreements presented to it, but only accept or reject them. In addition, rejection is generally considered to be most unlikely in practice, and has not occurred so far. Finally, although in theory the social partners may negotiate an agreement among themselves that differs from the initial Commission proposal that triggers the social partnership procedure, in practice the terms of the first three agreements have been very similar to the terms of the original Commission proposals. In summary, although the Commission may not amend social partner agreements prior to presenting them to Council, overall the influence of the Commission on the final form of EU legislation is enhanced relative to the influence it exerts through the 'normal' procedure.

Finally, adoption of a social partnership procedure would be expected to add to the power of the Commission via increasing the efficacy of legislation both by enlisting the expertise and credibility of the social partners and by facilitating the acceptance by employers and unions of EU legislation because legislation passed this way is, by its very nature, legislation to which both employers and unions have already agreed (Falkner, 1998, p.178).

While self-interest can explain Commission support for social partnership, however, it does not explain why the Commission was much more active in pursuing social partnership as an objective after 1985. To explain this we need to refer to the role of ideas, specifically the ideological convictions of the particular man who was President of the Commission during this period, Jacques Delors. Delors believed that equity, a moralised social order and economic success could not be guaranteed by the market alone, or by the state, but instead required dialogue between different groups, especially employers and unions, to reach clearer understandings of mutual needs about what had to be done, and in this way enable groups and public authorities to move ahead on the basis of 'dynamic compromise' (Ross, 1995a). In addition, Delors took a special interest in social policy, defined social partnership as an essential component of the social dimension, and ran a Commission that was more supportive of the social partners than previously. Delors himself took a personal interest in launching and nourishing the social dialogue, and it is at least conceivable that without Delors at its head the Commission would not have put forward the idea of adopting and adapting the Belgian procedure of translating social partner agreements into law. It is therefore reasonable to conclude that Delors' ideology and actions were a catalyst in the process that led to the adoption of the social partnership procedure, and that they were probably decisive in ensuring that it occurred in December 1991 rather than at some later date after QMV had already been extended to additional areas of social policy. On the other hand, one cannot conclude that without Delors a social partnership procedure would never have happened, as history suggests that the Commission would still have supported this sort of idea, albeit not so actively, and the self-interested incentive for UNICE to participate in the co-determination of EU social policy would remain strong once QMV was actually adopted for a substantial range of social policy areas.

Member States

The heads of government of EU Member States were involved in the causal sequence leading up to the adoption of the social partnership procedure at Maastricht in two ways. First, as participants in the 1991 IGC they were the negotiators at Maastricht and the signatories (or not) to the Social Protocol. Second, it was UNICE's perception earlier in 1991 that heads of government intended to extend QMV to new areas of social policy that led UNICE to reverse its opposition to binding agreements with trade unions on European employment and social policy. In consequence, it signed the 31 October Agreement with CEEP and the ETUC that formed the basis of the social partnership procedure, as this was incorporated almost unchanged into the Social Protocol, and subsequently into the Treaty of Amsterdam.

The chapter by Hugh Compston on the role of Member States shows that the decision by Member States at Maastricht to adopt the social partnership procedure can be explained almost entirely in terms of political self-interest, defined as the leadership interests and electoral interests of the heads of government of Member States. Most heads of government already knew from experience at national level that making employment and social policy by agreement with employers and trade unions facilitates the implementation of measures in this area and minimises political threats to the government arising from employer and/or trade union opposition to such measures. In addition, under the social partnership procedure the powers of Member States were not significantly less than under the 'normal' legislative procedure. Council accepted a convention that it may not amend the contents of a social partner agreement submitted to it for ratification, whereas it may amend legislation processed the 'normal' way, but it may still reject agreements presented to it and request the Commission to bring forward a more suitable proposal using the 'normal' legislative procedure, although in practice it seems unlikely that Council would ever reject a proposal supported by both employers and unions throughout the European Union. That the social partnership procedure also cuts the European Parliament out of the decision-making process altogether may also have seemed attractive to some.

The fact that the social partnership procedure was adopted at Maastricht but not earlier can be explained largely but not totally in terms of self-interest by the removal of two major barriers in 1991. First, the British opt-out from the Social Protocol meant that the inclusion of the procedure could not be vetoed by Britain. The refusal of British Prime Minister John Major to accept a watered-down version of the Social Chapter left the way open for the social partnership procedure to be included in a stronger package of social policy. Major's refusal to sign was clearly motivated by self-interest, as acceptance would have endangered his position as Prime Minister (Lange, 1993, p.236). However, the vehement opposition within the Conservative Party to EU-level social policy and social partnership cannot be attributed entirely to self-interest but is at least partly due to the popularity of neoliberal ideology within the party (Dorey, forthcoming). Without this, Major might well have been able to accept the watered-down Dutch version of the Social Chapter – although one might equally argue that in these circumstances he might have been able to accept the stronger version too. In short, ideology may well have made a difference, although it is impossible to be certain.

The significance of the second barrier to come down can be understood more directly in terms of self-interest: the social partner agreement of October 1991 signalled the end of business opposition to binding agreements with trade unions at EU level. This meant that the social partnership procedure would not be a dead letter and minimised political attacks on governments on this issue by business and allied political parties. The chapter by Compston also shows that the positive positions of Member States on QMV in social policy during the lead-up to Maastricht, which led to UNICE signing the 31 October 1991 Agreement, can be explained entirely in terms of self-interest. The richer countries wished to harmonise social policy to prevent investment being lost to other countries with lower social standards and therefore lower costs for business, which would threaten the higher social standards of the richer countries by creating stronger incentives to cut non-wage labour costs. Admittedly this theory would lead one to expect Germany and the Netherlands to have been more supportive of the extension of QMV in social policy prior to Maastricht than they in fact were, but they did sign in the end, consistent with its prediction. The poorer countries, which had lower social standards and therefore stood to lose competitiveness if minimum EU social standards were raised against their will using QMV in Council, agreed to QMV because these potential losses were controlled due to the limited scope of the extension of QMV, and offset by promises of additional cohesion funding. In addition, the substantial financial benefits already being received by the poorer countries from the EU made it unlikely that their heads of government would take the political risk of vetoing the entire Maastricht package due to their objections to certain aspects of the Social Protocol. Britain, of course, opted out. All these dynamics were foreseeable as possibilities in October 1991, when UNICE made its decision to sign the agreement with the ETUC and CEEP on the basis that there was a good chance that QMV would be extended at Maastricht to new areas of social policy.

Council ratification of the three social partner agreements presented to it so far can be explained very largely in terms of self-interest, as the content of these tended to converge on existing Council preferences due to two interrelated factors. The first of these was the concern of employers not to agree to a text with stronger provisions than Council would pass using the 'normal' legislative procedure, while the second was the concern of the ETUC not to agree to a text with weaker provisions than the Council would otherwise pass. Although, as noted earlier, there is a perception that at times the ETUC agreed to weaker social provision than this logic would predict, there is no evidence that agreements were radically weaker as a consequence.

Conclusion: self-interest dominant but not wholly determinant

To sum up, the actions of the major policy actors in the development and operation of social partnership at EU level can be explained almost entirely in terms of self-interest. The positions and actions of UNICE, CEEP and the ETUC in relation to the establishment of the social partnership procedure can be explained completely in terms of self-interest, although the positions of the ETUC on specific issues handled by the social partnership procedure cannot be completely explained this way. Equally, the self-interested support of the Commission for social partnership was amplified by the ideological convictions of its President, Jacques Delors. The positions of Member State heads of government can also be explained in terms of self-interest apart from Britain's implacable opposition, which has to be attributed at least in part to the distinctive neoliberal ideology of the British Conservative Party.

This suggests that the role of ideas is marginal, contrary to Falkner's emphasis on the role of concepts such as the 'social dimension' and 'European social model' as principled ideas with high normative validity (Falkner, 1998, p.202). Instead, we see the role of ideas as being mainly limited to being the medium through which the dynamics of self-interest are played out. We accept that ideas such as 'social partnership' and 'European social model' did constitute focal points for argumentation, as did the Belgian model for the social partnership procedure, but the above analysis suggests that apart from the social convictions of Jacques Delors and the clash between the neoliberal ideas of British Conservatives and the more moderate views of other Member States, ideas are essentially epiphenomenal. Of interest is the fact that the debate over EMU does not appear to have had a significant impact on the causal sequence leading up to adoption of the social partnership procedure beyond its significance as another step in the Single Market process, which mainly appears to have affected the dynamics of social partnership via the concern of trade unions and some Member States over the possibility of social dumping.

Our analysis of social partnership bears some striking conclusions for the debate on the causes of European integration. One well trodden aspect of this debate concerns the extent to which states, and the central EU institutions in partnership with other agents such as societal interests, are agents of integration, and the relative balance between these actors. A second, related debate about integration concerns the extent to which 'economic' or 'social' factors best explain the behaviour of actors in the integration process. Our study of EU-level social partnership has something to contribute to both of these debates, but most particularly to the second.

There can be little doubt that the development of EU-level social partnership does involve the role of societal interests in the integration process in partnership with the EU institutions, although it is important not to overemphasise its significance in this case. Certainly, the establishment of the procedure is an important precedent in that it is an alternative route to EU legislation. Yet to date, almost ten years after the historic October 1991 social partner agreement, employers have refused to negotiate more often than they have agreed, and on the whole their involvement owes more to a change of strategy in pursuit of their objective of putting a brake on social policy than to a change in belief system. Throughout, the involvement of employers has been characterised by pragmatic self-interest, and there is no sign yet of social partnership being the 'thin end of the wedge' to further social legislation. This scenario is somewhat challenging to those accounts of the integration process which place importance on the role of institutions, ideas, policy learning and language as a means of understanding the integration process. These accounts hold that the actions of policy actors are shaped by the political institutions in which they participate, with iterative contact between actors and exposure to ideas, rules, procedures and language shaping the way actors behave and respond over time, akin to a process of socialisation. Here, the richness and diversity of accounts is significant. Thus, 'historical institutionalism' holds that the very belief systems and goals of policy actors are shaped by these processes. Added to this are the effects of 'path dependency' in conditioning present and future actions, that is, the impact of the history of working together and of previous decisions and courses of action taken. 'Rational choice' institutionalism, on the other hand, sees the conditioning effect upon actors of institutional incentives as being limited to influencing their strategies, rather than the very goals of actors. That is, actors retain an identity of 'self-interest' in their purposive behaviour, and make firm choices. Only the way in which they try to achieve their objectives is influenced by the institutional umbrellas in which they participate.

The analysis we have undertaken is clearly much more supportive of explanations of political behaviour based on a keen sense of self-interest. Where 'institutionalism' can be employed at all, our analysis clearly lends itself more to confirming 'rational choice' variants of institutionalism. Actors may have changed their strategies as a result of anticipated political decisions, but not their belief systems. Neither Member States nor employers appear to have lost sight at all of their interests as a result of their participation within political institutions, whether these be the institution of social partnership, the patronage of the European Commission, or the Council of Ministers.

The fact that the social partnership procedure has existed for nearly a decade makes it a good point at which to evaluate whether there is evidence of policy-oriented learning between actors as a result of their iterative interactions. The basis of this account, provided by Sabatier and Jenkins Smith (1988), holds that over time 'secondary' aspects of policy actors' belief systems, such as beliefs about the appropriate ways of achieving core values, begin to change as a result of interaction with the ideas put forward by others that contest their interest, 'rival belief systems' and learning to live with compromises imposed upon them by political institutions. It is this aspect of social partnership which the Commission clearly hopes will bring results. In this connection it seems clear that social *dialogue*, which does afford actors the chance to explore the views of others within their policy arena and enable interpersonal chemistry to develop, was a crucial precondition for the 31 October Agreement to be signed by the social partners. However, there is no sign of an escalation of social partnership at the inter-sectoral level, or of a change in the pragmatic self-interest that informs the participation of employers, or of a lengthening of the leashes upon which the social partners act at the behest of their members. Some explanations for actions are quirky and defy categorisation or elaborate theorising. For example, a conversation between two well-placed individuals during a plane ride resulted in a promise to reconsider a position on an issue on behalf of one organisation. At the sectoral level, whilst there is indisputably an increase in activity of social dialogue and of agreements concluded between social partners, the significance of these agreements is open to question and, as Tina Weber shows, participation on the part of employers is most frequently based upon reactive reasons and informed strategy making.

Our findings lead us to a simple, but stark, conclusion. Pragmatic self-interest very largely explains the behaviour of all of the actors in the social partnership policy process, and the outcomes we find today. Yet ideas do play a role in inflecting the causal dynamics set up by the interplay of perceived self-interest, and our study demonstrates that at times they are a key factor in influencing decisions by policy-makers. At the same time we need to recognise that decisions are also influenced by the specificities of the personalities involved, directly or indirectly. The best single predictive guide to EU-level social partnership, however, is an understanding of the self-interested incentives that face decision-makers in the specific organisations involved.

Appendix 1: the Legal Basis of the Social Partnership Procedure in the Treaty of Amsterdam

Note: Although the term 'social partnership procedure' has no basis in law or common usage, it is employed in this study as a concise label for the procedure using which social partner agreements may be implemented by means of Council decisions, as outlined below.

Article 137 (ex Article 118)

1. With a view to achieving the objectives of Article 136, the Community shall support and complement the activities of the Member States in the following fields:
   - improvement in particular of the working environment to protect workers' health and safety;
   - working conditions;
   - the information and consultation of workers;
   - the integration of persons excluded from the labour market, without prejudice to Article 150;
   - equality between men and women with regard to labour market opportunities and treatment at work.
2. To this end, the Council may adopt, by means of directives, minimum requirements for gradual implementation, having regard to the conditions and technical rules obtaining in each of the Member States. Such directives shall avoid imposing administrative, financial and legal constraints in a way which would hold back the creation and development of small and medium-sized undertakings.

   The Council shall act in accordance with the procedure referred to in Article 251 after consulting the Economic and Social Committee and the Committee of the Regions.

   The Council, acting in accordance with the same procedure, may adopt measures designed to encourage cooperation between Member States through initiatives aimed at improving knowledge, developing exchanges of information and best practices, promoting innovative approaches and evaluating experiences in order to combat social exclusion.
3. However, the Council shall act unanimously on a proposal from the Commission, after consulting the European Parliament, the Economic and Social Committee and the Committee of the Regions, in the following areas:
   - social security and social protection of workers;
   - protection of workers where their employment contract is terminated;
   - representation and collective defence of the interests of workers and employers, including co-determination, subject to paragraph 6;

- conditions of employment for third-country nationals legally residing in Community territory;
- financial contributions for promotion of employment and job-creation, without prejudice to the provisions relating to the Social Fund.

4. A Member State may entrust management and labour, at their joint request, with the implementation of directives adopted pursuant to paragraphs 2 and 3. In this case, it shall ensure that, no later than the date on which a directive must be transposed in accordance with Article 249, management and labour have introduced the necessary measures by agreement, the Member State concerned being required to take any necessary measure enabling it at any time to be in a position to guarantee the results imposed by that directive.

5. The provisions adopted pursuant to this Article shall not prevent any Member State from maintaining or introducing more stringent protective measures compatible with this Treaty.

6. The provisions of this Article shall not apply to pay, the right of association, the right to strike or the right to impose lockouts.

Article 138 (ex Article 118a)

1. The Commission shall have the task of promoting the consultation of management and labour at Community level and shall take any relevant measure to facilitate their dialogue by ensuring balanced support for the parties.

2. To this end, before submitting proposals in the social policy field, the Commission shall consult management and labour on the possible direction of Community action.

3. If, after such consultation, the Commission considers Community action advisable, it shall consult management and labour on the content of the envisaged proposal. Management and labour shall forward to the Commission an opinion or, where appropriate, a recommendation.

4. On the occasion of such consultation, management and labour may inform the Commission of their wish to initiate the process provided for in Article 139. The duration of the procedure shall not exceed nine months, unless the management and labour concerned and the Commission decide jointly to extend it.

Article 139 (ex Article 118b)

1. Should management and labour so desire, the dialogue between them at Community level may lead to contractual relations, including agreements.

2. Agreements concluded at Community level shall be implemented either in accordance with the procedures and practices specific to management and labour and the Member States or, in matters covered by Article 137, at the joint request of the signatory parties, by a Council decision on a proposal from the Commission.

   The Council shall act by qualified majority, except where the agreement in question contains one or more provisions relating to one of the areas referred to in Article 137(3), in which case it shall act unanimously.

Appendix 2: the 1996 Parental Leave Directive

Council Directive 96/34/EC of 3 June 1996 on the framework agreement on parental leave concluded by UNICE, CEEP and the ETUC

Official Journal L 145, 19/06/1996 p.0004–0009
CONSLEG – 96L0034 – 16/01/1998 – 11 p.
Amended by 397L0075 (OJ L 010 16.01.98 p.24)
THE COUNCIL OF THE EUROPEAN UNION,
Having regard to the Agreement on social policy, annexed to the Protocol (No. 14) on social policy, annexed to the Treaty establishing the European Community, and in particular Article 4 (2) thereof,
Having regard to the proposal from the Commission,

1. Whereas on the basis of the Protocol on social policy, the Member States, with the exception of the United Kingdom of Great Britain and Northern Ireland (hereinafter referred to as 'the Member States'), wishing to pursue the course mapped out by the 1989 Social Charter have concluded an Agreement on social policy amongst themselves;

2. Whereas management and labour may, in accordance with Article 4 (2) of the Agreement on social policy, request jointly that agreements at Community level be implemented by a Council decision on a proposal from the Commission;

3. Whereas paragraph 16 of the Community Charter of the Fundamental Social Rights of Workers on equal treatment for men and women provides, inter alia, that 'measures should also be developed enabling men and women to reconcile their occupational and family obligations';

4. Whereas the Council, despite the existence of a broad consensus, has not been able to act on the proposal for a Directive on parental leave for family reasons, as amended on 15 November 1984;

5. Whereas the Commission, in accordance with Article 3 (2) of the Agreement on social policy, consulted management and labour on the possible direction of Community action with regard to reconciling working and family life;

6. Whereas the Commission, considering after such consultation that Community action was desirable, once again consulted management and labour on the substance of the envisaged proposal in accordance with Article 3 (3) of the said Agreement;

7. Whereas the general cross-industry organisations (UNICE, CEEP and the ETUC) informed the Commission in their joint letter of 5 July 1995 of their desire to initiate the procedure provided for by Article 4 of the said Agreement;

8. Whereas the said cross-industry organisations concluded, on 14 December

1995, a framework agreement on parental leave; whereas they have forwarded to the Commission their joint request to implement this framework agreement by a Council Decision on a proposal from the Commission in accordance with Article 4 (2) of the said Agreement;

9. Whereas the Council, in its Resolution of 6 December 1994 on certain aspects for a European Union social policy; a contribution to economic and social convergence in the Union, asked the two sides of industry to make use of the possibilities for concluding agreements, since they are as a rule closer to social reality and to social problems; whereas in Madrid, the members of the European Council from those States which have signed the Agreement on social policy welcomed the conclusion of this framework agreement;

10. Whereas the signatory parties wanted to conclude a framework agreement setting out minimum requirements on parental leave and time off from work on grounds of force majeure and referring back to the Member States and/or management and labour for the definition of the conditions under which parental leave would be implemented, in order to take account of the situation, including the situation with regard to family policy, existing in each Member State, particularly as regards the conditions for granting parental leave and exercise of the right to parental leave;

11. Whereas the proper instrument for implementing this framework agreement is a Directive within the meaning of Article 189 of the Treaty; whereas it is therefore binding on the Member States as to the result to be achieved, but leaves them the choice of form and methods;

12. Whereas, in keeping with the principle of subsidiarity and the principle of proportionality as set out in Article 3b of the Treaty, the objectives of this Directive cannot be sufficiently achieved by the Member States and can therefore be better achieved by the Community; whereas this Directive is confined to the minimum required to achieve these objectives and does not go beyond what is necessary to achieve that purpose;

13. Whereas the Commission has drafted its proposal for a Directive, taking into account the representative status of the signatory parties, their mandate and the legality of the clauses of the framework agreement and compliance with the relevant provisions concerning small and medium-sized undertakings;

14. Whereas the Commission, in accordance with its Communication of 14 December 1993 concerning the implementation of the Protocol on social policy, informed the European Parliament by sending it the text of the framework agreement, accompanied by its proposal for a Directive and the explanatory memorandum;

15. Whereas the Commission also informed the Economic and Social Committee by sending it the text of the framework agreement, accompanied by its proposal for a Directive and the explanatory memorandum;

16. Whereas clause 4 point 2 of the framework agreement states that the implementation of the provisions of this agreement does not constitute valid grounds for reducing the general level of protection afforded to workers in the field of this agreement. This does not prejudice the right of Member States and/or management and labour to develop different

legislative, regulatory or contractual provisions, in the light of changing circumstances (including the introduction of non-transferability), as long as the minimum requirements provided for in the present agreement are complied with;

17. Whereas the Community Charter of the Fundamental Social Rights of Workers recognises the importance of the fight against all forms of discrimination, especially based on sex, colour, race, opinions and creeds;

18. Whereas Article F (2) of the Treaty on European Union provides that 'the Union shall respect fundamental rights, as guaranteed by the European Convention for the Protection of Human Rights and Fundamental Freedoms signed in Rome on 4 November 1950 and as they result from the constitutional traditions common to the Member States, as general principles of Community law';

19. Whereas the Member States can entrust management and labour, at their joint request, with the implementation of this Directive, as long as they take all the necessary steps to ensure that they can at all times guarantee the results imposed by this Directive;

20. Whereas the implementation of the framework agreement contributes to achieving the objectives under Article 1 of the Agreement on social policy,

HAS ADOPTED THIS DIRECTIVE:

Article 1
Implementation of the framework agreement
The purpose of this Directive is to put into effect the annexed framework agreement on parental leave concluded on 14 December 1995 between the general cross-industry organisations (UNICE, CEEP and the ETUC).

Article 2
Final provisions

1. The Member States shall bring into force the laws, regulations and administrative provisions necessary to comply with this Directive by 3 June 1998 at the latest or shall ensure by that date at the latest that management and labour have introduced the necessary measures by agreement, the Member States being required to take any necessary measure enabling them at any time to be in a position to guarantee the results imposed by this Directive. They shall forthwith inform the Commission thereof.

2. The Member States may have a maximum additional period of one year, if this is necessary to take account of special difficulties or implementation by a collective agreement. They must forthwith inform the Commission of such circumstances.

3. When Member States adopt the measures referred to in paragraph 1, they shall contain a reference to this Directive or be accompanied by such reference on the occasion of their official publication. The methods of making such reference shall be laid down by Member States.

Article 3
This Directive is addressed to the Member States.
Done at Luxembourg, 3 June 1996.

Annex
FRAMEWORK AGREEMENT ON PARENTAL LEAVE

PREAMBLE

The enclosed framework agreement represents an undertaking by UNICE, CEEP and the ETUC to set out minimum requirements on parental leave and time off from work on grounds of force majeure, as an important means of reconciling work and family life and promoting equal opportunities and treatment between men and women.

ETUC, UNICE and CEEP request the Commission to submit this framework agreement to the Council for a Council Decision making these minimum requirements binding in the Member States of the European Community, with the exception of the United Kingdom of Great Britain and Northern Ireland.

I. GENERAL CONSIDERATIONS

1. Having regard to the Agreement on social policy annexed to the Protocol on social policy, annexed to the Treaty establishing the European Community, and in particular Articles 3(4) and 4(2) thereof;

2. Whereas Article 4(2) of the Agreement on social policy provides that agreements concluded at Community level shall be implemented, at the joint request of the signatory parties, by a Council decision on a proposal from the Commission;

3. Whereas the Commission has announced its intention to propose a Community measure on the reconciliation of work and family life;

4. Whereas the Community Charter of Fundamental Social Rights stipulates at point 16 dealing with equal treatment that measures should be developed to enable men and women to reconcile their occupational and family obligations;

5. Whereas the Council Resolution of 6 December 1994 recognises that an effective policy of equal opportunities presupposes an integrated overall strategy allowing for better organisation of working hours and greater flexibility, and for an easier return to working life, and notes the important role of the two sides of industry in this area and in offering both men and women an opportunity to reconcile their work responsibilities with family obligations;

6. Whereas measures to reconcile work and family life should encourage the introduction of new flexible ways of organising work and time which are better suited to the changing needs of society and which should take the needs of both undertakings and workers into account;

7. Whereas family policy should be looked at in the context of demographic changes, the effects of the ageing population, closing the generation gap and promoting women's participation in the labour force;

8. Whereas men should be encouraged to assume an equal share of family responsibilities, for example they should be encouraged to take parental leave by means such as awareness programmes;

9. Whereas the present agreement is a framework agreement setting out minimum requirements and provisions for parental leave, distinct from maternity leave, and for time off from work on grounds of force majeure,

and refers back to Member States and social partners for the establishment of the conditions of access and detailed rules of application in order to take account of the situation in each Member State;

10. Whereas Member States should provide for the maintenance of entitlements to benefits in kind under sickness insurance during the minimum period of parental leave;

11. Whereas Member States should also, where appropriate under national conditions and taking into account the budgetary situation, consider the maintenance of entitlements to relevant social security benefits as they stand during the minimum period of parental leave;

12. Whereas this agreement takes into consideration the need to improve social policy requirements, to enhance the competitiveness of the Community economy and to avoid imposing administrative, financial and legal constraints in a way which would impede the creation and development of small and medium-sized undertakings;

13. Whereas management and labour are best placed to find solutions that correspond to the needs of both employers and workers and must therefore have conferred on them a special role in the implementation and application of the present agreement,

THE SIGNATORY PARTIES HAVE AGREED THE FOLLOWING:

II. CONTENT

Clause 1: Purpose and scope

1. This agreement lays down minimum requirements designed to facilitate the reconciliation of parental and professional responsibilities for working parents.

2. This agreement applies to all workers, men and women, who have an employment contract or employment relationship as defined by the law, collective agreements or practices in force in each Member State.

Clause 2: Parental leave

1. This agreement grants, subject to clause 2.2, men and women workers an individual right to parental leave on the grounds of the birth or adoption of a child to enable them to take care of that child, for at least three months, until a given age up to 8 years to be defined by Member States and/or management and labour.

2. To promote equal opportunities and equal treatment between men and women, the parties to this agreement consider that the right to parental leave provided for under clause 2.1 should, in principle, be granted on a non-transferable basis.

3. The conditions of access and detailed rules for applying parental leave shall be defined by law and/or collective agreement in the Member States, as long as the minimum requirements of this agreement are respected. Member States and/or management and labour may, in particular:

(a) decide whether parental leave is granted on a full-time or part-time basis, in a piecemeal way or in the form of a time-credit system;

(b) make entitlement to parental leave subject to a period of work qualification and/or a length of service qualification which shall not exceed one year;

(c) adjust conditions of access and detailed rules for applying parental leave to the special circumstances of adoption;

(d) establish notice periods to be given by the worker to the employer when exercising the right to parental leave, specifying the beginning and the end of the period of leave;

(e) define the circumstances in which an employer, following consultation in accordance with national law, collective agreements and practices, is allowed to postpone the granting of parental leave for justifiable reasons related to the operation of the undertaking (e.g. where work is of a seasonal nature, where a replacement cannot be found within the notice period, where a significant proportion of the workforce applies for parental leave at the same time, where a specific function is of strategic importance). Any problem arising from the application of this provision should be dealt with in accordance with national law, collective agreements and practices;

(f) in addition to (e), authorise special arrangements to meet the operational and organisational requirements of small undertakings.

4. In order to ensure that workers can exercise their right to parental leave, Member States and/or management and labour shall take the necessary measures to protect workers against dismissal on the grounds of an application for, or the taking of, parental leave in accordance with national law, collective agreements or practices.

5. At the end of parental leave, workers shall have the right to return to the same job or, if that is not possible, to an equivalent or similar job consistent with their employment contract or employment relationship.

6. Rights acquired or in the process of being acquired by the worker on the date on which parental leave starts shall be maintained as they stand until the end of parental leave. At the end of parental leave, these rights, including any changes arising from national law, collective agreements or practice, shall apply.

7. Member States and/or management and labour shall define the status of the employment contract or employment relationship for the period of parental leave.

8. All matters relating to social security in relation to this agreement are for consideration and determination by Member States according to national law, taking into account the importance of the continuity of the entitlements to social security cover under the different schemes, in particular health care.

Clause 3: Time off from work on grounds of force majeure

1. Member States and/or management and labour shall take the necessary measures to entitle workers to time off from work, in accordance with national legislation, collective agreements and/or practice, on grounds of force majeure for urgent family reasons in cases of sickness or accident making the immediate presence of the worker indispensable.

2. Member States and/or management and labour may specify the conditions of access and detailed rules for applying clause 3.1 and limit this entitlement to a certain amount of time per year and/or per case.

Clause 4: Final provisions

1. Member States may apply or introduce more favourable provisions than those set out in this agreement.

2. Implementation of the provisions of this agreement shall not constitute

valid grounds for reducing the general level of protection afforded to workers in the field covered by this agreement. This shall not prejudice the right of Member States and/or management and labour to develop different legislative, regulatory or contractual provisions, in the light of changing circumstances (including the introduction of non-transferability), as long as the minimum requirements provided for in the present agreement are complied with.

3. The present agreement shall not prejudice the right of management and labour to conclude, at the appropriate level including European level, agreements adapting and/or complementing the provisions of this agreement in order to take into account particular circumstances.

4. Member States shall adopt the laws, regulations and administrative provisions necessary to comply with the Council decision within a period of two years from its adoption or shall ensure that management and labour introduce the necessary measures by way of agreement by the end of this period. Member States may, if necessary to take account of particular difficulties or implementation by collective agreement, have up to a maximum of one additional year to comply with this decision.

5. The prevention and settlement of disputes and grievances arising from the application of this agreement shall be dealt with in accordance with national law, collective agreements and practices.

6. Without prejudice to the respective role of the Commission, national courts and the Court of Justice, any matter relating to the interpretation of this agreement at European level should, in the first instance, be referred by the Commission to the signatory parties who will give an opinion.

7. The signatory parties shall review the application of this agreement five years after the date of the Council decision if requested by one of the parties to this agreement.

Done at Brussels, 14 December 1995.

Appendix 3: the 1997 Part-time Work Directive

Council Directive 97/81/EC of 15 December 1997 concerning the Framework Agreement on part-time work concluded by UNICE, CEEP and the ETUC - Annex: Framework agreement on part-time work

Official Journal L 014, 20/01/1998 p.0009–0014
CONSLEG – 97L0081 – 05/05/1998 – 13 p.
Amendments:
Amended by 398L0023 (OJ L 131 05.05.98 p.10)
Text:
COUNCIL DIRECTIVE 97/81/EC of 15 December 1997 concerning the Framework Agreement on part-time work concluded by UNICE, CEEP and the ETUC
THE COUNCIL OF THE EUROPEAN UNION,
Having regard to the Agreement on social policy annexed to the Protocol (No. 14) on social policy, annexed to the Treaty establishing the European Community, and in particular Article 4(2) thereof,
Having regard to the proposal from the Commission,

1. Whereas on the basis of the Protocol on social policy annexed to the Treaty establishing the European Community, the Member States, with the exception of the United Kingdom of Great Britain and Northern Ireland (hereinafter referred to as 'the Member States'), wishing to continue along the path laid down in the 1989 Social Charter, have concluded an agreement on social policy;
2. Whereas management and labour (the social partners) may, in accordance with Article 4(2) of the Agreement on social policy, request jointly that agreements at Community level be implemented by a Council decision on a proposal from the Commission;
3. Whereas point 7 of the Community Charter of the Fundamental Social Rights of Workers provides, inter alia, that 'the completion of the internal market must lead to an improvement in the living and working conditions of workers in the European Community. This process must result from an approximation of these conditions while the improvement is being maintained, as regards in particular (. . .) forms of employment other than open-ended contracts, such as fixed-term contracts, part-time working, temporary work and seasonal work';
4. Whereas the Council has not reached a decision on the proposal for a Directive on certain employment relationships with regard to distortions of competition (1), as amended (2), nor on the proposal for a Directive on certain employment relationships with regard to working conditions (3);
5. Whereas the conclusions of the Essen European Council stressed the

179

need to take measures to promote employment and equal opportunities for women and men, and called for measures with a view to increasing the employment-intensiveness of growth, in particular by a more flexible organisation of work in a way which fulfils both the wishes of employees and the requirements of competition;

6. Whereas the Commission, in accordance with Article 3(2) of the Agreement on social policy, has consulted management and labour on the possible direction of Community action with regard to flexible working time and job security;

7. Whereas the Commission, considering after such consultation that Community action was desirable, once again consulted management and labour at Community level on the substance of the envisaged proposal in accordance with Article 3(3) of the said Agreement;

8. Whereas the general cross-industry organisations, the Union of Industrial and Employers' Confederations of Europe (UNICE), the European Centre of Enterprises with Public Participation (CEEP) and the European Trade Union Confederation (ETUC) informed the Commission in their joint letter of 19 June 1996 of their desire to initiate the procedure provided for in Article 4 of the Agreement on social policy; whereas they asked the Commission, in a joint letter dated 12 March 1997, for a further three months; whereas the Commission complied with this request;

9. Whereas the said cross-industry organisations concluded, on 6 June 1997, a Framework Agreement on part-time work; whereas they forwarded to the Commission their joint request to implement this Framework Agreement by a Council decision on a proposal from the Commission, in accordance with Article 4(2) of the said Agreement;

10. Whereas the Council, in its Resolution of 6 December 1994 on prospects for a European Union social policy: contribution to economic and social convergence in the Union (4), asked management and labour to make use of the opportunities for concluding agreements, since they are as a rule closer to social reality and to social problems;

11. Whereas the signatory parties wished to conclude a framework agreement on part-time work setting out the general principles and minimum requirements for part-time working; whereas they have demonstrated their desire to establish a general framework for eliminating discrimination against part-time workers and to contribute to developing the potential for part-time work on a basis which is acceptable for employers and workers alike;

12. Whereas the social partners wished to give particular attention to part-time work, while at the same time indicating that it was their intention to consider the need for similar agreements for other flexible forms of work;

13. Whereas, in the conclusions of the Amsterdam European Council, the Heads of State and Government of the European Union strongly welcomed the agreement concluded by the social partners on part-time work;

14. Whereas the proper instrument for implementing the Framework Agreement is a Directive within the meaning of Article 189 of the Treaty;

whereas it therefore binds the Member States as to the result to be achieved, whilst leaving national authorities the choice of form and methods;

15. Whereas, in accordance with the principles of subsidiarity and proportionality as set out in Article 3(b) of the Treaty, the objectives of this Directive cannot be sufficiently achieved by the Member States and can therefore be better achieved by the Community; whereas this Directive does not go beyond what is necessary for the attainment of those objectives;

16. Whereas, with regard to terms used in the Framework Agreement which are not specifically defined therein, this Directive leaves Member States free to define those terms in accordance with national law and practice, as is the case for other social policy Directives using similar terms, providing that the said definitions respect the content of the Framework Agreement;

17. Whereas the Commission has drafted its proposal for a Directive, in accordance with its Communication of 14 December 1993 concerning the application of the Protocol (No. 14) on social policy and its Communication of 18 September 1996 concerning the development of the social dialogue at Community level, taking into account the representative status of the signatory parties and the legality of each clause of the Framework Agreement;

18. Whereas the Commission has drafted its proposal for a Directive in compliance with Article 2(2) of the Agreement on social policy which provides that Directives in the social policy domain 'shall avoid imposing administrative, financial and legal constraints in a way which would hold back the creation and development of small and medium-sized undertakings';

19. Whereas the Commission, in accordance with its Communication of 14 December 1993 concerning the application of the Protocol (No. 14) on social policy, informed the European Parliament by sending it the text of its proposal for a Directive containing the Framework Agreement;

20. Whereas the Commission also informed the Economic and Social Committee;

21. Whereas Clause 6.1 of the Framework Agreement provides that Member States and/or the social partners may maintain or introduce more favourable provisions;

22. Whereas Clause 6.2 of the Framework Agreement provides that implementation of this Directive may not serve to justify any regression in relation to the situation which already exists in each Member State;

23. Whereas the Community Charter of the Fundamental Social Rights of Workers recognises the importance of the fight against all forms of discrimination, especially based on sex, colour, race, opinion and creed;

24. Whereas Article F(2) of the Treaty on European Union states that the Union shall respect fundamental rights, as guaranteed by the European Convention for the Protection of Human Rights and Fundamental Freedoms and as they result from the constitutional traditions common to the Member States, as general principles of Community law;

25. Whereas the Member States may entrust the social partners, at their

joint request, with the implementation of this Directive, provided that the Member States take all the necessary steps to ensure that they can at all times guarantee the results imposed by this Directive;

26. Whereas the implementation of the Framework Agreement contributes to achieving the objectives under Article 1 of the Agreement on social policy,

HAS ADOPTED THIS DIRECTIVE:

Article 1

The purpose of this Directive is to implement the Framework Agreement on part-time work concluded on 6 June 1997 between the general cross-industry organisations (UNICE, CEEP and the ETUC) annexed hereto.

Article 2

1. Member States shall bring into force the laws, regulations and administrative provisions necessary to comply with this Directive not later than 20 January 2000, or shall ensure that, by that date at the latest, the social partners have introduced the necessary measures by agreement, the Member States being required to take any necessary measures to enable them at any time to be in a position to guarantee the results imposed by this Directive. They shall forthwith inform the Commission thereof.

Member States may have a maximum of one more year, if necessary, to take account of special difficulties or implementation by a collective agreement.

They shall inform the Commission forthwith in such circumstances.

When Member States adopt the measures referred to in the first sub-paragraph, they shall contain a reference to this Directive or shall be accompanied by such reference on the occasion of their official publication. The methods of making such a reference shall be laid down by the Member States.

2. Member States shall communicate to the Commission the text of the main provisions of domestic law which they have adopted or which they adopt in the field governed by this Directive.

Article 3

This Directive shall enter into force on the day of its publication in the Official Journal of the European Communities.

Article 4

This Directive is addressed to the Member States.

Done at Brussels, 15 December 1997.

(1) OJ C 224, 8.9.1990, p.6.
(2) OJ C 305, 5.12.1990, p.8.
(3) OJ C 224, 8.9.1990, p.4.
(4) OJ C 368, 23.12.1994, p.6.

Annex

Union of Industrial and Employers' Confederations of Europe
European Trade Union Confederation
European Centre of Enterprises with Public Participation

Framework Agreement on Part-Time Work

PREAMBLE

This Framework Agreement is a contribution to the overall European strategy on employment. Part-time work has had an important impact on employment in recent years. For this reason, the parties to this agreement have given priority attention to this form of work. It is the intention of the parties to consider the need for similar agreements relating to other forms of flexible work.

Recognising the diversity of situations in Member States and acknowledging that part-time work is a feature of employment in certain sectors and activities, this Agreement sets out the general principles and minimum requirements relating to part-time work. It illustrates the willingness of the social partners to establish a general framework for the elimination of discrimination against part-time workers and to assist the development of opportunities for part-time working on a basis acceptable to employers and workers.

This Agreement relates to employment conditions of part-time workers recognising that matters concerning statutory social security are for decision by the Member States. In the context of the principle of non-discrimination, the parties to this Agreement have noted the Employment Declaration of the Dublin European Council of December 1996, wherein the Council inter alia emphasised the need to make social security systems more employment-friendly by 'developing social protection systems capable of adapting to new patterns of work and of providing appropriate protection to people engaged in such work'. The parties to this Agreement consider that effect should be given to this Declaration.

ETUC, UNICE and CEEP request the Commission to submit this Framework Agreement to the Council for a decision making these requirements binding in the Member States which are party to the Agreement on social policy annexed to the Protocol (No. 14) on social policy annexed to the Treaty establishing the European Community.

The parties to this Agreement ask the Commission, in its proposal to implement this Agreement, to request that Member States adopt the laws, regulations and administrative provisions necessary to comply with the Council decision within a period of two years from its adoption or ensure (1) that the social partners establish the necessary measures by way of agreement by the end of this period. Member States may, if necessary to take account of particular difficulties or implementation by collective agreement, have up to a maximum of one additional year to comply with this provision.

Without prejudice to the role of national courts and the Court of Justice, the parties to this agreement request that any matter relating to the interpretation of this agreement at European level should, in the first instance, be referred by the Commission to them for an opinion.

GENERAL CONSIDERATIONS

1. Having regard to the Agreement on social policy annexed to the Protocol (No. 14) on social policy annexed to the Treaty establishing the European Community, and in particular Articles 3(4) and 4(2) thereof;

2. Whereas Article 4(2) of the Agreement on social policy provides that agreements concluded at Community level may be implemented, at the joint request of the signatory parties, by a Council decision on a proposal from the Commission;

3. Whereas, in its second consultation document on flexibility of working time and security for workers, the Commission announced its intention to propose a legally binding Community measure;

4. Whereas the conclusions of the European Council meeting in Essen emphasised the need for measures to promote both employment and equal opportunities for women and men, and called for measures aimed at 'increasing the employment intensiveness of growth, in particular by more flexible organisation of work in a way which fulfils both the wishes of employees and the requirements of competition';

5. Whereas the parties to this agreement attach importance to measures which would facilitate access to part-time work for men and women in order to prepare for retirement, reconcile professional and family life, and take up education and training opportunities to improve their skills and career opportunities for the mutual benefit of employers and workers and in a manner which would assist the development of enterprises;

6. Whereas this Agreement refers back to Member States and social partners for the arrangements for the application of these general principles, minimum requirements and provisions, in order to take account of the situation in each Member State;

7. Whereas this Agreement takes into consideration the need to improve social policy requirements, to enhance the competitiveness of the Community economy and to avoid imposing administrative, financial and legal constraints in a way which would hold back the creation and development of small and medium-sized undertakings;

8. Whereas the social partners are best placed to find solutions that correspond to the needs of both employers and workers and must therefore be given a special role in the implementation and application of this Agreement.

THE SIGNATORY PARTIES HAVE AGREED THE FOLLOWING:

Clause 1: Purpose

The purpose of this Framework Agreement is:

(a) to provide for the removal of discrimination against part-time workers and to improve the quality of part-time work;

(b) to facilitate the development of part-time work on a voluntary basis and to contribute to the flexible organisation of working time in a manner which takes into account the needs of employers and workers.

Clause 2: Scope

1. This Agreement applies to part-time workers who have an employment contract or employment relationship as defined by the law, collective agreement or practice in force in each Member State.

2. Member States, after consultation with the social partners in accordance with national law, collective agreements or practice, and/or the social partners at the appropriate level in conformity with national industrial relations practice may, for objective reasons, exclude wholly or partly from the terms of this Agreement part-time workers who work on a casual basis. Such exclusions should be reviewed periodically to establish if the objective reasons for making them remain valid.

Clause 3: Definitions

For the purpose of this agreement:

1. The term 'part-time worker' refers to an employee whose normal hours of work, calculated on a weekly basis or on average over a period of employment of up to one year, are less than the normal hours of work of a comparable full-time worker.

2. The term 'comparable full-time worker' means a full-time worker in the same establishment having the same type of employment contract or relationship, who is engaged in the same or a similar work/occupation, due regard being given to other considerations which may include seniority and qualifications/skills.Where there is no comparable full-time worker in the same establishment, the comparison shall be made by reference to the applicable collective agreement or, where there is no applicable collective agreement, in accordance with national law, collective agreements or practice.

Clause 4: Principle of non-discrimination

1. In respect of employment conditions, part-time workers shall not be treated in a less favourable manner than comparable full-time workers solely because they work part time unless different treatment is justified on objective grounds.

2. Where appropriate, the principle of pro rata temporis shall apply.

3. The arrangements for the application of this clause shall be defined by the Member States and/or social partners, having regard to European legislation, national law, collective agreements and practice.

4. Where justified by objective reasons, Member States after consultation of the social partners in accordance with national law, collective agreements or practice and/or social partners may, where appropriate, make access to particular conditions of employment subject to a period of service, time worked or earnings qualification. Qualifications relating to access by part-time workers to particular conditions of employment should be reviewed periodically having regard to the principle of non-discrimination as expressed in Clause 4.1.

Clause 5: Opportunities for part-time work

1. In the context of Clause 1 of this Agreement and of the principle of non-discrimination between part-time and full-time workers:

(a) Member States, following consultations with the social partners in accordance with national law or practice, should identify and review obstacles of a legal or administrative nature which may limit the opportunities for part-time work and, where appropriate, eliminate them;

(b) the social partners, acting within their sphere of competence and through the procedures set out in collective agreements, should identify and review obstacles which may limit opportunities for part-time work and, where appropriate, eliminate them.

2. A worker's refusal to transfer from full-time to part-time work or vice versa should not in itself constitute a valid reason for termination of employment, without prejudice to termination in accordance with national law, collective agreements and practice, for other reasons such as may arise from the operational requirements of the establishment concerned.

3. As far as possible, employers should give consideration to:

(a) requests by workers to transfer from full-time to part-time work that becomes available in the establishment;

(b) requests by workers to transfer from part-time to full-time work or to increase their working time should the opportunity arise;

(c) the provision of timely information on the availability of part-time and full-time positions in the establishment in order to facilitate transfers from full-time to part-time or vice versa;

(d) measures to facilitate access to part-time work at all levels of the enterprise, including skilled and managerial positions, and, where appropriate, to facilitate access by part-time workers to vocational training to enhance career opportunities and occupational mobility;

(e) the provision of appropriate information to existing bodies representing workers about part-time working in the enterprise.

Clause 6: Provisions on implementation

1. Member States and/or social partners may maintain or introduce more favourable provisions than set out in this agreement.

2. Implementation of the provisions of this Agreement shall not constitute valid grounds for reducing the general level of protection afforded to workers in the field of this agreement. This does not prejudice the right of Member States and/or social partners to develop different legislative, regulatory or contractual provisions, in the light of changing circumstances, and does not prejudice the application of Clause 5.1 as long as the principle of non-discrimination as expressed in Clause 4.1 is complied with.

3. This Agreement does not prejudice the right of the social partners to conclude, at the appropriate level, including European level, agreements adapting and/or complementing the provisions of this Agreement in a manner which will take account of the specific needs of the social partners concerned.

4. This Agreement shall be without prejudice to any more specific Community provisions, and in particular Community provisions concerning equal treatment or opportunities for men and women.

5. The prevention and settlement of disputes and grievances arising from the application of this Agreement shall be dealt with in accordance with national law, collective agreements and practice.

6. The signatory parties shall review this Agreement, five years after the date of the Council decision, if requested by one of the parties to this Agreement.

(1) Within the meaning of Article 2(4) of the Agreement on social policy of the Treaty establishing the European Community.

Appendix 4: the 1999 Fixed-Term Work Directive

Council Directive 1999/70/EC of 28 June 1999 concerning the framework agreement on fixed-term work concluded by ETUC, UNICE and CEEP

Official Journal L 175, 10/07/1999 p.0043–0048
Text:
THE COUNCIL OF THE EUROPEAN UNION,
Having regard to the Treaty establishing the European Community, and in particular Article 139(2) thereof,
Having regard to the proposal from the Commission,
Whereas:

1. Following the entry into force of the Treaty of Amsterdam the provisions of the Agreement on social policy annexed to the Protocol on social policy, annexed to the Treaty establishing the European Community have been incorporated into Articles 136 to 139 of the Treaty establishing the European Community;

2. Management and labour (the social partners) may, in accordance with Article 139(2) of the Treaty, request jointly that agreements at Community level be implemented by a Council decision on a proposal from the Commission;

3. Point 7 of the Community Charter of the Fundamental Social Rights of Workers provides, inter alia, that 'the completion of the internal market must lead to an improvement in the living and working conditions of workers in the European Community. This process must result from an approximation of these conditions while the improvement is being maintained, as regards in particular forms of employment other than open-ended contracts, such as fixed-term contracts, part-time working, temporary work and seasonal work';

4. The Council has been unable to reach a decision on the proposal for a Directive on certain employment relationships with regard to distortions of competition(1), nor on the proposal for a Directive on certain employment relationships with regard to working conditions(2);

5. The conclusions of the Essen European Council stressed the need to take measures with a view to 'increasing the employment-intensiveness of growth, in particular by a more flexible organisation of work in a way which fulfils both the wishes of employees and the requirements of competition';

6. The Council Resolution of 9 February 1999 on the 1999 Employment Guidelines invites the social partners at all appropriate levels to negotiate agreements to modernise the organisation of work, including flexible working arrangements, with the aim of making undertakings produc-

tive and competitive and achieving the required balance between flexibility and security;

7. The Commission, in accordance with Article 3(2) of the Agreement on social policy, has consulted management and labour on the possible direction of Community action with regard to flexible working time and job security;

8. The Commission, considering after such consultation that Community action was desirable, once again consulted management and labour on the substance of the envisaged proposal in accordance with Article 3(3) of the said Agreement;

9. The general cross-industry organisations, namely the Union of Industrial and Employers' Confederations of Europe (UNICE), the European Centre of Enterprises with Public Participation (CEEP) and the European Trade Union Confederation (ETUC), informed the Commission in a joint letter dated 23 March 1998 of their desire to initiate the procedure provided for in Article 4 of the said Agreement; they asked the Commission, in a joint letter, for a further period of three months; the Commission complied with this request extending the negotiation period to 30 March 1999;

10. The said cross-industry organisations on 18 March 1999 concluded a framework agreement on fixed-term work; they forwarded to the Commission their joint request to implement the framework agreement by a Council Decision on a proposal from the Commission, in accordance with Article 4(2) of the Agreement on social policy;

11. The Council, in its Resolution of 6 December 1994 on 'certain aspects for a European Union social policy: a contribution to economic and social convergence in the Union' (3), asked management and labour to make use of the opportunities for concluding agreements, since they are as a rule closer to social reality and to social problems;

12. The signatory parties, in the preamble to the framework agreement on part-time work concluded on 6 June 1997, announced their intention to consider the need for similar agreements relating to other forms of flexible work;

13. Management and labour wished to give particular attention to fixed-term work, while at the same time indicating that it was their intention to consider the need for a similar agreement relating to temporary agency work;

14. The signatory parties wished to conclude a framework agreement on fixed-term work setting out the general principles and minimum requirements for fixed-term employment contracts and employment relationships; they have demonstrated their desire to improve the quality of fixed-term work by ensuring the application of the principle of non-discrimination, and to establish a framework to prevent abuse arising from the use of successive fixed-term employment contracts or relationships;

15. The proper instrument for implementing the framework agreement is a directive within the meaning of Article 249 of the Treaty; it therefore binds the Member States as to the result to be achieved, whilst leaving them the choice of form and methods;

16. In accordance with the principles of subsidiarity and proportionality as set out in Article 5 of the Treaty, the objectives of this Directive cannot be sufficiently achieved by the Member States and can therefore be better achieved by the Community; this Directive limits itself to the minimum required for the attainment of those objectives and does not go beyond what is necessary for that purpose;
17. As regards terms used in the framework agreement but not specifically defined therein, this Directive allows Member States to define such terms in conformity with national law or practice as is the case for other Directives on social matters using similar terms, provided that the definitions in question respect the content of the framework agreement;
18. The Commission has drafted its proposal for a Directive, in accordance with its Communication of 14 December 1993 concerning the application of the agreement on social policy and its Communication of 20 May 1998 on adapting and promoting the social dialogue at Community level, taking into account the representative status of the contracting parties, their mandate and the legality of each clause of the framework agreement; the contracting parties together have a sufficiently representative status;
19. The Commission informed the European Parliament and the Economic and Social Committee by sending them the text of the agreement, accompanied by its proposal for a Directive and the explanatory memorandum, in accordance with its communication concerning the implementation of the Protocol on social policy;
20. On 6 May 1999 the European Parliament adopted a Resolution on the framework agreement between the social partners;
21. The implementation of the framework agreement contributes to achieving the objectives in Article 136 of the Treaty,

HAS ADOPTED THIS DIRECTIVE:

Article 1

The purpose of the Directive is to put into effect the framework agreement on fixed-term contracts concluded on 18 March 1999 between the general cross-industry organisations (ETUC, UNICE and CEEP) annexed hereto.

Article 2

Member States shall bring into force the laws, regulations and administrative provisions necessary to comply with this Directive by 10 July 1999, or shall ensure that, by that date at the latest, management and labour have introduced the necessary measures by agreement, the Member States being required to take any necessary measures to enable them at any time to be in a position to guarantee the results imposed by this Directive. They shall forthwith inform the Commission thereof.

Member States may have a maximum of one more year, if necessary, and following consultation with management and labour, to take account of special difficulties or implementation by a collective agreement. They shall inform the Commission forthwith in such circumstances.

When Member States adopt the provisions referred to in the first paragraph, these shall contain a reference to this Directive or shall be accompanied by such reference at the time of their official publication. The procedure for such reference shall be adopted by the Member States.

Article 3
This Directive shall enter into force on the day of its publication in the Official Journal of the European Communities.
Article 4
This Directive is addressed to the Member States.
Done at Luxembourg, 28 June 1999.
(1) OJ C 224, 8.9.1990, p.6. and OJ C 305, 5.12.1990, p.8.
(2) OJ C 224, 8.9.1990, p.4.
(3) OJ C 368, 23.12.1994, p.6.

Annex

ETUC-UNICE-CEEP FRAMEWORK AGREEMENT ON FIXED-TERM WORK

PREAMBLE
This framework agreement illustrates the role that the social partners can play in the European employment strategy agreed at the 1997 Luxembourg extraordinary summit and, following the framework agreement on part-time work, represents a further contribution towards achieving a better balance between 'flexibility in working time and security for workers'.

The parties to this agreement recognise that contracts of an indefinite duration are, and will continue to be, the general form of employment relationship between employers and workers. They also recognise that fixed-term employment contracts respond, in certain circumstances, to the needs of both employers and workers.

This agreement sets out the general principles and minimum requirements relating to fixed-term work, recognising that their detailed application needs to take account of the realities of specific national, sectoral and seasonal situations. It illustrates the willingness of the social partners to establish a general framework for ensuring equal treatment for fixed-term workers by protecting them against discrimination and for using fixed-term employment contracts on a basis acceptable to employers and workers.

This agreement applies to fixed-term workers with the exception of those placed by a temporary work agency at the disposition of a user enterprise. It is the intention of the parties to consider the need for a similar agreement relating to temporary agency work. This agreement relates to the employment conditions of fixed-term workers, recognising that matters relating to statutory social security are for decision by the Member States. In this respect the social partners note the Employment Declaration of the Dublin European Council in 1996 which emphasised, inter alia, the need to develop more employment-friendly social security systems by 'developing social protection systems capable of adapting to new patterns of work and providing appropriate protection to those engaged in such work'. The parties to this agreement reiterate the view expressed in the 1997 part-time agreement that Member States should give effect to this Declaration without delay. In addition, it is also recognised that innovations in occupational social protection systems are necessary in order to adapt them to current conditions, and in particular to provide for the transferability of rights.

The ETUC, UNICE and CEEP request the Commission to submit this framework agreement to the Council for a decision making these requirements binding in the Member States which are party to the Agreement on social policy annexed to the Protocol (No. 14) on social policy annexed to the Treaty establishing the European Community.

The parties to this agreement ask the Commission, in its proposal to implement the agreement, to request Member States to adopt the laws, regulations and administrative provisions necessary to comply with the Council Decision within two years from its adoption or ensure (1) that the social partners establish the necessary measures by way of agreement by the end of this period. Member States may, if necessary and following consultation with the social partners, and in order to take account of particular difficulties or implementation by collective agreement, have up to a maximum of one additional year to comply with this provision.

The parties to this agreement request that the social partners are consulted prior to any legislative, regulatory or administrative initiative taken by a Member State to conform to the present agreement.

Without prejudice to the role of national courts and the Court of Justice, the parties to this agreement request that any matter relating to the interpretation of this agreement at European level should in the first instance be referred by the Commission to them for an opinion.

GENERAL CONSIDERATIONS

1. Having regard to the Agreement on social policy annexed to the Protocol (No. 14) on social policy annexed to the Treaty establishing the European Community, and in particular Article 3.4 and 4.2 thereof;

2. Whereas Article 4.2 of the Agreement on social policy provides that agreements concluded at Community level may be implemented, at the joint request of the signatory parties, by a Council decision on a proposal from the Commission;

3. Whereas, in its second consultation document on flexibility in working time and security for workers, the Commission announced its intention to propose a legally-binding Community measure;

4. Whereas in its opinion on the proposal for a Directive on part-time work, the European Parliament invited the Commission to submit immediately proposals for directives on other forms of flexible work, such as fixed-term work and temporary agency work;

5. Whereas in the conclusions of the extraordinary summit on employment adopted in Luxembourg, the European Council invited the social partners to negotiate agreements to 'modernise the organisation of work, including flexible working arrangements, with the aim of making undertakings productive and competitive and achieving the required balance between flexibility and security';

6. Whereas employment contracts of an indefinite duration are the general form of employment relationships and contribute to the quality of life of the workers concerned and improve performance;

7. Whereas the use of fixed-term employment contracts based on objective reasons is a way to prevent abuse;

8. Whereas fixed-term employment contracts are a feature of employment in certain sectors, occupations and activities which can suit both employers and workers;

9. Whereas more than half of fixed-term workers in the European Union are women and this agreement can therefore contribute to improving equality of opportunities between women and men;

10. Whereas this agreement refers back to Member States and social partners for the arrangements for the application of its general principles, minimum requirements and provisions, in order to take account of the situation in each Member State and the circumstances of particular sectors and occupations, including the activities of a seasonal nature;

11. Whereas this agreement takes into consideration the need to improve social policy requirements, to enhance the competitiveness of the Community economy and to avoid imposing administrative, financial and legal constraints in a way which would hold back the creation and development of small and medium-sized undertakings;

12. Whereas the social partners are best placed to find solutions that correspond to the needs of both employers and workers and shall therefore be given a special role in the implementation and application of this agreement.

THE SIGNATORY PARTIES HAVE AGREED THE FOLLOWING

Purpose (clause 1)

The purpose of this framework agreement is to:

(a) improve the quality of fixed-term work by ensuring the application of the principle of non-discrimination;

(b) establish a framework to prevent abuse arising from the use of successive fixed-term employment contracts or relationships.

Scope (clause 2)

1. This agreement applies to fixed-term workers who have an employment contract or employment relationship as defined in law, collective agreements or practice in each Member State.

2. Member States after consultation with the social partners and/or the social partners may provide that this agreement does not apply to:

(a) initial vocational training relationships and apprenticeship schemes;

(b) employment contracts and relationships which have been concluded within the framework of a specific public or publicly-supported training, integration and vocational retraining programme.

Definitions (clause 3)

1. For the purpose of this agreement the term 'fixed-term worker' means a person having an employment contract or relationship entered into directly between an employer and a worker where the end of the employment contract or relationship is determined by objective conditions such as reaching a specific date, completing a specific task, or the occurrence of a specific event.

2. For the purpose of this agreement, the term 'comparable permanent worker' means a worker with an employment contract or relationship of indefinite duration, in the same establishment, engaged in the same or similar work/occupation, due regard being given to qualifications/skills. Where there is no comparable permanent worker in the same establishment, the comparison shall be made by reference to the applicable collective agreement, or where there is no applicable collective agreement, in accordance with national law, collective agreements or practice.

Principle of non-discrimination (clause 4)

1. In respect of employment conditions, fixed-term workers shall not be treated in a less favourable manner than comparable permanent workers solely because they have a fixed-term contract or relation unless different treatment is justified on objective grounds.
2. Where appropriate, the principle of pro rata temporis shall apply.
3. The arrangements for the application of this clause shall be defined by the Member States after consultation with the social partners and/or the social partners, having regard to Community law and national law, collective agreements and practice.
4. Period-of-service qualifications relating to particular conditions of employment shall be the same for fixed-term workers as for permanent workers except where different length of service qualifications are justified on objective grounds.

Measures to prevent abuse (clause 5)

1. To prevent abuse arising from the use of successive fixed-term employment contracts or relationships, Member States, after consultation with social partners in accordance with national law, collective agreements or practice, and/or the social partners, shall, where there are no equivalent legal measures to prevent abuse, introduce in a manner which takes account of the needs of specific sectors and/or categories of workers, one or more of the following measures:
(a) objective reasons justifying the renewal of such contracts or relationships;
(b) the maximum total duration of successive fixed-term employment contracts or relationships;
(c) the number of renewals of such contracts or relationships.
2. Member States after consultation with the social partners and/or the social partners shall, where appropriate, determine under what conditions fixed-term employment contracts or relationships:
(a) shall be regarded as 'successive';
(b) shall be deemed to be contracts or relationships of indefinite duration.

Information and employment opportunities (clause 6)

1. Employers shall inform fixed-term workers about vacancies which become available in the undertaking or establishment to ensure that they have the same opportunity to secure permanent positions as other workers. Such information may be provided by way of a general announcement at a suitable place in the undertaking or establishment.
2. As far as possible, employers should facilitate access by fixed-term workers to appropriate training opportunities to enhance their skills, career development and occupational mobility.

Information and consultation (clause 7)

1. Fixed-term workers shall be taken into consideration in calculating the threshold above which workers' representative bodies provided for in national and Community law may be constituted in the undertaking as required by national provisions.
2. The arrangements for the application of clause 7.1 shall be defined by Member States after consultation with the social partners and/or the social partners in accordance with national law, collective agreements or practice and having regard to clause 4.1.

3. As far as possible, employers should give consideration to the provision of appropriate information to existing workers' representative bodies about fixed-term work in the undertaking.

Provisions on implementation (clause 8)

1. Member States and/or the social partners can maintain or introduce more favourable provisions for workers than set out in this agreement.
2. This agreement shall be without prejudice to any more specific Community provisions, and in particular Community provisions concerning equal treatment or opportunities for men and women.
3. Implementation of this agreement shall not constitute valid grounds for reducing the general level of protection afforded to workers in the field of the agreement.
4. The present agreement does not prejudice the right of the social partners to conclude at the appropriate level, including European level, agreements adapting and/or complementing the provisions of this agreement in a manner which will take note of the specific needs of the social partners concerned.
5. The prevention and settlement of disputes and grievances arising from the application of this agreement shall be dealt with in accordance with national law, collective agreements and practice.
6. The signatory parties shall review the application of this agreement five years after the date of the Council decision if requested by one of the parties to this agreement.

18 March 1999

(1) Within the meaning of Article 2.4 of the Agreement on social policy annexed to the Protocol (No. 14) on social policy annexed to the Treaty establishing the European Community.

Notes

1 ETUC and European Social Partnership: a Third Turning-Point?

1 Calculated as a weighted average for the 15 current EU Member States, and Norway and Switzerland, without Spain, Portugal, Greece and Luxembourg.
2 Calculated as the unweighted average for the 15 current EU Member States.
3 Weighted average for the current 15 EU Member States, calculated from OECD, 'Statistical Compendium', Economic Outlook data.
4 ETUC release to the press, Brussels, 13 November 1978, cited in Grote, 1987, p.247.
5 In 1978 the German unions had started a major campaign for shorter hours in the crisis-ridden steel sector. A year later, with the support of British, Belgian, Dutch, plus some more ambivalent support from Italian and French unions, they succeeded in making the struggle for the 35-hour working week, without a reduction in weekly wages, the first-ever European campaign issue. At this time the DGB-TUC axis dictated ETUC policies (Groux *et al.*, 1993, p.57). The campaign had many reluctant followers, for instance in Italy and Scandinavia.
6 The Belgian central organisations, represented in the National Labour Council and assisted by an independent chairperson, can negotiate general agreements on labour and social policy issues. These agreements are turned into law by the parliament and provide the basis for sectoral bargaining in the bipartite Joint Industry Councils, with binding effects even on non-organised employers (Van Ruysseveldt and Visser, 1996).

2 European Employers: Social Partners?

1 For an overview of these organisations, see Greenwood (1997).
2 See European Commission (1993a).
3 Indeed, ETUC officials said that as late as the morning of 31 October 1991, the day UNICE signed up to the Maastricht negotiation provisions, they 'would not have believed that the day would have closed with the conclusion of a document which provided for the possibility of European framework agreements' (Buschak and Kallenbach, 1998, p. 171).
4 On the employer side this included UNICE for the private sector and CEEP for the public sector. The trade union side only included the ETUC.
5 Although these agreements are generally perceived as being loosely worded, this is not UNICE's perception, which was that they were surprisingly detailed and precise, resulting from hard negotiations, word by word

and line by line. They define the 'common ground' on which employers and trade unions are prepared to stand, thus helping the legislators
to put forward legislative proposals that have a better chance of being
accepted.

6 This is, however, non-binding, with no more force than a joint opinion since the parties merely undertake to 'invite' their respective members
to take certain actions and there is no obligation on anyone to accept
this invitation. This outcome respected the wish of CEEP to restrict the
agreement to this 'soft' status.

7 See Corbett (1993) for the various actors' initial positions.

8 Indeed, the expectation of a Labour victory at the UK general election
was so great that this was one of the main reasons why the governments of the other Member States consented to the twin-track approach
for social policy at Maastricht, as they only expected it to be a very
temporary arrangement (IDS European Report, 1992; Forster, 1995).

9 UNICE's view was that the ETUC did not want to negotiate on this
issue because it had a hidden agenda, namely that their main concern
was not the lack of information and consultation in multinational companies, but that they saw and continue to see EWCs as the first step
towards creation of pan-European trade unionism, leading eventually
to pan-European collective bargaining and possible industrial action within
multinational companies.

10 UEAPME would have two seats, but no veto. It remains to be seen
whether UEAPME will be a signatory to the agreements, although UNICE
is committed to convincing the ETUC and CEEP.

3 The Impact of the Social Dialogue Procedure on the Powers of European Union Institutions

1 The term 'social dialogue' refers to a number of different circumstances
and practices: from the consultation launched when the Community
was set up, to the commitment to tripartite approaches during the 1970s,
via the autonomous dialogue, the so-called Val Duchesse process under
the auspices of the Commission in the spirit of Article 118b of the
Single European Act, to the developments stimulated by implementation of the social policy agreement. The notion of 'the social dialogue'
cumulatively embraces these various forums where the European social
partners come together and these endeavours towards dialogue and, in
some cases, negotiations. The two related elements: (a) the participation of labour and management in European-level decision-making and
(b) a dialogue between management and labour at the European level,
make up the concept of the social dialogue. Although the term has
been used to describe a range of different processes and institutional
arrangements since the inception of the European Communities, it essentially revolves around three specific aspects: (a) the process which
has developed since 1984–5 involving talks between the Commission
and the three intersectoral associations of European trade unions and
employers, ETUC, UNICE and CEEP, as well as talks amongst ETUC,

UNICE and CEEP by themselves without the Commission; (b) agreements, both formal and informal, involving representatives of unions and employers at the sectoral level; and (c) developments in European-level information and consultation within multinational companies.

2 The new chapter on social policy states first that Protocol No. 14 on social policy annexed to the European Community Treaty and the Agreement on social policy attached thereto shall be repealed. The provisions of the Agreement on social policy are then added to Articles 136–45 of the European Community Treaty. The Amsterdam Treaty was signed by the Member States on 2 October 1997 and entered into force on 1 May 1999. See further Betten (1998).

3 The social dialogue project was launched by Delors, the former president of the Commission. He initiated in 1985 at Val Duchesse talks between UNICE, ETUC and CEEP, the three European organisations who represent the main national interprofessional employer and trade union confederations.

4 True, this monopoly is restricted in some exceptional cases. The Council, for example, can on its own initiate legislation regarding the introduction of the third stage of Economic and Monetary Union (Art. 121(3)) and in the area of state aid (Art. 88(2)). The Parliament is entitled to draw up proposals for election of its members (Article 190(4)). Moreover, the Council (Art. 208 EC and Art. 14(4) TEU), the EP (Art. 192(2) EC) and a Member State (Art. 115 EC) may request the Commission to submit proposals in certain areas. Further, the Commission shares the power of initiative with the Member States within the Common Foreign and Security Policy (Art. 22 TEU), Police and Judicial Co-operation (Art. 42 TEU) and the EC asylum and immigration policy chapter (Art. 67 EC). In addition, although the Commission has the formal monopoly of initiative, no more than 10 per cent of all proposals appear to originate as 'spontaneous Commission initiatives'. Considerably more emerge from requests by Member States, the Council or industry (Peterson, 1999, p.59).

5 For example, such consultations in the case of the fixed-term work agreement were not completed until 42 months after initiation of the social dialogue procedure (European Parliament, 1999b, p.17).

6 The Economic and Social Committee argues that it is not clear from Article 138(4) that social partners may initiate the negotiation only after the second phase of the consultation, i.e. when a Commission proposal is already on the table (Economic and Social Committee, 1994, consideration 4.1.2). The Committee suggested that there are advantages in allowing the social partners to initiate the negotiation after the first consultation, before the Commission proposal is tendered. Further, it points out that even before the Commission considers a possible direction of Community action in the social policy field, and independent of the consultation of the social partners as prescribed by Article 138 EC on social policy, the social partners may initiate the social dialogue autonomously (consideration 4.1.3). In accordance with Article 139 EC, this autonomous social dialogue may lead to contractual relations, including agreements.

7   See the Commission initiative in connection with the second-stage consultation of management and labour, pursuant to Article 3(3) of the Agreement on social policy, on the flexibility of working time and security for workers (forms of work other than full-time, open-ended employment) of 9 April 1996 (PE 220.571).

8   Insofar as the two sides enjoy autonomy granted to them by virtue of Article 139 EC, any topic of interest to both may be subjected to negotiation, regardless of whether the resulting agreement receives or fails to receive the sanction of European Union law (European Trade Union Institute, 1992, p.85). However, the negotiating parties to an agreement to be implemented through legislation under article 139(2) EC must ensure that the subject of discussion remains within the remit of Article 137 EC (Commission of the European Communities, 1998a, p.16).

9   See also Lapeyre (1996, p.121).

10 These criteria are as follows: (a) organisations should be cross-industry or relate to specific sectors or categories and be organised at European level; (b) they should consist of organisations which are themselves an integral and recognised part of Member State social partner structures and with the capacity to negotiate agreements, and which are representative of all Member States, as far as possible; (c) they should have adequate structures to ensure their effective participation in the consultation process.

11 Case T-135/96, Union Europeenne de l'Artisanat et des Petites et Moyennes Entreprises (UEAPME) v. Council, ECR [1998] II-2335, considerations 75–7.

12 For an extensive assessment of these criteria see above.

13 Case T-135/96, Union Europeenne de l'Artisanat et des Petites et Moyennes Entreprises (UEAPME) v. Council, ECR [1998] II-2335, considerations 84–90.

14 See further on this matter the discussion on the role of the European Parliament below.

15 For an opposite view see Mazey and Richardson (1999, p.123) who argue that any notion that any one set of interests can dominate the EU policy process over a long period of time is unfounded. They are of the opinion that the degree of competition between EU institutions themselves, and between EU institutions and Member States, is so intense that it is impossible for any actor (public or private) to consistently control the trajectory of the policy game.

16 Framework agreement on parental leave [1996] OJ L145/6, clause 2.3(3).

17 See clause 2.2 of this agreement the reference to which is contained in note 4.

18 See clauses 4.4 in both agreements.

19 The principle of non-discrimination referred to in clauses 4.1 in both agreements is applied only to 'employment conditions' while any issues to do with the statutory legislation of social security are excluded.

20 Expression taken from Vobruba (1995, p.312).

21 However, in its recent Communication on social dialogue, the Commission declared that it would also provide political support for the

parties to the social dialogue (Commission of the European Communities, 1998a, p.16). This statement has not been further elaborated.

22 The Commission explicitly acknowledged that it couldn't intervene in the negotiation (Commission, 1998, p.12).

23 See Council Directive 94/45/EC of 22 September 1994 on the establishment of a European Works Council or a procedure in Community-scale undertakings and Community-scale groups of undertakings for the purposes of informing and consulting employees, OJ L 254/64 of 30 September 1994 and Council Directive 97/80/EC of 15 December 1997; on the burden of proof in cases of discrimination based on sex, OJ L 14/6 of 20 January 1998.

24 The social partners also declined to negotiate on the Commission proposal concerning the combating of sexual harassment at work, but the Commission has not yet come forward with a proposal for a directive on the subject.

25 As regards the Council amendments concerning the Commission proposal for the works council directive referred to in note 23 see Boockmann (1998, p.232). As regards the Council's amendments to the Commission proposal for the burden of proof directive referred in note 23, see Council common position no. 37/97 adopted on 24 July 1997 with a view to the adoption of the Council Directive on the burden of proof in cases of discrimination based on sex, OJ C307/6, 8 October 1997, pp.10–12.

26 Compare the Commission's original proposal on parental leave (OJ C333/6 of 9 December 1983, as amended in OJ C316/6 of 27 November 1984) with the social partners' agreement on the subject referred to in note 4. For this purpose see Falkner (1998, p.123).

27 See for comparison the Commission proposals for: (1) Directive on certain employment relationships with regard to working conditions COM (90) 228; OJ C224 of 8 September 1990, p.4; (2) Directive on certain employment relationships with regard to distortions of competition COM (90) 228; OJ C 224 of 8 September 1990, p.6; (3) Directive supplementing the measures to encourage improvements in the safety and health at work of temporary workers COM (90) 228; OJ C 224 of 8 September 1990, p.8, amended by COM(90) 533; OJ C 305 of 5 December 1990, p.12. See also Falkner (1998, p.141).

28 Recently, the European Parliament adopted significant amendments to the Commission proposal concerning the working time directive in the course of the co-decision procedure (European Social Dialogue: Newsletter from the European Commission: Employment and Social Affairs DG/D, No. 12, December 1999, p.1).

29 See Bercusson's (1992, p.185) thesis about the social dialogue as negotiation 'in shadow of law'.

30 Under the term 'political entrepreneur' I mean the ability of the Commission to behave as a leader or an informal agenda-setter, influencing and advancing the integration process by tabling new and innovative proposals which command the assent of the Member States and nudge the Union in a more integrative direction. For general discussion see e.g. Nugent (1995).

31 See for reference note 26.
32 See also, Europe, Agence internationale d'information pour la presse, 21 September 1994, p.7.
33 Case T-135/96, Union Europeenne de l'Artisanat et des Petites et Moyennes Entreprises (UEAPME) v. Council, ECR [1998] II-2335, paragraph 89.
34 Case C-300/89 Commission v. Council [1991] ECR I-2867, paragraph 20; Case 138/79 Roquettes Freres v. Council [1980] ECR 3333, paragraph 33; and Case 139/79 Maizena v. Council [1980] ECR 3393, paragraph 34.
35 In one of its declarations from that period, the ETUC stated that: 'Democratisation of European institutions is indispensable in order to prevent them becoming bodies on which ministers, officials and diplomats have more power of decision than the democratically elected members of the European Parliament. Major reforms are needed to equip the European Parliament with true legislative powers in order to find solution to the problems which are within the European competence and which can only be solved at that level' (European Trade Union Confederation, 'Declaration on European Union' [1984]).
36 See also the European Parliament (1995, consideration 35) Resolution on the White paper on European social policy as well as the related report (European Parliament, 1994c, p.15).

4   The Intergovernmental Dimension of EU Social Partnership

1 I would like to thank the practitioners and experts in Brussels who made time to answer my questions: Yves Chretien, Reinhart Eisenberg, Joelle Hivonnet, Jackie Morin and Daniel Vaughan-Whitehead.
2 I would like to thank the practitioners and experts in Dublin who made time to discuss the role of Ireland in the passage of the Social Protocol, in particular Brigid Laffan, Dermott McCarthy and Bobby McDonagh.
3 The Fixed-Term Work Framework Agreement was 'regarded favourably by all delegations' at the Labour and Social Affairs Council meeting of 25 May 1999 but could not be formally adopted at that meeting because the mandatory six-week period for national parliaments to examine the proposed legislation had not yet elapsed. It was formally adopted without debate at the Culture/Audiovisual Council meeting of 28 June 1999.

5   The European Sectoral Social Dialogue

1 EIRO is managed by the European Foundation for the Improvement of Living and Working Conditions in Dublin (www.eiro.eurofound.ie).
2 'The European Sectoral Social Dialogue: the Dawn of a New Era?', Conference on the UK and the European Social Dimension organised by the Faculty of Law, Leeds University, Leeds, November 1997.

References

Addison, J.T. and S. Siebert (1994) 'Recent Developments in Social Policy in the New European Union', *Industrial and Labour Relations Review*, vol. 48, no. 1, pp.5–27.

Baglioni, G. and C.J. Crouch (eds) (1990) *European Industrial Relations: the Challenge of Flexibility*, London: Sage.

Barnouin, B. (1986) *The European Labour Movement and European Integration*, London: Frances Pinter.

Bercusson, B. (1992) 'Maastricht; a Fundamental Change in European Labour Law', *Industrial Relations Journal*, vol. 23, pp.177–90.

Bercusson, B. (1994) 'The Dynamics of European Labour Law after Maastricht', *Industrial Law Journal*, vol. 23, no. 1, pp.1–31.

Bercusson, B. (1996) *European Labour Law*, London: Butterworths.

Bercusson, B. and J.J. van Dijk (1995) 'The Implementation of the Protocol and Agreement on Social Policy of the Treaty on European Union', *The International Journal of Comparative Labour Law and Industrial Relations*, vol. 11, no. 1, pp.3–30.

Berger, S. and H. Compston (eds) (forthcoming) *Policy Concertation and Social Partnership in Western Europe: Lessons for the 21st Century*, Oxford: Berghahn.

Betten, L. (1998) 'The Democratic Deficit of Participatory Democracy in Community Social Policy', *European Law Review*, vol. 23, no. 1, pp.20–36.

Bislev, S. (1992) 'Social Security and Health', in Lise Lyck (ed.), *Denmark and EC Membership Evaluated*, London: Pinter.

Blair, A. (1999) *Dealing with Europe*, Aldershot: Ashgate.

Blanpain, R. and C. Engels (1997) *European Labour Law*, 4th edn, The Hague: Kluwer.

Boockmann, B. (1998) 'Agenda Control by Interest Groups in EU Social Policy', *Journal of Theoretical Politics*, vol. 10, no. 2, pp.215–36.

Boyer, R. (1996) 'Hypothesis Revisited: Globalization but Still the Century of Nations', in S. Berger and R. Dore (eds), *National Diversity and Global Capitalism*, Ithaca, NY: Cornell University Press, pp.29–59.

Branch, A. (1997) 'Throwing the Baby out with the Bathwater? Liberal Intergovernmentalism, Neofunctionalism and the Institutionalisation of European-level Collective Bargaining', Nuffield College, Oxford, MPhil thesis.

Bull, M.J. (1992) 'The Corporatist Ideal-type and Political Exchange', *Political Studies*, vol. 40, no. 2, pp.255–72.

Bulletin of the European Communities, 1985–1991.

Busch, K. (1996) 'Wieviel Europa brauchen die Gewerkschaften?', in A. Maurer and B. Thiele (eds), *Legitimitätsprobleme und Demokratisierung der Europäischen Union*, Marburg: Schüren, pp.97–111.

Buschak, W. and V. Kallenbach (1998) 'The European Trades Union Confederation', in W.E. Lecher and H-W. Platzer (eds), *European Union – European Industrial Relations? Global Challenges, National Developments and Transnational Dynamics*, London: Routledge.

Carley, M. (1993) 'Social Dialogue', in M. Gold (ed.), *The Social Dimension: Employment Policy in the European Community*, London: Macmillan.

Christiansen, T. (1997) 'Tensions of European Governance: Politicised Bureaucracy and Multiple Accountability in the European Commission', *Journal of European Public Policy*, vol. 4, no. 1, pp.73–90.

Coldrick, P. (1990) 'Collective Bargaining in the New Europe', *Personnel Management*, vol. 22, no. 10, pp. 58–61.

Commission of the European Communities (DGX Information) (1984) *The European Trade Union Confederation*, Luxembourg: Office for Official Publications of the European Communities.

Commission of the European Communities (1989) *Communication from the Commission Concerning its Action Programme Relating to the Implementation of the Community Charter of Basic Social Rights for Workers*, COM (89) 568 final, Brussels, 29 November 1989, Luxembourg: Office for Official Publications of the European Communities.

Commission of the European Communities (1990) *Employment in Europe*, Luxembourg: Office for Official Publications of the European Communities.

Commission of the European Communities (1993a) *Communication Concerning the Application of the Agreement on Social Policy*, presented by the Commission to the Council and to the European Parliament, COM (93) 600 final, 14 December 1993, Luxembourg: Office for Official Publications of the European Communities.

Commission of the European Communities (1993b) 'Growth, Competitiveness, Employment: the Challenges and Ways Forward into the 21st Century: White Paper', *Bulletin EC*, Supplement, 6, Luxembourg: Office for Official Publications of the European Communities.

Commission of the European Communities (1996a) *Commission Communication Concerning the Development of the Social Dialogue at Community Level*, COM (96) 448 final, Brussels, 18 September 1996, Luxembourg: Office for Official Publications of the European Communities.

Commission of the European Communities (1996b) *Proposal for a Council Directive 97/80/EC on the Burden of Proof in Cases of Discrimination Based on Sex*, COM (96) 340, Luxembourg: Office for Official Publications of the European Communities.

Commission of the European Communities (1996c) *Proposals for a Council Directive on the Framework Agreement Concluded by UNICE, CEEP and ETUC on Parental Leave*, COM (96) 26, Luxembourg: Office for Official Publications of the European Communities.

Commission of the European Community (1996d) 'Social Dialogue – The Situation in the Community in 1995', *Social Europe*, 2/95, Luxembourg: Office for Official Publications of the European Communities.

Commission of the European Communities (1997a) 'Status Report 1996', *European Social Dialogue Newsletter*, special issue.

Commission of the European Communities (1997b) *Proposal for a Council Directive Concerning the Framework Agreement on Part-time Work Concluded by UNICE, CEEP and the ETUC*, COM (97) 392, Brussels, 23 July 1997, Luxembourg: Office for Official Publications of the European Communities.

Commission of the European Communities (1998a) *Communication on Adapting and Promoting the Social Dialogue at Community Level*, COM (98) 322 of

20 May 1998, Luxembourg: Office for Official Publications of the European Communities.

Commission of the European Communities (1998b) *Proposal for a Council Directive Establishing a General Framework for Informing and Consulting Employees in the European Community*, COM (98) 612, 11 November 1998, Luxembourg: Office for Official Publications of the European Communities.

Commission of the European Communities (1998c) 'Status Report on the Social Dialogue 1997', *European Social Dialogue*, June 1998, Luxembourg: Office for Official Publications of the European Communities.

Commission of the European Communities (1998d) *Recommendation for the Broad Guidelines of the Economic Policy of the Member States and the Community*, DG II, COM (98) 144 final, Luxembourg: Office for Official Publications of the European Communities.

Commission of the European Communities (2000) *Industrial Relations in Europe*, DGV, Luxembourg: Office for Official Publications of the European Communities.

Commission of the European Communities (DGV Employment, Industrial Relations and Social Affairs) (undated) *European Social Dialogue Joint Opinions*, Luxembourg: Office for Official Publications of the European Communities.

Community Charter of the Fundamental Social Rights of Workers (1989) *Social Europe 1/92*.

Compston, H. (forthcoming) 'Social Partnership, Welfare State Regimes and Working Time in Europe', in B. Ebbinghaus and P. Manow (eds), *Varieties of Welfare Capitalism*, London: Routledge.

Corbett, R. (1993) *The Treaty of Maastricht – From Conception to Ratification: a Comprehensive Reference Guide*, Harlow: Longman Current Affairs.

Corbett, R. (1998) *The European Parliament's Role in Closer EU Integration*, Basingstoke: Macmillan.

Cram, L. (1997) *Policy-making in the European Union: Conceptual Lenses and the Integration Process*, London: Routledge.

Cullen, H. and E. Campbell (1998) 'The Future of Social Policy-making in the European Union', in P. Craig and C. Harlow (eds), *Lawmaking in the European Union*, London: Kluwer, pp.262–84.

Culture/Audiovisual Council, 28 June 1999, Press Release, Press: 206, No. 9409/99.

Dang-Nguyen, G., V. Schneider and R. Werle (1994) 'Corporate Actor Networks in European Policy Making: Harmonising Telecommunications Policy', MPIFG Discussion Paper 93/4, Koeln: Max Planck Institut für Gesellschaftsforschung.

Danish Government (1992) 'Memorandum from the Danish Government', reprinted in F. Laursen and S. Vanhoonacker (eds), *The Intergovernmental Conference on Political Union*, Maastricht: European Institute of Public Administration.

Delors, J. (2000) 'Das europäische Gesellschaftsmodell und der Sozialen Dialog in Europa', in E. Piehl and H-J. Timman (eds), *Der Europäische Beschäftigungspakt. Entstehungsprozeß und Perspektiven*, Baden-Baden: Nomos, pp.103–12.

De Ruyt, J. (1987) *L'Acte Unique Européen*, Bruxelles: Editions de l'Université de Bruxelles.

Dinan, D. (1994) *Ever Closer Union?* Colorado: Lynne Rienner.

Dølvik, J.E. (1997) 'Redrawing Boundaries of Solidarity? ETUC, Social Dialogue and the Europeanisation of Trade Unions in the 1990s', ARENA Report No. 5/97, Oslo: Arena.

Dølvik, J.E. (1999) *An Emerging Island? ETUC, Social Dialogue and the Europeanisation of the Trade Unions in the 1990s*, Brussels: ETUI.

Dølvik, J.E. (2000) 'Building Regional Structures: ETUC and the European Industry Federations', *Transfer – European Review of Labour and Research*, vol. 6, no. 1.

Dorey, P. (forthcoming) 'Britain in the 1990s: the Absence of Policy Concertation', in S. Berger and H. Compston (eds), *Policy Concertation and Social Partnership in Western Europe: Lessons for the 21st Century*, Oxford: Berghahn.

Earnshaw, D. and D. Judge (1995) 'Early Days: the European Parliament, Co-decision and the European Union Legislative Process Post-Maastricht', *Journal of European Public Policy*, vol. 2, no. 4, pp.624–49.

Ebbinghaus, B. and A. Hassel (1999) 'Striking Deals: Concertation in the Reform of Continental European Welfare States', Discussion Paper 99–3, Max Planck Institute for the Study of Societies.

Ebbinghaus, B. and J. Visser (1997) 'European Labor and Transnational Solidarity: Challenges, Pathways, and Barriers', in J. Klausen and L.A. Tilly (eds), *European Integration in Social and Historical Perspective: 1850 to the Present*, Lanham, MD: Rowman & Littlefield, pp.195–221.

Ebbinghaus, B. and J. Visser (1999) 'When Institutions Matter: Union Growth and Decline in Western Europe, 1950–1995', *European Sociological Review*, vol. 15, no. 2, pp.1–24.

Ebbinghaus, B. and J. Visser (2000) *Trade Unions in Western Europe Since 1945*, London: Macmillan.

Economic and Social Committee (1994) *Opinion on the Communication Concerning the Application of the Agreement on Social Policy presented by the Commission to the Council and to the European Parliament*, OJ C397/40, Luxembourg: Office for Official Publications of the European Communities.

Economic and Social Committee (1999) *The ESC: a Bridge between Europe and Civil Society*, Luxembourg: Office for Official Publications of the European Communities.

Economic and Social Committee (2000) *ESC Presentation Pamphlet* (http://www.esc.eu.int/en/org/welcome.htm).

Economist, The (1991) 14 December.

Edinger, Lewis J. (1993) 'Pressure Group Politics in West Germany', in Jeremy Richardson (ed.), *Pressure Groups*, Oxford: Oxford University Press.

EIRO (European Industrial Relations Observatory) (1999) *Social Partners reach draft framework agreement on fixed term contracts* (http://www.eiro.eurofound.ie).

EIRO (European Industrial Relations Observatory) database, www.eiro.eurofound.ie, Dublin.

ETUC (1991) *VIIth Statutory Congress: Report on Activities 88/90*, Brussels: ETUC.

ETUC (1999a) 'General Trade Union Policy Resolution', IX Statutory Congress of the European Trade Union Confederation, Brussels: ETUC (mimeo).

ETUC (1999b) 'Towards a European System of Industrial Relations', XI ETUC Congress, Helsinki 1999, Brussels: ETUC (mimeo).

ETUC, CEEP, UNICE (1993) 'Proposals by the Social Partners for the Implementation of the Agreement annexed to the Protocol on Social Policy of the Treaty on European Union', mimeo.

Eurochambres (1996) 'The Development of the Social Dialogue at Community Level', position paper, 18 December 1996, Brussels.

Eurochambres (1998) 'Eurochambres and the European Social Dialogue', position paper, 5 November 1998, Brussels.

Eurocommerce (1998) 'Adapting and Promoting the Social Dialogue at Community Level', position paper, 25 November 1998, Brussels.

European Industrial Relations Review (1992) 'The Social Dialogue – Eurobargaining in the Making?', no. 220.

European Industrial Relations Review (1994) 'Information and Consultation Talks Fail', no. 243.

European Industrial Relations Review (1997a) 'Atypical Working in Europe: Part One', no. 282.

European Industrial Relations Review (1997b) 'Commission Launches Debate on National-level Information and Consultation', no. 282.

European Industrial Relations Review (1997c) 'UEAPME Objects to Part-time Working Agreement', no. 283.

European Industrial Relations Review (1997d) 'Second Consultation Paper on National Information and Consultation', no. 287.

European Industrial Relations Review (1998) 'UEAPME Challenge Rejected', no. 295.

European Industrial Relations Review (1999) 'UNICE-UEAPME Co-operation Deal', no. 300.

European Parliament (1986) *Resolution on the Role of the Social Partners in the Labor Market*, OJ C322/52, Luxembourg: Office for Official Publications of the European Communities.

European Parliament (1988a) *Resolution on the Democratic Deficit in the European Community*, OJ C187/229, Luxembourg: Office for Official Publications of the European Communities.

European Parliament (1988b) *Resolution on the Role of the Two Sides of Industry in the Community*, OJ C309/104, Luxembourg: Office for Official Publications of the European Communities.

European Parliament (1991) *Resolution on the Enhancement of Democratic Legitimacy in the Context of the Intergovernmental Conference on Political Union*, OJ C129/134, Luxembourg: Office for Official Publications of the European Communities.

European Parliament (1994a) *Resolution on the New Social Dimension of the Treaty on European Union*, OJ C77/30, Luxembourg: Office for Official Publications of the European Communities.

European Parliament (1994b) *Resolution on the Application of the Agreement on Social Policy*, OJ C205/86, Luxembourg: Office for Official Publications of the European Communities.

European Parliament (1994c) *Report on the White Paper on European Social Policy – a Way Forward for the Union*, Rapporteur: Jesús Cabezón Alonso, A4–122/94, Luxembourg: Office for Official Publications of the European Communities.

European Parliament (1994d) *Resolution on the Social Protocol agreed at Maastricht*, OJ C176/159, Luxembourg: Office for Official Publications of the European Communities.

European Parliament (1995) *Resolution on the White paper on European Social Policy – a Way Forward for the Union*, OJ C43/63, Luxembourg: Office for Official Publications of the European Communities.

European Parliament (1996a) *Resolution on the Commission Proposal for a Council Directive on the Framework Agreement Concluded by UNICE, CEEP and ETUC on parental leave*, OJ C96/284, Luxembourg: Office for Official Publications of the European Communities.

European Parliament (1996b) *Report on the Commission Proposal for a Council Directive on the Framework Agreement Concluded by UNICE, CEEP and ETUC on Parental Leave*, Rapporteur: Mrs Anne-Karin Glase, A4-0064/96, Luxembourg: Office for Official Publications of the European Communities.

European Parliament (1996c) *Report on Participation of Citizens and Social Players in the Union's Institutional System*, Rapporteur: Philippe Herzog, A4-338/96, Luxembourg: Office for Official Publications of the European Communities.

European Parliament (1997a) *Resolution on the Commission Proposal for a Council Directive Concerning the Framework Agreement on Part-time Work Concluded by UNICE, CEEP and ETUC*, A4-352/97, Luxembourg: Office for Official Publications of the European Communities.

European Parliament (1997b) *Resolution on the Commission Communication Concerning the Development of the Social Dialogue at Community Level*, OJ C286/338, 22 September 1997, Luxembourg: Office for Official Publications of the European Communities.

European Parliament (1998) *Report on the Communication from the Commission on Adapting and Promoting the Social Dialogue at Community Level*, A4-392/98, 30 October 1998, Luxembourg: Office for Official Publications of the European Communities.

European Parliament (1999a) *Resolution on the Commission Proposal for a Council Directive Concerning the Framework Agreement on Fixed-Time Work Concluded by UNICE, CEEP and the ETUC*, OJ C279/430, 1 October 1999, Luxembourg: Office for Official Publications of the European Communities.

European Parliament (1999b) *Report on the Commission Proposal for a Council Directive Concerning the Framework Agreement on Fixed-Term Work Concluded by UNICE, CEEP and the ETUC*, A4-261/99, 30 April 1999, Luxembourg: Office for Official Publications of the European Communities.

European Trade Union Confederation (April 1991) 'Economic and Monetary Union: ETUC Submission to Intergovernmental Conference' (Brussels: unpublished).

European Trade Union Institute (1992) 'The European Dimensions of Collective Bargaining after Maastricht', Brussels: European Trade Union Institute.

Fajertag, G. and P. Pochet (eds) (2000) *Social Pacts in Europe*, 2nd edn, Brussels: OSE/ETUI.

Falkner, G. (1993) 'Sozialpartnerliche Politikmuster und Europäische Integration', in E. Tálos (ed.), *Sozialpartnerschaft. Kontinuität und Wandel eines Modells*, Vienna: Verlag für Gesellschaftskritik, pp.79–101.

Falkner, G. (1996a) 'European Works Councils and the Maastricht Social Agreement: Towards a New Policy Style?', *Journal of European Public Policy*, vol. 3, no. 2, pp.192–208.

Falkner, G. (1996b) 'The Maastricht Protocol on Social Policy: Theory and Practice', *Journal of European Social Policy*, vol. 6, no. 1, pp.1–16.

Falkner, G. (1998) *EU Social Policy in the 1990s: Towards a Corporatist Policy Community*, London and New York: Routledge.

Ferner, A. and R. Hyman (1992) *Industrial Relations in the New Europe*, Oxford: Blackwell.

Forster, A. (1995) 'Empowerment and Constraint: Britain and the Negotiation of the Treaty on European Union', University of Oxford, DPhil thesis.

Gabaglio, E. (1992) 'Die Sozialpartner: direkte Protagonisten der Europäischen Integration', *Soziales Europea*, 2/1992, pp.13–16.

Garrett, G. and G. Tsebelis (1996) 'An Institutional Critique of Intergovernmentalism', *International Organisations*, vol. 50, no. 2, pp.269–99.

Garrett, G. and B. Weingast (1993) 'Ideas, Interests and Institutions: Constructing the European Community's Internal Market', in J. Goldstein, and R.O. Keohane (eds), *Ideas and Foreign Policy: Beliefs, Institutions and Political Change*, London: Cornell University Press.

Goetschy, J. (1996) 'ETUC: the Construction of European Unionism', in P. Leisink, J. Van Leemput and J. Vilrokx (eds), *The Challenges to Trade Unions in Europe: Innovation or Adaption?* London: Elgar.

Goldstein, J. and R.O. Keohane (1993) 'Ideas and Foreign Policy: an Analytical Framework', in J. Goldstein and R.O. Keohane (eds), *Ideas and Foreign Policy: Beliefs, Institutions and Political Change*, London: Cornell University Press.

Gorges M.J. (1996) *Euro-corporatism?* Lanham: University Press of America.

Grant, C. (1994) *Delors: Inside the House that Jacques Built*, London: Nicholas Brealey Publishing.

Greek Government (1992) 'Greek Memorandum: Contribution to the Discussions on Progress Towards Political Union, Brussels, 15 May 1990', reprinted in F. Laursen and S. Vanhoonacker (eds) (1992) *The Intergovernmental Conference on Political Union*, Maastricht: European Institute of Public Administration.

Green Cowles, M. (1995) 'Setting the Agenda for the New Europe: the ERT and EC 1992', *Journal of Common Market Studies*, vol. 33, no. 4, pp.501–26.

Greenwood, J. (1997) *Representing Interests in the European Union*, Basingstoke: Macmillan.

Grote, J. (1987) *Tripartism and European Integration: Mutual Transfers, Osmotic Exchanges, or Frictions between the 'National' and the 'Transnational'. Trade Unions Today and Tomorrow*, Maastricht: Presses Interuniversitaire, pp.231–56.

Groux, G., R. Mouriaux and J.M. Pernot (1993) 'L'euroéanisation du mouvement syndical: La Confédération européenne des syndicals', *Le mouvement social*, vol. 163, pp.41–68.

Hall, M. (1994) 'Industrial Relations and the Social Dimension of European Integration: Before and After Maastricht' in R. Hyman and A. Ferner (eds), *New Frontiers in European Industrial Relations*, Oxford: Basil Blackwell.

Hall, P. (1993) 'Pluralism and Pressure Politics in France', in J. Richardson (ed.) *Pressure Groups*, Oxford: Oxford University Press.

Harlow, C. (1992) 'A Community of Interests? Making the Most of European Law', *The Modern Law Review*, vol. 55, pp.331–50.

Hassel, A. (1999) 'Bündnisse für Arbeit: Nationale Handlungsfähigkeit im europäischen Regimewettbewerb', Discussion Paper 99–5, Max Planck Institute for the Study of Societies.

Heclo, H. and H. Madsen (1987) *Policy and Politics in Sweden*, Philadelphia: Temple University Press.

Hepple, B. (1994) *Europe Social Dialogue – Alibi or Opportunity*, London: The Institute of Employment Rights.

Hobsbawm, E. (1994) *Age of Extremes: the Short Twentieth Century, 1914–1991*, London: Abacus.

Hodges, M. and W. Wallace (eds) (1981) *Economic Divergence in the European Community*, London: The Royal Institute of International Affairs.

Hornung-Draus, R. (1998) 'European Employer Organisations: Structure and Recent Developments', *Industrielle Beziehungen*, vol. 5, no. 2.

IDS European Report (1992) 'Social Europe After the Summit', no. 362.

ILO (1997) 'Industrial Relations, Democracy and Social Stability', *World Labour Report 1997–98*, Geneva: International Labour Office.

Irish Times, The (1991) 4 December; 9 December; 10 December; 11 December; 12 December; 13 December.

John, P. (1998) *Analysing Public Policy*, London and New York: Pinter.

Johnson, D. (1996) 'The Impact of the Nordic Countries on EU Social Policy', in L. Miles (ed.), *The European Union and the Nordic Countries*, London: Routledge.

Keller, B. and B. Sörries (1998) 'The New Social Dialogue: Procedural Structuring, First Results and Perspectives', in *Industrial Relations Journal – European Annual Review 1997*, Oxford: Blackwell.

Keller, B. and B. Sörries (1999) 'The New European Social Dialogue: Old Wine in New Bottles?', *Journal of European Social Policy*, vol. 9, no. 2, pp.111–25.

Kirchner, E. (1992) *Decision-Making in the European Community*, Manchester: Manchester University Press.

Kohl, H. and F. Mitterand (1992) letter addressed to Andreotti, reprinted in F. Laursen and S. Vanhoonacker (eds) (1992) *The Intergovernmental Conference on Political Union*, Maastricht: European Institute of Public Administration.

Kohler-Koch, B. and H-W. Platzer (1986) 'Tripartismus – Bedingungen und Perspektiven des sozialen Dialogs in der EG', *Integration*, 4/1986, pp.173–88.

Labour and Social Affairs Council, 15 December 1997, Press Release, Press: 396, No. 13370/97.

Labour and Social Affairs Council, 25 May 1999, Press Release, Press: 164, No. 8439/99.

Lange, P. (1991) 'The Politics of the Social Dimension', in A.M. Sbragia (ed.), *Europolitics*, Washington: Brookings Institution.

Lange, P. (1993) 'Maastricht and the Social Protocol: Why Did They Do It?', *Politics and Society*, vol. 21, no. 1, pp.5–36.

Lapeyre, J. (1996) 'First Round of European Negotiations on Key Issues for Equal Opportunities and Equal Treatment', *Transfer*, vol. 2, no. 1, pp.121–4.

Laursen, F. (1992) 'Denmark and European Political Union', in F. Laursen and S. Vanhoonacker (eds), *The Intergovernmental Conference on Political Union*, Maastricht: European Institute of Public Administration.

Lecher, W.E. (1994) *Trade Unions in European Union*, London: Lawrence and Wishart.

Majone, G. (1996) 'The European Commission as Regulator', in M. Giandomenico (ed.), *Regulating Europe*, London: Routledge, pp.61–79.

March, J.G. and J.P. Olsen (1989) *Rediscovering Institutions*, New York: The Free Press.

Marin, M. (1988) 'Guidelines on the Development of the Community's Social Policy', *Europe*, Document no. 1498 of 19 March 1988.

Martin, A. and G. Ross (1999) 'In the Line of Fire: the Europeanization of European Labor', in A. Martin and G. Ross (eds), *The Brave New World of European Labor*, New York: Berghahn, pp.312–67.

Martinez Lucio, M. (forthcoming) 'Spain in the 1990s: Strategic Concertation', in S. Berger and H. Compston (eds), *Policy Concertation and Social Partnership in Western Europe: Lessons for the 21st Century*, Oxford: Berghahn.

Mazey, S. and J. Richardson (1999) 'Interests', in L. Cram, D. Dinan and N. Nugent (eds), *Developments in the European Union*, Basingstoke: Macmillan, pp.105–29.

Miller, K.E. (1993) *Denmark: a Troubled Welfare State*, Oxford: Westview Press.

Milward, A.S. (1992) *The European Rescue of the Nation State*, London: Routledge.

Moravcsik, A. (1998) *The Choice for Europe*, London: UCL Press.

Mosley, H. (1990) 'The Social Dimension of European Integration', *International Labour Review*, vol. 129, pp.147–63.

Nugent, N. (1991) *The Government and Politics of the European Community*, 2nd edn, London: Macmillan.

Nugent, N. (1995) 'The Leadership Capacity of the European Commission', *Journal of European Public Policy*, vol. 2, no. 4, pp.603–23.

Organisation for Economic Cooperation and Development (1998) 'Key Employment Policy Challenges Faced by OECD Countries', in Labour Market and Social Policy Occasional Papers, 31, Paris: Organisation for Economic Cooperation and Development.

Peters, B.G. (1992) 'Bureaucratic Politics and Institutions of the European Community', in A. Sbragia (ed.), *Euro-Politics: Institutions and Policymaking in the 'New' European Community*, Washington: The Brookings Institution, pp.75–122.

Peterson, J. (1999) 'The Santer Era: the European Commission in Normative, Historic and Theoretical Perspective', *Journal of European Public Policy*, vol. 6, no. 1, pp.46–65.

Pierson, P. and S. Leibfried (1995) 'The Dynamics of Social Policy Integration', in S. Leibfried and P. Pierson (eds), *European Social Policy*, Washington: Brookings.

Platzer, H.W. (1991) *Gewerkschaftspolitik ohne Grenzen? Die transnationale Zusammenarbeit der Gewerkschaften im Europa der 90er*, Bonn: Dietz.

Pochet, P. (1998) 'Les pactes sociaux en Europe dans les années 1990', *Sociologie du Travail*, vol. 40, no. 2, pp.173–90.

Pollack, M. (1997) 'The Commission as an Agent', in N. Nugent (ed.), *At the Heart of the Union: Studies of the European Commission*, Basingstoke: Macmillan, pp.109–28.

Portuguese Ministry of Foreign Affairs (1992) 'Memorandum from the Portuguese Delegation: Political Union with a View to the Intergovernmental

Conference, Lisbon, 30 November 1990', reprinted in F. Laursen and S. Vanhoonacker (1992) (eds), *The Intergovernmental Conference on Political Union*, Maastricht: European Institute of Public Administration.

Presidency Conclusions of European Council Meetings: 1985 IGC (*Bull.EC 12-1985*, pp.11–14), The Hague June 1986 (*Bull.EC 6-1986*, pp.7–12), London December 1986 (*Bull.EC 12-1986*, pp.7–13), Brussels June 1987 (*Bull.EC 6-1987*, pp.7–13), Copenhagen December 1987 (*Bull.EC 12-1987*, pp.7–9), Brussels February 1988 (*Bull.EC 2-1988*, pp.8ff), Hanover June 1988 (*Bull.EC 6-1988*, pp.164–8), Rhodes December 1988 (*Bull.EC 12-1988*, pp.8–11), Madrid June 1989 (*Bull.EC 6-1989*, pp.8–13), Strasbourg December 1989 (*Bull.EC 12-1989*, pp.8–16), Dublin April 1990 (*Bull.EC 4-1990*, pp.7–11), Dublin June 1990 (*Bull.EC 6-1990*, pp.8–22), Rome October 1990 (*Bull.EC 10-1990*, pp.7–10), Rome December 1990 (*Bull.EC 12-1990*, pp.8–14), Luxembourg June 1991 (*Bull.EC 6-1991*), pp.8–14.

Purcell, J. (1993) 'The End of Institutional Industrial Relations', *The Political Quarterly*, vol. 64, pp.6–23.

Ramsay, H. (1995) 'Euro-unionism and the Great Auction: an Assessment of the Prospects for the European Labour Movement Post-Maastricht', in P. Cressey and B. Jones (eds), *Work and Employment in Europe: a New Convergence?* London: Routledge.

Reding, V. (1993) 'Report of the Committee on Social Affairs, Employment and the Working Environment of the European Parliament on the New Social Dimension of the Maastricht Treaty', EP Doc. A3-247/93, 1 September 1993, Luxembourg: Office for Official Publications of the European Communities.

Regini, M. (1984) 'The Conditions for Political Exchange: How Concertation Emerged and Collapsed in Italy and Great Britain', in J.H. Goldthorpe (ed.), *Order and Conflict in Contemporary Capitalism*, Oxford: Clarendon Press, pp.124–42.

Rein, M. and D. Schon (1991) 'Frame-reflective Policy Discourse', in P. Wagner, C.H. Weiss, B. Whitrock and H. Wollman (eds), *Social Sciences and Modern States: Experiences and Theoretical Crossroads*, Cambridge: Cambridge University Press, pp.262–89.

Rhodes, M. (1992) 'The Future of the "Social Dimension": Labour Market Regulation in Post-1992 Europe', *Journal of Common Market Studies*, vol. 30, no. 1, pp.23–51.

Rhodes, M. (1993) 'The Social Dimension after Maastricht: Setting a New Agenda for the Labour Market', *The International Journal of Comparative Labour Law and Industrial Relations*, vol. 9, no. 4, pp.297–325.

Rhodes, M. (1995) 'A Regulatory Conundrum: Industrial Relations and the Social Dimension,' in S. Leibfried and P. Pierson (eds), *European Social Policy: Between Fragmentation and Integration*, Washington, DC: Brookings Institution, pp.78–122.

Ross, G. (1995a) *Jacques Delors and European Integration*, Cambridge: Polity Press.

Ross, G. (1995b) 'Assessing the Delors Era and Social Policy', in S. Leibfried and P. Pierson (eds), *European Social Policy: Between Fragmentation and Integration*, Washington, DC: The Brookings Institution.

Ross, G. and A. Martin (1998) 'European Integration and the Europeanization of Labor', Centro de Estudios Avanzados en Ciencias Sociales Working Paper 1998/126.

Sabatier, P. and H. Jenkins Smith (1988) 'Policy Change and Policy Oriented Learning', *Western Political Quarterly*, vol. 21, pp.123–277.

Schneider, V., G. Dang-Nguyen and R. Werle (1994) 'Corporate Actor Networks in European Policy-making: Harmonising Telecommunications Policy', *Journal of Common Market Studies*, vol. 32, no. 4, pp.473–98.

Schmitter, P.C. (1981) 'Interest Intermediation and Regime Governability in Contemporary Western Europe and North America', in S. Berger (ed.), *Organizing Interests in Western Europe*, Cambridge: Cambridge University Press.

Schmitter, P.C. (1983) 'Neo-Corporatism, Consensus, Governability, and Democracy in the Management of Crisis in Contemporary Advanced Industrial-Capitalist Societies', Paper for Organisation for Economic Cooperation and Development conference on Social Dialogue and Consensus, Paris.

Sciarra, S. (1993) 'European Social Policy and Labour Law: Challenges and Perspectives', in Academy of European Law (ed.), *Collected Courses of the Academy of European Law*, vol. IV, book I, pp.301–40.

Shalev, M. (1992) 'The Resurgence of Labour Quiescence', in M. Regini (ed.), *The Future of Labour Movements*, London: Sage, pp.102–32.

Silvia, S.J. (1991) 'The Social Charter of the European Community: a Defeat for European Labour', *Industrial and Labor Relations Review*, vol. 44, no. 4, pp.626–43.

Slomp, H. (forthcoming) 'The Netherlands in the 1990s: Towards "Flexible Corporatism" in the Polder Model', in S. Berger and H. Compston (eds), *Policy Concertation and Social Partnership in Western Europe: Lessons for the 21st Century*, Oxford: Berghahn.

Smyrl, M.E. (1998) 'When (and How) do the Commission's Preferences Matter?', *Journal of Common Market Studies*, vol. 36, no. 1, pp.79–99.

Stöckl, I. (1986) *Gewerkschaftsausschüsse in der EG*, Kehl: N.P. Engel.

Streeck, W. (1984) 'Neo-Corporatist Industrial Relations and the Economic Crisis in West Germany', in J.H. Goldthorpe (ed.), *Order and Conflict in Contemporary Capitalism*, Oxford: Clarendon Press, pp.291–314.

Streeck, W. (1994) 'European Social Policy after Maastricht: the "Social Dialogue" and "Subsidiarity"', *Economic and Industrial Democracy*, vol. 15, pp.151–78.

Streeck, W. (1995) 'Neo-voluntarism: a New European Social Policy Regime?', *European Law Journal*, vol. 1, no. 1, pp.31–59.

Streeck, W. (1996) 'Neo-voluntarism: a New European Social Policy Regime?', in G. Marks et al. (eds), *Governance in the European Union*, London: Sage, pp.64–94.

Streeck, W. (1997) 'Citizenship under Regime Competition: the Case of the European Works Councils', Florence, European University Institute/Schuman Centre, Jean Monnet Chair Paper 97/42.

Streeck, W. and P. Schmitter (1991) 'From National Corporatism to Transnational Pluralism: Organized Interests in the Single European Market', *Politics and Society*, vol. 19, no. 2, pp.133–64.

Streeck, W. and J. Visser (1998) 'An Evolutionary Dynamic of Trade Union Systems', Discussion Paper 98–4, Max Planck Institute for the Study of Societies.

Streeck, W. and S. Vitols (1995) 'The European Community: Between Mandatory Consultation and Voluntary Information', in J. Rogers and W. Streeck (eds), *Works Councils*, Chicago: University of Chicago Press, pp.243–82.

Streit, M. and W. Mussler (1994) 'The Economic Constitution of the European Community – from Rome to "Maastricht"', Paper presented at the conference 'European Law in Context: Constitutional Dimensions of European Economic Integration', Badia Fiesolana, Italy, 14–15 November.

Teague, P. (1989a) 'European Community Labour Market Harmonisation', *Journal of Public Policy*, vol. 9, no. 1, pp.1–34.

Teague, P. (1989b) *The European Community: The Social Dimension. Labour Market Policies for 1992*, London: Kogan Page.

'The Single European Act', in *Treaty on European Union and Treaty Establishing the European Community*, Luxembourg: Office for Official Publications of the European Communities.

Traxler, F. (1996) 'Collective Bargaining in the OECD: Developments, Preconditions and Effects', *European Journal of Industrial Relations*, vol. 4, no. 2, pp.207–26.

'Treaty Establishing the European Communities (signed in Rome on 25 March 1957)', in *Treaty on European Union and Treaty Establishing the European Community*, Luxembourg: Office for Official Publications of the European Communities.

'Treaty Establishing the European Community' (Treaty of Amsterdam), Luxembourg: Office for Official Publications of the European Communities.

'Treaty on European Union (signed in Maastricht on 7 February 1992)', in *Treaty on European Union and Treaty Establishing the European Community*, Luxembourg: Office for Official Publications of the European Communities.

Tsoukalis, L. (1992) *The New European Economy: the Politics and Economics of Integration*, Oxford: Oxford University Press.

Tsoukalis, L. (1997) *The New European Economy Revisited*, Oxford: Oxford University Press.

Tudyka, K., T. Etty and M. Sucha (1978) *Mach ohne grenzen und grenzenlose Ohnmacht. Arbeitsnehmerbewußtsein und die bedingungen gewerkschaftliche Gegenstrategien im multinationalen Konzernen*, Frankfurt a/M: Campus.

Tyszkiewicz, Z. (1999) 'The European Social Dialogue, 1985–1998: a Personal View', in E. Gabaglio and R. Hoffmann (eds), *European Trade Union Yearbook 1998*, Brussels: ETUI, pp.35–47.

UEAPME (1997) 'UEAPME Position Paper on the Green Paper of the European Commission "Partnership for a New Organisation of Work"', Brussels, November 1997.

UNICE (1994) 'Comments on the Green Paper on European Social Policy – Options for the Future', position paper, Brussels, 30 April 1994.

UNICE (1995) 'Parental leave agreement meets business needs better than a directive', press release, Brussels, 14 December 1995.

UNICE (1997a) 'Agreement on part-time work responds to companies' needs better than a directive', press release, Brussels, 6 June 1997.

UNICE (1997b) 'UNICE Council of Presidents approves agreement on part-time work and calls on the European Council to build a competitive Europe', press release, 6 June 1997.

UNICE (1997c) 'Second stage of social partner consultation on prevention of sexual harassment at work', UNICE response, 22 July 1997.

UNICE (1998a) 'UNICE will not opt for negotiations on information and consultation at national level', press release, Brussels, 16 March 1998.

UNICE (1998b) 'UNICE and UEAPME sign co-operation agreement', press release, Brussels, 4 December 1998.

UNICE (1999) 'Freeing Europe's employment potential: European social policy on the eve of 2000 seen by companies', position paper.

van der Wee, H. (1986) *Prosperity and Upheaval: the World Economy 1945–1980*, London: Viking.

Van Ruysveldt, J. and J. Visser (1996) 'Weak Corporatisms Going Different Ways? Industrial Relations in the Netherlands and Belgium', in J. Van Ruysveldt and J. Visser (eds), *Industrial Relations in Europe*, London: Sage, pp.205–64.

Vilar, E. (1997) *Modalités de fonctionnement du dialogue social européen dans le cadre de l'accord sur la politique sociale*, Brussels: UEAPME.

Visser, J. (1999) 'Concertation: the Art of Making Social Pacts', in E. Gabaglio and R. Hoffmann (eds), *European Trade Union Yearbook 1998*, Brussels: ETUI, pp.217–32.

Visser, J. and B. Ebbinghaus (1992) 'Making the Most of Diversity? European Integration and Transnational Organization of Labour', in J. Greenwood, J. Grote and K. Ronit (eds), *Organized Interests and the European Community*, London: Sage, pp.206–37.

Visser, J. and A.C. Hemerijck (1997) *'A Dutch Miracle'. Job Growth, Welfare Reform, and Corporatism in the Netherlands*, Amsterdam: Amsterdam University Press.

Vobruba, G. (1995) 'Social Policy on Tomorrow's Euro-corporatist Stage', *Journal of European Social Policy*, vol. 5, pp.303–15.

Wallerstein, M., M. Golden and P. Lange (1997) 'Unions, Employers' Associations, and Wage-Setting Institutions in Northern and Central Europe, 1950–1992', *Industrial and Labour Relations Review*, vol. 50, no. 3, pp.379–401.

Weber, M. (1948) 'The Social Psychology of the World Religions', in H.H. Gerth and C. Wright Mills (eds), *From Max Weber*, London: Routledge and Kegan Paul.

Weiss, M. (1992) 'The Significance of Maastricht for European Community Social Policy', *The International Journal of Comparative Labour Law and Industrial Relations*, vol. 8, no. 1, pp.3–14.

Wendon, B. (1998) 'The Commission as Image-venue Entrepreneur in EU Social Policy', *Journal of European Public Policy*, vol. 5, no. 2, pp.339–53.

Western, B. (1997) *Between Class and Market: Postwar Unionization in the Capitalist Democracies*, Princeton, NJ: Princeton University Press.

Wise, M. and R. Gibb (1993) *Single Market to Social Europe*, New York: Longman.

Wittrock, P. and H. Wollman (eds) (1991) *Social Sciences and Modern States: National Experiences and Theoretical Crossroads*, Cambridge: Cambridge University Press, pp.262–89.

Wright, V. (1992) *The Government and Politics of France*, London: Unwin Hyman.

Index